LIVING IN THE WORLD

Living in the World

How Conservative Mennonites Preserved the Anabaptism

of the Sixteenth Century

By

Ronald C. Jantz

WIPF & STOCK · Eugene, Oregon

LIVING IN THE WORLD
How Conservative Mennonites Preserved the Anabaptism of the Sixteenth Century

Copyright © 2020 Ronald C. Jantz. All rights reserved. Except for brief quotations in critical publications or reviews, no part of this book may be reproduced in any manner without prior written permission from the publisher. Write: Permissions, Wipf and Stock Publishers, 199 W. 8th Ave., Suite 3, Eugene, OR 97401.

Wipf & Stock
An Imprint of Wipf and Stock Publishers
199 W. 8th Ave., Suite 3
Eugene, OR 97401

www.wipfandstock.com

PAPERBACK ISBN: 978-1-7252-7357-3
HARDCOVER ISBN: 978-1-7252-7358-0
EBOOK ISBN: 978-1-7252-7359-7

Manufactured in the U.S.A.

The painting on the cover is by Marie Birckholtz-Bestvater, "Mennonite Farm and Windmill", oil painting. The original is held in the Mennonite Library and Archives Art Collection, North Newton, KS. Permission to use this image on the book cover has been granted by the Mennonite Library and Archives, Bethel College, North Newton, KS.
The image of Menno Simons is in the public domain. See https://commons.wikimedia.org/

wiki/File:PieterHolsteyn-MennoSimons1622.jpg

For My Family

and in Memory of

Martin and Lucille (Koehn) Jantz

The regenerated do not go to war nor fight. They are the children of peace who have beaten their swords into plowshares and their spears into pruning hooks and know of no war. They give to Caesar the things that are Caesar's and to God the things that are God's.

My dear reader, if the poor, ignorant world with an honest heart accepted this our hated and despised doctrine, which is not of us but of Christ, and faithfully obeyed it, they could well change their deadly swords into plowshares and their spears into pruning hooks, level their gates and walls, dismiss their executioners and henchmen.

Menno Simons

This is clear that we shall not punish our enemies by the power of the magistracy, but shall do good toward them for all the evil they commit against us. Yea, even if he take our goods by force, or desires to take them, we shall not resist this evil. If anyone take our goods by mistake, it is our duty to tell him of it in true love; for he did not wish to do it and is thankful if we tell him of it.

John Holdeman

Table of Contents

AUTHOR'S PREFACE	1
PART ONE - THE EUROPEAN EXPERIENCE	13
CHAPTER ONE, Emergence of the Anabaptists	17
CHAPTER TWO, Menno Simons — The Former Priest	29
CHAPTER THREE, The World of the Dutch Mennonites	43
CHAPTER FOUR, Living with the Czars	55
CHAPTER FIVE, Surviving Lenin and Stalin	69
CHAPTER SIX, From Ostrog to Lone Tree, Kansas	77
PART TWO - NONRESISTANCE AND A PEOPLE APART	91
CHAPTER SEVEN, Building the Church	93
CHAPTER EIGHT, The Holdemans and Schleitheim	105
CHAPTER NINE, Nonresistance	113
CHAPTER TEN, Separation from the World	123
CHAPTER ELEVEN, The Holdeman People Today	133
CHAPTER TWELVE, Epilogue	147
APPENDIX ONE, The Kansas Ostrogers	150
APPENDIX TWO, Dutch-Prussian Family Names	158

Table of Contents

APPENDIX THREE, Holdeman Congregations   165

ABBREVIATIONS   172

BIBLIOGRAPHY   173

INDEX OF SUBJECTS   189

List of Figures

1	A Dutch Windmill	20
2	The Martyrdom of Jan Smit	24
3	Menno Simons	30
4	Holy Roman Emperor Charles V	32
5	Schönsee Old Flemish Church	37
6	Mennonite Farm and Windmill in Prussia	46
7	Frederick II, King of Prussia	48
8	Czar Alexander II of Russia	56
9	A Mennonite Headstone	65
10	Vladimir Lenin - Russian Communist Leader	70
11	A Mennonite Residence in Oklahoma Territory	83
12	A Residence on the Treeless Plains of Kansas	85
13	Abandoned Farm Dalhart, Texas. 1938	89
14	Floyd Koehn Serving in the South Pacific - September, 1943	119
15	A Sketch of a Young Holdeman Family	136
16	The Parallel Lives of the Schmidt and Jantz Families, from Przechowka to Lone Tree	157
17	The Ratzlaff, Richert, Schmidt, and Wedel Families of Przechowka	162
18	The Unrau (Unruh), Jantz, Ratzlaff, and Schmidt Families of Przechowka	163
19	The Becker, Jantz, Ratzlaff, and Schmidt Families of Przechowka	164

List of Maps

1. The Sketch of the Netherlands shows Witmarsum in Friesland, the birthplace of Menno Simons, and Groningen, the home of the Groningen Old Flemish Society in the Seventeenth Century (map by the author). 31
2. The Congregations of the Groningen Old Flemish in Prussia (Przechowka, Jeziorka, and Schönsee) Superimposed on Modern State Boundaries(map by the author.) 36
3. A Map of Central Europe ca. 1500 Showing the Holy Roman Empire. 42
4. The map sketch shows the trek of the Mennonites from the Przechowka communities to South Russia (map by the author). 51
5. Ostrog, Chortitza and Molotschna Located in Modern Ukraine (map by the author) 53
6. The Village of Leeleva (Lileva) Front Row: Tobias Voth, Henry Schmidt, Tobias Schmidt, Henry Jantz, Tobias Boese, Henry Penner, Peter Wedel, Henry Unruh Top Row: Edward Bettner, John Jantz, John Dekker, Tobias Boese, Ferinaud Kass, Benjamin Boese, Carl Mueller 61
7. Congregations of the Church of God in Christ, Mennonite in Kansas (map by the author). 104
8. Congregations of the Church of God in Christ, Mennonite in Kansas (map by the author). 166
9. Congregations of the Church of God in Christ, Mennonite in the Southeast United States (map by the author). 167
10. Congregations of the Church of God in Christ, Mennonite in the Western United States (map by the author). 168
11. Congregations of the Church of God in Christ, Mennonite in Oklahoma and Texas (map by the author). 169
12. Congregations of the Church of God in Christ, Mennonite in the Upper Midwest of the United States (map by the author). 170
13. Congregations of the Church of God in Christ, Mennonite in the Northeast of the United States (map by the author). . . . 171

List of Photos

1 A Mennonite Home in Karolswalde (photo courtesy of Dale Schrag) 58
2 The Family of B. B. Janz in 1914 72
3 Tobias A. Unruh 79
4 The S.S. Vaderland landed in Philadelphia on December 26, 1874. 81
5 The Halstead Milling Company 87
6 The Halstead Co-op in 2019, Viewed from the Same Vantage Point as the Halstead Mill in 1877 (photgraph by the author). . 88
7 John Holdeman Gravestone (photograph by the author). 100

List of Tables

1	Frequency of Mennonite Family Names (N=4,960)	160
2	Frequency of Mennonite Family Names in the *Messenger of Truth*, 2017–2018.	161
3	Genealogy Numbering System	161

Author's Preface

ARLY IN THE 1520S, ANABAPTISM became a recognizable Reformation movement in three areas — Switzerland, South Germany, and the Netherlands. In this narrative, we focus on the Netherlands and the work of Menno Simons, the person who ultimately lent his name to the religion whose members are called Mennonites. In these pages, the reader will be able to experience the religious adventure of Anabaptism and appreciate the core principles of nonconformity and nonresistance. We trace these early movements to modern times in which a little known group of Mennonites brought a unique way of life to the Great Plains of America.

The Anabaptists were a gathering of common people without a religious hierarchy, basing their faith and practice on the New Testament, rejecting both infant baptism and participation in warfare.[1] In the ensuing religious turmoil of the sixteenth and seventeenth centuries, the Mennonite religion emerged in response to the state-mandated faith of the ruling authorities. The Mennonites were one of three related but distinct groups that emerged from the Anabaptist movement of the sixteenth century.[2]

Through this ethnographic and historical account, we trace a small group of disciplined people who had very strong ideas about living a life that was centered on the teachings of Jesus. These people who lived together, migrated together, and worshipped together have also been united through bonds of kinship, sharing a relatively few family names of Dutch-Prussian origin. Through multiple migrations and transformations, the descendants of the Groningen Old Flemish in Prussia and the Ostrogers in Russia arrived in the United States and embraced the teachings of John Holdeman, becoming the Church of God in Christ, Mennonite.

In this text, we hope to impart an understanding of the culture and beliefs of these people and, for society, a message of why they live their lives as they do. Foremost in their belief system is the foundational religious principle of

---

[1] Smith, *Story*, 1–2.
[2] These three groups included the Hutterites from South Germany and Austria; the Swiss Brethren from Switzerland and South Germany; and the Mennonites from the Netherlands and North Germany. See Hostetler, *Hutterite Society*, 8.

AUTHOR'S PREFACE

nonresistance, a practice that is derived from the words of Jesus as spoken in the Gospel of Matt. 5:39 — *But I say to you, Do not resist an evildoer. But if anyone strikes you on the right cheek, turn the other also.*[3]

In the Reformation of the early 1500s, a small group of radicals, lesser known than such notables as Luther and Calvin, rejected the state-church collaboration. The early Anabaptists and the later Mennonites believed that Jesus' commandment requires the renunciation of warfare and other compulsive means in the furtherance of political and social ends.[4] In practicing nonresistance, these humble people have sought to separate themselves from the evil of the world, living in relatively isolated, rural communities and avoiding involvement in worldly society. However, adherence to this practice has caused the Mennonites much grief with government and religious authorities and the citizenry of the countries they hoped to call home, resulting in an adversarial and, at times, a symbiotic relationship.

In living a nonresistant faith and separating from the world, this committed group of people has confronted royalty, religious authorities, and rulers of Europe in order to preserve their way of life. Today, they exist and thrive as a cultural enclave in the rural communities of the Great Plains, evidence of their success in separating from the world.[5] Although they honor and obey worldly governments, as apostle Paul indicated, their citizenship is in heaven (Phil. 3:20 — *But our citizenship is in heaven, and it is from there that we are expecting a Savior, the Lord Jesus Christ*). In striving to live according to Christ's commandments, their traditional culture conveys a message to modern society about humility, modesty, generosity, and peaceful living. In turn, they ask the people of the world to let them be Mennonite.

Although many readers will find it difficult to understand or relate to the religion of these conservative Mennonites, it will be hard not to acknowledge the message their way of life presents to the non-Mennonites of the world. In writing about Mennonite ethics, Abraham Toews has eloquently summarized how these people have lived for over 400 years.[6]

> Instead of being led by the spirit of this world they aim to follow God's spirit. To keep away from the voices of the world they band together and live in their own villages . . . When they clash with the cultural, political and religious views of their

---

[3] Unless otherwise noted, all Biblical quotations are from the *HarperCollins Study Bible*, New Revised Standard Version.

[4] Crous, "Nonresistance," 897.

[5] The Great Plains is a broad expanse of prairie in America and Canada located west of the Mississippi River. This vast area includes the states of Kansas, Nebraska, North Dakota, and South Dakota and portions of Alberta, Saskatchewan, and Manitoba. The Mennonites who are the subject of this text found the Great Plains ideal for settling because of the agricultural and wheat growing potential.

[6] Toews, *Mennonite Ethics*, 209–10.

neighbors they base their actions on the literal interpretation of Acts 1:14 and Acts 2:42 — *They devoted themselves to the apostles' teaching and to fellowship, to the breaking of bread and to prayer.* Their judgment is correct when they say they do not "belong to this world". They have developed a frugality, sobriety, honesty, truthfulness and an all-embracing dutifulness which, in the form of mutual aid, goes to all continents.

It is fair to say that many of the principles of sixteenth century Anabaptism have been preserved in these small close-knit groups. Depending on how one counts, we can conclude that Anabaptist principles have survived in conservative Mennonite communities for over fifteen generations. Kauffman reports that this persistence could have only been possible by people compromising with the real world.[7] Although there may have been some weakening of commitment, these pages will show how conservative Mennonites have maintained their adherence to the historic Anabaptist principles. While assimilating into modern society, they are constantly reassessing what belongs to the world, facing new ethical demands while also striving to maintain their practices of nonresistance and separation from the world.

The Structures of this Book

This book is best thought of as a cultural history albeit an unusual hybrid – part history, part culture, part national identity and, in the end, part message to the American people. As such, it belongs to the genre of Mennonite literature but also should appeal more widely to the general public. Much of today's writing about Mennonite culture deals with the more progressive Mennonite groups. In this narrative, we focus on conservative Mennonites and follow C. Henry Smith's classification in which he designates "conservative" as including the Church of God in Christ, Mennonite and the Kleine Gemeinde, also known as the Evangelical Mennonite Church since 1952. These conservatives are recognized by worldly people as having rigid dress regulations, requiring beards for men and the head covering for women, and typically using avoidance and shunning for fallen-away members.[8] In this text, we build on the work of Abe Unruh[9] and Clarence Hiebert[10] who have both described the life and times of one of the most conservative Mennonite groups, the Holdeman people or, more formally, the Church of God in Christ, Mennonite (CGCM). The origins of the modern day Holdeman Church can

---

[7] Kauffman, *Anabaptists*, 27.
[8] Smith, *Story*, 744.
[9] Unruh, *Helpless Poles*.
[10] Hiebert, *Holdeman People*.

AUTHOR'S PREFACE

be traced back to the Groningen Old Flemish in the Netherlands and the Ostrogers[11] who settled in the province of Volhynia, now part of the Ukraine.

In what follows, we provide a narrative history of this small group of Mennonites and trace their journeys from Holland to Prussia, to Russia, and finally to America. The book is organized into two major sections. In Part One, the European Experience, I introduce the reader to the Anabaptism of the sixteenth century. The assertion in this book is that the Anabaptist principles defined in the sixteenth century can be clearly found in the doctrines and practices of the modern-day Church of God in Christ, Mennonite. Building on this premise, I follow the Mennonites in their migrations through Europe, highlighting their encounters with kings, princes, nobles, and various religious leaders. I introduce the culture and kinship relationships, offering unique insight into a religious group that has stayed together and migrated together for over 400 years. We discuss life in the twentieth century, how these rural people settled the Great Plains and, more tragically, the unfortunate circumstances that fell upon those who remained in Russia.

In Part Two, we explore the core Anabaptist principles of "nonresistance" and "nonconformity" in more detail and learn about the early adherents who were commonly labeled *Wiedertäufer* or rebaptizers. I introduce the Holdeman people, examining how the Anabaptist principles have become part of their church doctrines and practices. In the twentieth century, the Holdemans found themselves in quite a different culture, faced with the need to assimilate and confronting the modern challenges of education and the use of technology. In this environment, they were forced to reinvent themselves, at times relaxing or even abandoning some of their earlier practices. In this context, we consider the question of how the core principles of Anabaptism have been preserved and how, or if, the Holdeman people will be able to maintain their ethno-religious identity into the future.

In his study of five Mennonite denominations, Kauffman has used an empirical methodology to examine various characteristics in order to trace the historic origins and development of these churches.[12] In this narrative, I use a more qualitative approach to describe the culture of the Church of God in Christ, Mennonite, using Holdeman voices from the *Messenger of Truth*[13] and their conference reports as a means to understand their approach to life and their everyday religion.[14] The Holdemans can be rightly thought of as

---

[11]In this text, I follow Hiebert's approach in using the term "Ostroger" to designate the small group of Mennonites who resided near the city of Ostrog, Volhynia province in nineteenth century Russia. See Hiebert, *Holdeman People*, 47, note no. 22.

[12]Kauffman, *Anabaptists*, 31.

[13]The *Messenger of Truth* is the newsletter of the Holdeman Church. The text of the *Messenger of Truth* is available for the years 1941 through 2018 via a CD published by Gospel Publishers.

[14]Ammerman, "Studying," 219–38.

dedicated genealogists and many have traced their family history from Russia to the Great Plains of America. The challenge in this text was to integrate these informal and diverse sources and related historical material in order to portray their culture, practices, and adherence to Anabaptist principles.

For the historian, piecing together a narrative from these various artifacts — diaries, documents, genealogies, records — is like the archaeologist who finds fragments of pottery buried in the ruins of an ancient civilization. There can rarely be conclusive proof about how people lived; the archaeologist can only hope to assemble enough fragments of civilization to show trends, support theories and to engage in intelligent guesswork. Where there is evidence of fire, the archaeologist can reasonably conclude that an early civilization formed social groups, began to use language and used fire for other "civilized" purposes such as cooking and making weapons.

Thus in my own endeavors as an "archaeologist", I have found resources that suggest that many of the ancestral names cited in this text originated in the Netherlands. The *Mennonite Encyclopedia* identifies family names of the conservative Mennonites as Dutch or Dutch-Prussian. The descendants of the Groningen Old Flemish who trekked from Prussia to Russia and ultimately settled in the Great Plains are almost exclusively of Dutch origin. Earlier research and genealogical studies have found that these people lived in isolated groups and shared a relatively few surnames. Today, the family names of these Mennonites are easily recognizable in the congregations of the Holdeman and Kleine Gemeinde churches. Typical family names include Giesbrecht, Jantz, Koehn, Loewen, Ratzlaff, Reimer, Schmidt, and Unruh. These surnames provide a method to trace the travels of the group through 400 years of history. In this process, the story of the Dutch-Prussian Mennonites who originated in a congregation known as the Groningen Old Flemish Society gradually emerges. In broad strokes, these perpetual migrants moved from Holland to Prussia and Royal Poland in the eighteenth century and, in the early nineteenth century, to the region of Volhynia near the city of Ostrog, today part of the Ukraine. The villages in Volhynia that are of most interest in this history are what is known as the Karolswalde circuit although some hearty souls moved at times to the communities of south Russia — Chortitza and Molotschna.

Introspection and Self-Reflection

Through the use of historical resources, published research, archival records, family genealogies, and an extensive database, I have hopefully created a picture for readers that is not only interesting but also provides some understanding of the historical context and culture of a relatively unknown group of people. These conservative Mennonites have maintained their unity

AUTHOR'S PREFACE

and allegiance to a few basic principles over a span of four hundred years. It is a story unique in many ways but also one that has meaning for us all. Scott Momaday's quote surely has resonance for readers:[15]

> There is a great good in returning to a landscape that has had extraordinary meaning in one's life. It happens that we return to such places in our minds irresistibly. There are certain villages and towns, mountains and plains that, having seen them, walked in them, lived in them, even for a day, we keep forever in the mind's eye. They become indispensable to our well-being; they define us and we say: I am who I am because I have been there, or there.

This historical narrative has been, in many ways, a returning to a landscape that has great meaning for me. What the reader will find in the following pages are the results of many years of personal research. My intent was to weave together historical events and personal stories, showing how events have affected these European sojourners and how they responded to the circumstances of the day. In the end, I wanted to convey an interesting story about a unique group whose culture, practices, and ethics hold a message for a modern society enmeshed in political chaos and one that is being rapidly transformed by technology and social media. As such, it is hoped that this book will appeal to the larger community of Mennonites and to the general reader who wants to understand the Mennonite neighbors in his or her community.

In similar genres, authors have taken the opportunity to reflect on involvement in their emerging narrative.[16,17] This cultural history would not have been possible without my own experience in rural Kansas, growing up in a family that was part of the Holdeman community. My parents were, for a brief period, members of the Holdeman Grace Mennonite Church in Halstead, Kansas. Our family reunions were an odd mixture of cousins, aunts, and uncles who were both inside and outside of various Holdeman congregations in Kansas, Louisiana, Mississippi, and Oklahoma. These experiences in my early years have provided both an intimacy and a degree of distance in writing about the Holdeman people.

Although no longer a part of the Holdeman community, I have often returned in my internal musings to think of myself as an ethnic Mennonite, pondering how my views of war, government, and religion have been formed by these early experiences in a conservative rural culture. These sentiments are similar to what is eloquently expressed by Theodore Reik:[18]

---

[15]Momaday, "Revisiting," 118.
[16]Toews, *Problem*, 5.
[17]Loewen, *Diaspora*, x–xiv.
[18]Winland, "Quest," 113.

AUTHOR'S PREFACE

A man can prefer to be together with others and even avoid his own people: he can feel estranged from them — but he can never be a stranger to them. The very intimacy of the experience, which is nothing but common memories that have become unconscious excludes the possibility of cutting a tie that was formed, not alone by the same blood, but by the same rhythm of living.

The first real consciousness of my heritage came through a booklet from the 1970 Abraham Schmidt reunion that my mother gave to me.[19] There were fascinating references to places in Russia and the accounting of hazardous journeys to the United States in the 1870s. There was even a hand drawn map of a village in Russia called Leeleva that revealed the homes and surnames of many of the early settlers. From that point on, I was compelled to find out more but not recognizing or understanding the driving force behind my search. After many years of historical and genealogical research, I have concluded that this history is as much a part of me as the events that occur in my natural life. If I did not understand the events in Europe and the many encounters with government and religious authorities, the resulting gap would be very much like one who suffers from amnesia.

The People of the Prussian Villages

There is little published literature about the people of the Church of God in Christ, Mennonite. For many reasons, the Holdeman Mennonites do not write about themselves or the history of their origins in Prussia. These people had no reason to seek new knowledge and their spiritual needs were satisfied in the Bible and a few other texts such as the *Martyr's Mirror* by Thieleman Jansz Van Braght and *The Mirror of Truth* by John Holdeman. However, the many published genealogies do provide brief historical accounts that help in capturing a more complete view of the life of the Holdeman people.

Family names and specific individuals in the Prussian and Russian communities provide a means of following the movements of the conservative Mennonites. In Appendix One, we trace several families from the seventeenth century settlements in Prussia to Russia and finally to Lone Tree, located in McPherson County, Kansas. Through a series of connecting ancestor charts, the reader will see 400 years of an unbroken chain of kinship relationships.

Appendix Two clarifies the methodology for identifying people and, for the early settlers, locating them in the Przechowka communities. To identify specific members of these groups, I have used an abbreviation system for those who lived in Przechowka and who are listed in the *Church Records of the Old*

---

[19]Schmidt, et al., *History*.

AUTHOR'S PREFACE

Flemish or Groningen Mennonisten Societaet in Przechowko, West Prussia.[20] For those who are listed in this resource, I have combined their numeric ID with the three letter designation *prz*. A few examples will illustrate this convention. In Figure 17 of Appendix Two, we see Benjamin Wedel (b. 7 August 1766) with the designation *prz261*. Benjamin is listed on page 13 of the Przechowka Kirchen Buch with the note that he was elected minister on October 20, 1790. Cornels Jantz has the designation *prz528* and his wife Trincke Ratzlaff has the designation *prz160* (See Appendix Two, Figure 19). Trincke Unrau (Figure 18 of Appendix Two) has the designation *prz976*. If readers have a copy of the Przechowka church record, they can easily locate these people by using the PRZ designations. I also have occasion to refer to the Mennonites who made the long trek to south Russia and established the village of Alexanderwohl. For people who are referenced in the Alexanderwohl church book, I use an ALX designation.[21]

It is useful at times to cite genealogy records in the early periods to illustrate connections and clarify dates. To facilitate this process, I have developed an extensive database of Prussian, Russian, and Holdeman Mennonites – some 6200 individuals. Each person in this database is assigned a unique identification which designates his or her generation and the position in the family. This approach is explained in more detail in Appendix Two with examples.

Thoughts for the Reader

Underlying this work is the effort to describe and learn how a small, conservative group of Mennonites has changed over a broad expanse of time. The goal has not been to suggest that these people change their practices but rather to acknowledge and admire their adaptability and way of life while also informing an unfamiliar public that there are different ways of living in a chaotic world. As the title suggests, an overriding question relates to how this conservative group has followed the practices set out by the early Anabaptists. The doctrines of nonresistance and nonconformity have been used to shed light on this question. In addition, the voices that emerge from their own literature are used to understand their adherence to the less obvious practices such as the ban, foot washing, and voluntary membership in the church.

Yet these people and their way of life have stirred controversy regarding the responsibilities of citizenship. They adhere to the two kingdom doctrine, being in the world but not of the world.[22] As such they withdraw from

---

[20] Pankratz and Unruh, *Church Records*.
[21] Duerksen and Duerksen, *Church Book*.
[22] Perry Bush provides an excellent description of the two kingdom ethic and theology.

AUTHOR'S PREFACE

all worldly systems and ask God to deal with the evil in the world. In an editorial about citizenship in the *Messenger of Truth*, Brother Edwin Hughes clarifies the Holdeman doctrine — *We must totally and completely renounce our allegiance to this world and its prince, Satan.*[23] So, it is fair to ask how these conservative Mennonites interpret their citizenship role and how they give back to a society that grants them special privileges such as not having to serve in the military. Mennonite scholars and theologians have debated this issue and the last chapter will shed some light on this important question. In the end, it is hoped that the values that emerged from a small group of radicals in the sixteenth century can still have meaning in our modern culture.

In this final thought for the reader, I hope to capture the essence of this book. What I have written may not satisfy many of the potential readers. The text is not academic. As such, it lacks a theoretical framework. Others may find issue in how I have used genealogical resources to characterize this small, vibrant community of conservative Mennonites. Finally, the focus on culture and change in the modern world has taken me into political and social issues. However, I believe this book meets the call for a richer understanding of religion and falls into a category that Kniss has labeled crosscurrents — the study of a religious group that is often unseen or ignored in the mainstream of religious scholarship.[24]

Acknowledgement

This book is a synthesis of sources from historians, archivists, and Mennonite scholars who have studied Anabaptism and Mennonite history from many different perspectives. I first want to acknowledge two authors who have preceded me and who have provided much of the inspiration for this book. Abe J. Unruh's book, *The Helpless Poles*, is in many ways addressed to the Holdeman people and tells the story of hardships, drudgery and suffering of their forefathers. Clarence Hiebert's book, *The Holdeman People*, is based on his dissertation and describes the origins, evolution, and life of the Holdeman Mennonites. I am also grateful for my mother's candid portrayal of living in and out of the Holdeman community. Her insights and experiences helped me create a much richer picture of Holdeman life.

"Although sovereign over both, God endowed two orders, two kingdoms, for the ruling of human society. One sphere of activity was the world of secular activity and culture of all humans, to be ruled over by the state. The second kingdom was the church, the world of spiritual activity, mission, and discipline. In this kingdom, Christians carried out the divine mandates applicable only to themselves as citizens of this spiritual realm". See Bush, *Two Kingdoms*, 6.

[23]Hughes, "Citizenship," 4–5.
[24]Kniss, "Against," 351–66.

AUTHOR'S PREFACE

Several of the life stories related in this text are derived from genealogies. Two of the most notable family histories are the *J.A.R. Schmidt Family and Descendants* and *The Genealogy and History of Jacob H. and Carolina Nightingale Schmidt*. In addition, I want to thank Phyllis and Donald Krueger for sharing their Koehn and Schmidt family trees on the Ancestry website. Their research has been very useful in helping me fill in some of the gaps in the database of Holdeman people, briefly discussed in Appendix Two. For my research, two institutions were critical in supplying the resources that are essential for any scholarly endeavor — the Rutgers University Libraries and the Mennonite Library and Archives of North Newton, Kansas.

I am beholden to many who accepted my invitation to be an informal reader of the manuscript. My brother, Ray Jantz, offered many critical comments that helped me clarify the transitions of Prussia from a province in Royal Poland to the three partitions of the Polish-Lithuanian Commonwealth at the end of the eighteenth century. My colleague at Rutgers University Libraries, Grace Agnew, provided generous comments based on her deep knowledge of Russia. Dr. Jim Niessen, World History Librarian at Rutgers University Libraries, helped clarify the European history context in which the Mennonites suffered and, at times, prospered. I want to thank Dr. Mark Jantzen of Bethel College in Newton, Kansas for clarifying the origins of Swiss and Dutch Anabaptism. My older brother, Dr. Richard Jantz, anthropologist at the University of Tennessee, shared helpful insights on the origins of the Holdeman people in Kansas.

I cannot possibly acknowledge all those with whom I have corresponded over the past many years. Perhaps the best I can do is acknowledge the citizens of the rural communities in the Great Plains and specifically the town where I grew up – Halstead, Kansas. In this community, I enjoyed a freedom and informal relationship with many of the people whose ancestors lived the journey from Prussia to Russia and, at last, to America.

AUTHOR'S PREFACE

Ronald C. Jantz
Librarian Emeritus
Rutgers University
Spring, 2020

PART ONE

Introduction

HIS BOOK PORTRAYS THE LIVES of a small group of conservative Mennonites beginning in the Netherlands of the sixteenth century. The early Dutch Anabaptists and their descendants, the conservative Mennonites, represent a way of life that is, in a sense, an act of resistance against the predominant American way of being Christian.[1] In living a nonresistant faith and separating from the world, this committed group of people has confronted kings, bishops, and czars in order to preserve their way of life. Although they honor and obey worldly governments, as apostle Paul indicated (Phil. 3:20), their citizenship is in heaven. In striving to reestablish a primitive Christianity and live according to Christ's commandments, this unique culture conveys a message to modern society about humility, modesty, generosity, and peaceful living. In turn, they ask the people of the world to let them be Mennonite.

The European Experience

Part One provides the reader with a view of four hundred years of conservative Mennonite history, beginning in the sixteenth century in Holland with the Anabaptists and proceeding through Prussia and Russia, culminating in the mass migration of Russian Mennonites to America and the establishment of settlements in Kansas, Oklahoma, South Dakota, and Canada.

Stepping back from the details for a moment, we can see how these perpetual migrants adapted to quite different circumstances over 400 years. In the middle of the sixteenth century, the Dutch Anabaptists settled primarily in the northern provinces of the Netherlands, hoping to remain outside the reach of the Spanish Catholic authorities. Unfortunately, the persecution at

---

[1] Cornelius Dyck argues that in Dutch Anabaptism we have the sharpest rejection of historic Christianity experienced anywhere in both doctrine and practice. See Dyck, "Place of Tradition," 34–49.

the hands of Charles V and his son, Philip II, intensified, bringing death and imprisonment to many Dutch Mennonites. Seeking a land that would offer peace and prosperity, the Mennonites fled in large numbers to Royal Poland and the Vistula river delta. In the political and religious turmoil spawned by the Reformation, these migrants found a patchwork of jurisdictions in Poland and Prussia. Some authorities branded the Mennonites as heretics while many local Catholic bishops and Lutheran councils granted them permission to settle outside the cities and in the more rural areas in exchange for the economic benefits they provided.[2] In the 1700s, the hardy Mennonites worked to clear the swamplands along the Vistula using their Dutch knowledge of dikes and windmills. During much of the eighteenth century, they transformed a watery wasteland between the Vistula river and Danzig into productive farmlands.[3]

Although Poland experienced great territorial expansion during the Reformation, much of their land was lost in the partitions of 1772, 1773, and 1795 in which Danzig and Warsaw became part of Prussia and Volhynia was transferred to Russia.[4] After some seventy years, Mennonite disagreements with the Catholic authorities and the German kings resulted in a major exodus from Prussia to Russia in the late eighteenth and early nineteenth centuries. For a time in Russia, it appeared that these conservative Mennonites might have found a permanent home, however Czar Alexander II insisted that they must participate in the military. The Czar's edict resulted in the migration to America where they became pioneers, homesteading on the prairies of the Great Plains, speaking Plattdeutsch[5] and surviving the hardships of the dust bowl days and severe economic recession. Sam Schmidt helps us remember what it was like at the beginning in settling on the desolate Kansas prairies of the late nineteenth century.[6]

> Living in a two-room sod house, gathering cow chips, corn and sunflower stalks for kindling to cook with, farming with horses, milking cows and keeping chickens and ducks. Storing apples and potatoes in a specially prepared hole dug in the ground with a small opening; which was left to cover and uncover. Milk, butter and cream were kept cool by tying on a rope and letting them down into the well to the water.

---

[2] Klassen, *Mennonites in Early Modern Poland*, 6–11.
[3] Klassen, *Mennonites in Early Modern Poland*, 29–31.
[4] Krahn, "Poland," 199.
[5] Plattdeutsch is a West Germanic language spoken mainly in Northern Germany and the northeastern part of the Netherlands. The Mennonites who were descended from the Dutch of the sixteenth century carried Plattdeutsch to various communities in Canada and the Great Plains of the United States. There are many variant spellings including Plattdietsch and Plattdütsch. This text will use the German spelling of "Plattdeutsch". See https://en.wikipedia.org/wiki/Low_German#Outside_Europe_and_the_Mennonites.
[6] Schmidt and Caldwell, *Genealogy and History*, 172.

A modern writer experiencing the tall grass prairies of Kansas captures what must have been the emotional experience of these hardy Mennonite pioneers.[7]

> a wilderness of perfect solitude. There are no politics here, only peace; no sadness, only hope; no doubt, only certainty. Not a house, not a fence, not a single human sign, only you; alone at last and at one with everything.

In Part One, the first six chapters, we follow the Dutch Mennonites from northern Holland to Prussia and then to Russia. In these migrations, they encountered rulers and religious authorities and struggled with their own doctrines, splitting into Flemish, Frisian, and Old Flemish congregations. After nearly one hundred years in Russia, the most impoverished groups emigrated to America while the more prosperous Mennonites chose to stay in Russia. Unfortunately, the Russian Mennonites, the unfortunate souls who chose not to emigrate to America, ultimately experienced a great human tragedy in the years during and following World War I.

---

[7] Macgregor, "American Rhapsody," 22.

CHAPTER ONE

Emergence of the Anabaptists

LTHOUGH THIS WORK is an investigation and a story, it also represents an assertion about a small group of people — the Groningen Old Flemish whose descendants ultimately became through many twists and turns the Holdeman people of the Great Plains. The assertion is that these people have preserved the basic tenets of Anabaptism through four hundred years of turbulent history — a feat that is likely unique in religious cultural history. In many ways, the Holdeman people are the spiritual descendants of the early Anabaptists.

For much of their history, Mennonites have not been permitted to live their lives as they saw fit. For over three hundred years in Europe, this marginalized group lived on the fringes of established culture, outside the political system and beyond the protections of the early modern states. Most cities and states declared the Mennonites unwelcome as heretics. In urban areas, Mennonites, like Jews, remained alien non-citizens but were tolerated because of their economic contributions.[1] Throughout this period, Mennonites clung tenaciously to their core beliefs, among these the commitment to nonresistance and separation from the world.[2]

The sixteenth century was a time of creativity and change but also one of uncertainty and anxiety about what the future would bring. Policies governing religion were at the center of this cauldron of change. The Anabaptist movement was, in effect, a continuation of the Protestant Reformation by those who felt that Martin Luther and Ulrich Zwingli[3] did not go far enough. The Anabaptists sought the restoration of primitive Christianity and a

---

[1] Urry, *Mennonites*, 41.

[2] The doctrine of separation from the world is derived from several scriptural passages in the New Testament including 1 John 2:15 — *Love not the world, neither the things that are in the world. If any man love the world, the love of the Father is not in him.*

[3] Ulrich Zwingli, along with Luther and Calvin, was a leader of the Protestant Reformation and did not approve of general religious toleration, advocating instead for the creation of a state church. See Horsch, *Mennonites in Europe*, 3.

return to the Scriptures for guidance in everyday life.[4] However, Luther and Zwingli supported the state in which rulers did not tolerate dissent from the established church.

The Peace of Augsburg, signed between Protestant princes and the Holy Roman Emperor in 1555, bound subjects to follow their ruler's religion, resulting in renewed persecution of Mennonite groups. The Anabaptists or re-baptizers and other cursed sects were excluded from this religious peace and considered heretics.[5,6]

The religious movement known as Anabaptism was founded in 1525 by Conrad Grebel and Felix Manz in Zurich, Switzerland. In this city, a small group of earnest Christians responded to what they believed was a divine call to establish a community of believers who were committed to adult baptism as a confession of faith.[7] This radical departure from current religious practice met with bitter opposition from the Zurich Council who represented both the government and the clergy. The Anabaptists were considered heretics who had committed both civic and ecclesiastical crimes.

The early Anabaptists comprised a cultural melting pot of priests, monks, laymen, scholars, artisans, farmers, and peasants. This varied cast of religious radicals differed among themselves and there was no single identity or movement. They were neither Catholic nor Protestant and these outcasts soon found their beliefs and practices created enemies among the authorities.[8] The church and government powers did not distinguish between the varieties of Anabaptists - some peaceful, some insurrectionist, and some militant.[9] New laws were passed against the practice of adult baptism resulting in harsh punishments of the adherents — imprisonment, torture, and death.[10] To practice Anabaptism and re-baptize adults was considered blasphemy and the heretics were summarily given the death sentence.[11] However, laws do not always serve to change human behavior and the Anabaptist movement spread rapidly to Germany and Holland.

---

[4] The Anabaptists adhered to a theological doctrine that the Christian scriptures were the sole infallible source of authority for Christian faith and practice, frequently referred to as *sola scriptura*. See Weaver, *Becoming Anabaptist*, 51.

[5] Urry, *Mennonites*, 22.

[6] Neff, "Augsburg Confession," 187.

[7] Kauffman and Harder, *Anabaptists*, 19.

[8] Weaver, *Becoming Anabaptist*, 18.

[9] In the autumn of 1533, the fanatical sect of the Münsterite Anabaptists arose in the Netherlands. Much has been written about the Münsterites who advocated a violent and militant form of Anabaptism. As a result, the emerging peaceful group of Anabaptists were also labeled as revolutionaries and subject to drastic persecution measures. See Horsch, *Mennonites in Europe*, 218.

[10] Smith, *Story of the Mennonites*, 10–12.

[11] Krahn, *Dutch Anabaptism*, 165.

Anabaptism Defined

The Anabaptist movement can be thought of as one of the most significant and momentous events of Reformation times, holding promise in today's world as a model for a new type of Christian society. Mast writes with a poetic flair:

> *From the very beginning Anabaptism was experienced as an invasion of perception, whether as a shadow that provoked fear or a light that brought freedom. An event . . . that burst into the social landscape of early sixteenth century continental Europe as the dawning of a new day, the rising of "the morning star" and a leaving of "the shadows of this world."*[12]

In the view of sixteenth century church and state authorities, the Anabaptist movement was one of the most tragic in the history of Christianity. The early Anabaptists were highly political, agreeing to pay taxes but also denying the authorities the right to restrict religious practice.[13] Infant baptism, the use of carnal weapons, and the oath were all called into question. There is, however, reason to believe that many of the great principles that are so essential to democracy — freedom of conscience, separation of church and state, and voluntarism in religion — were ultimately derived from this sixteenth century movement.[14] The Anabaptists became advocates of the institutional separation of church and state and were alone among the sixteenth century reformers to break with the medieval structure of the the established church.[15]

The term "Anabaptist" (German: *Wiedertäufer*) originated in a Greek word meaning "rebaptizer". This label appeared in the early sixteenth century but was never used by the Anabaptists themselves since it was associated with criminal behavior by the religious authorities of the time.[16] Understanding the origins of Anabaptism is essential for us to understand the culture and practice of conservative Mennonites as they struggled to adapt to the policies of kings, nobles, and bishops of the church. The Waldensians, fifteenth century precursors to the Anabaptists, were outspoken critics of the established Church, stating that a church with secular power was an intolerable contradiction. However, many of the early scholars and critics such as Dante and Luther wanted to only remove the abuses rather than create a new type of Christianity. Luther merely reversed the Roman claim

---

[12] Biesecker-Mast, *Peristence*, 21.
[13] Klaassen, "Anabaptist Critique," 218–30.
[14] Bender, "Anabaptist Vision," 3–14.
[15] Estep, *Anabaptist Story*, 261.
[16] Clasen, *Anabaptism*, 12–13.

that the church should have primacy over the government, thereby retaining the symbiotic relationship between church and state. In contrast, Anabaptists recognized the importance of government but clearly distinguished its function from that of the church. "The church should not claim to exercise the functions of the state and the state should not seek to exercise the functions of the church".[17]

Although living in a world ruled by a Catholic prince, the early Anabaptists rebelled against the traditional sacraments. The bread and the wine of the Last Supper were ordinary foods with no special magic. Since God is everywhere, there was no need for sacred places. Sacred people, such as priests, and sacred holidays were no longer important since all the faithful worshipers and all days were considered equal. The sacraments were interpreted as visible symbols, not having any supernatural potence. The radicals risked life and limb in their commitment to a direct, spiritual communion with God.[18,19]

Figure 1: A Dutch Windmill

A look back some 400 years ago to the early Anabaptist radicals in Switzerland will help us understand how closely the beliefs of the modern Holdeman Mennonites resemble the foundational principles of Anabaptism. The Anabaptists of the sixteenth century envisioned a new form of society, a movement that began in 1525 and spread throughout Western Europe – Switzerland, Moravia, many parts of Germany, and the Netherlands. The early Anabaptists were totally decentralized, breaking into small and sometimes hostile groups who held different opinions on almost every subject.[20]

Early Leaders

The Anabaptists experienced much persecution involving torture and execution during the early and middle years of the sixteenth century. In the 1520s, Zurich, Switzerland was a hotbed of radicals whose ideas about infant baptism were perhaps the most disturbing to religious authorities. Two of the most important early leaders of Anabaptism in Switzerland were Conrad

---

[17]Klaassen, "Anabaptist Critique," 226.

[18]Driedger, *Mennonite Identity*, 13.

[19]Weaver, *Becoming Anabaptist*, 12.

[20]Clasen, *Anabaptism*, xii-xvii.

Grebel and Felix Manz. Grebel was the son of a wealthy iron merchant and had attended university. His friends and teachers considered him a young man of brilliant intellect, upright character and of great ability.[21,22] Manz was the son of a Zurich priest and was highly educated, conversant in Latin, Greek, and some Herbrew. These two rebels were uncompromising in piety and courage, possessing a relentless zeal common to all the radicals in Zurich.[23] The first Anabaptist congregation was formed on January 21, 1525 in which Conrad Grebel baptized an adult priest, Georg Blaurock.[24] From this event onward, Anabaptism spread quickly throughout Switzerland, south Germany, and somewhat later to the Netherlands. Shortly thereafter, *Wiedertäufer* and various other appelations began to be used by authorities. Conrad Grebel became a victim of the plague and died in August, 1526. Felix Manz was executed on January 5, 1527.[25]

Michael Sattler has been called by both admirers and critics the most significant of the first generation leaders of Anabaptism.[26] He is the only martyr from south Germany whose story has been taken up by the Dutch Mennonite Martyrologies.[27] Sattler, born in 1495 near Freiburg, Germany, was an early leader in the Anabaptist movement. He was a learned man who was familiar with the original languages of the Bible. Early in adult life, he entered the monastery of St. Peter near Freiburg, Germany but soon found the moral conditions disappointing and left the cloister in 1523, marrying soon thereafter.[28]

Roman Catholic authorities targeted Sattler for his seditious activities, imprisoning him for eleven weeks prior to his trial on May 17, 1527. During this period, he and fellow prisoners were treated with the utmost cruelty. In his trial, the judges debated Sattler's sentence for about an hour and thirty minutes and then read his sentence in the hushed silence of the courtroom:

> Between the representatives of his Imperial Majesty and Michael Sattler judgment is passed that Michael Sattler shall be delivered

---

[21] However, prior to his embrace of Anabaptism, Grebel's life and early years at the University of Vienna were spiritually and morally debilitating. His immoral relations with women and participation in drunken student brawls were scandalous. See Estep, *Anabaptist Story,* 32–33.

[22] Yoder, "Conrad Grebel," 132–46. This article provides an excellent description of Grebel's more mature years as a young adult, his educational pursuits, and his gradual embrace of Anabaptism.

[23] Clasen, *Anabaptism,* 3–7.

[24] Blaurock surpassed both Grebel and Manz in the extent and effectiveness of early Anabaptist ministry. He spread the faith for two and a half years before he was executed for heresy. Blaurock was burned at the stake on September 6, 1529. See Estep, *Anabaptist Story,* 49.

[25] Yoder, *Legacy,* 27.

[26] Yoder, *Legacy,* 10.

[27] Yoder, *Legacy,* 67.

[28] Bender, "Sattler, Michael," 427.

to the executioner, who shall firstly cut out his tongue; then throw him on a cart and with red hot tongs tear pieces out of his body twice, and on the way to the place of execution make use of the tongs five times more in like manner. Thereupon he shall burn his body to ashes as an arch heretic.[29]

Sattler did not lose his composure and prayed for the judges while enduring the inhuman torture stipulated in the sentence. Sattler's wife was drowned a few days later in the Neckar river.

Dutch Anabaptists and Martyrs

As the reformation stirred the religious feelings of the Dutch people, the religious and state authorities intensified the persecution of the Anabaptists and the emerging Mennonite groups. The *Martyrs Mirror*, first published in 1660, remains today a popular book found in conservative Mennonite homes. The author, Thieleman Jansz Van Braght, has recorded some 1500 martyr accounts of which about half are Dutch.[30] In this cherished text, we can find evidence of Mennonite family names and how the early Anabaptist adherents resisted authorities in order to remain faithful to their convictions. Because of these faith commitments, the Anabaptists frequently ran afoul of the religious authorities, resulting in punishment for various infractions. The following accounts taken from the *Martyrs Mirror* will give the reader some insight into the religious persecutions that were pervasive in a sixteenth century Holland that was ruled by a Catholic king.[31]

In 1534, William Wiggers was brought to the Schagen castle in North Holland where he was imprisoned for eight days and then beheaded for his faith.[32] Another account tells of Pieter Jans and five others who were burned alive at the stake on March 20, 1549.[33] This punishment resulted from being rebaptized by Giles Aix-la-Chapelle and having joined the forbidden sect of the Anabaptists. The sentence reveals how the Anabaptists persisted, according to the authorities, in their pernicious views with regard to the sacraments of the holy church. The sentence as it was transcribed from the book of sentences of the city of Amsterdam reads as follows: "... *condemn said persons to be burnt by the executioner; and furthermore declare all their property confiscated for the benefit of his Imperial Majesty* ...".

In addition to the conventional methods of execution including beheading and burning at the stake, Dutch magistrates devised some of the most perverse

---

[29] Horsch, *Mennonites in Europe*, 72–77.
[30] Hiebert, *Holdeman People*, 24.
[31] Van Braght, *Martyrs Mirror*, 483.
[32] Van Braght, *Martyrs Mirror*, 442.
[33] Van Braght, *Martyrs Mirror*, 483.

schemes to intimidate Mennonites and prolong the agony. The martyrdom of Jan Smit is one example (Figure 2).[34] In 1572, Smit was taken prisoner in Amsterdam for his refusal to row in a boat on the Zuyder Zee since he did not want to be associated with military actions and he had no enemies. While in prison, he was examined and found to be of the Mennonistic religion. For this crime, he was sentenced to be suspended by one leg to the gallows until death ensued.[35,36]

In yet another account taken from the book of criminal sentences of the city of Amsterdam, we see how the Anabaptists refused to recant in order to escape persecution.

> In March of 1549, two brothers devised a scheme to free their friends from one of the dungeons in the city of Amsterdam. They knew the time had come for the execution of their friends, who were Anabaptists and members of the accursed Mennonite sect. Using the tools of their trade as sailors, they took a boat hook and crowbar, scaled the walls of the prison, smashed a window and began visiting each cell. Many were freed that night but one prisoner, Ellert Jans, refused the brothers' help since he had decided that his life had reached a zenith and he could reach no higher plateaus of happiness if he were to continue living. Subsequently on March 20, 1549, Ellert Jans was burned at the stake with seven other Anabaptists, all who had refused to recant. Pieter Jans and Gijsbert Jans were among this group as well as two women.

Jan Claesz was baptized by Menno Simons and beheaded for his faith on January 19, 1544. In a heartrending last message, Claesz writes to his children, Claes Jansz and Geertge Jansz, in which we see the emphasis of the Anabaptists to separate from the world. "Oh, look not to the multitude or the old custom, but to the little flock which is persecuted for the word of the Lord; . . . My dear children, surrender yourself to that which is good, and the Lord will give you understanding in all things."[37,38]

What the reader will find surprising is the role of women in the early Anabaptist movement, a position that seems contrary to apostle Paul's commandment (1 Cor. 14:34–35 — *Women should be silent in the churches. For they are not permitted to speak, but should be subordinate, as the law also*

---

[34] The *Martyrs Mirror* was first published in the Dutch language in 1660. The first English edition was published in 1837 and the book is in the public domain, available on the Internet Archive - https://archive.org/details/MartyrsMirror/mode/2up.
[35] Van Braght, *Martyrs Mirror*, 962–63.
[36] Zijpp, "Jan Smit (d. 1572)," para. 1.
[37] Van Braght, *Martyrs Mirror*, 468–69.
[38] Krahn, *Dutch Anabaptism*, 201–02.

says. *If there is anything they desire to know, let them ask their husbands at home. For it is shameful for a woman to speak in church.*) Anabaptist women seemed to enjoy more freedom of choice and expression than was the norm in the sixteenth century Netherlands. Only a few of their contributrions and stories have been told. Anna Jansz, one of the better known Anabaptist women, was drowned by the authorities on January 24, 1539 in Rotterdam.[39,40] In her short life, she composed a popular song entitled "I Have Heard the Trumpet Sounding" and left a poignant letter to her son Isaiah with these courageous words:[41]

> But if you hear of the existence of a poor, lowly, cast-out little company, that has been despised and rejected by the World, go join it. . . Do not fear people, forsake your life rather than depart from the Truth.

Although to us in the twenty-first century, these accounts from the *Martyrs Mirror* describe sentences uncomprehendingly harsh for the crime committed, these acts were unfortunately repeated many times against the Mennonites of Holland who were accused of being unbelievers and committing crimes against the holy sacraments. Gradually throughout the sixteenth century, the Mennonites were either driven underground or they moved to the

Figure 2: The Martyrdom of Jan Smit

northern regions of Holland which were out of reach of the Roman Catholic authorities. Throughout this period, life became very difficult for the Mennonites. To be a believer in adult baptism automatically implied a death sentence. To continue practicing their faith, Mennonite groups met in rural areas to hold their church services and to escape the notice of the authorities.

---

[39] Van Braght, *Martyrs Mirror*, 453.
[40] Joldersma and Grijp, *Elizabeth's Manly Courage*, 14–15.
[41] Joldersma and Grijp, *Elizabeth's Manly Courage*, 67.

The Schleitheim Confession

Michael Sattler presented the seven articles of a confession of faith to a conference on February 24, 1527. This presentation became known as the *Schleitheim Confession* and where we see the first formal expression of the core principles of Anabaptism.[42] The Schleitheim articles are Anabaptism's oldest confessional document and it is profoundly interesting that this document says nothing about God and Jesus Christ. The Confession deals only with those issues in which Anabaptism and the Reformation differ and it focuses primarily on relationships with the church and state.[43] The Schleitheim articles are summarized below:

> **adult baptism** *(Baptism shall be administered to all who have been instructed and give evidence of repentance and a change of life . . .)*;
>
> **all who partake of one bread** *(. . . shall be those who have been united by baptism)*;
>
> **administering the ban** *(Discipline and expulsion shall be used toward those who have surrendered their lives to the Lord . . . and yet stumble and fall into sin or are unexpectedly overtaken)*;
>
> **separation from the world and nonresistance** *(Separation is needful from all evil and wickedness which Satan has planted in the world. This includes abstinence from all use of the un-Christian, yea, Satanic weapons of violence)*;
>
> **participation in government** *(The civil government is an institution outside the perfection of God . . . In the Church of Christ no other means of correction are used than discipline through admonition and expulsion of him who has sinned)*;
>
> **a shared ministry** *(Ministers shall have the qualifications mentioned by the Apostle Paul)*;
>
> **oaths** *(Christ, the perfect teacher, forbade His disciples all oaths,*

---

[42] Michael Sattler is credited with being the principal author of the articles of the *Schleitheim Confession*. His work has been confirmed by comparing the text with other writings which are known to be by Sattler. See Baylor, *Radical Reformation*, 172. Footnote no. 1.

[43] Blanke, "Anabaptism and the Reformation," 65.

whether true or false).[44]

The Varieties of Anabaptism

Ultimately, the reforms triggered by Zwingli and the Anabaptists in Switzerland and south Germany were carried by various advocates and publications to the Netherlands.[45] The *Schleitheim Confession* did have impact on the Dutch Anabaptist movement. We know that there was much contact between the southern and northern Anabaptists. Krahn indicates that the early writings of the Swiss and South German Anabaptists were in use in the Low Countries. Similarly, the writings of the Low Countries had great influence in the South.[46]

Certainly, the Anabaptist vision throughout the years has been one that embraced a willingness to "be in conflict with the powers that be." Grimsrud summarizes the key characteristics that have remained constant over hundreds of years including the refusal to participate in war, rejection of infant baptism, and a deep suspicion toward government and state power dynamics.[47] These same characteristics appear in a demographic study of the larger group of Mennonites by Leo Driedger and Howard Kauffman. In their "Anabaptism Scale", these researchers report on the original Anabaptist beliefs that are still held by Mennonites today in rural, village, and town communities. Across these categories, roughly 75 percent of the respondents agreed to the following statements: baptism is not proper for children, Christians should not take part in war, and Christians cannot in good conscience perform some tasks of government.[48]

The *Schleitheim Confession* focused on the differences between Anabaptism and the established churches. The objective of these early radicals was the restoration of the true apostolic church, establishing a genuine practice of the discipleship of Christ and separation from the world. In subsequent centuries, the varying social, economic, and political environments led to differences of interpretation in both doctrine and practice.[49] Of the Dutch Anabaptists, the Groningen Old Flemish adhered to the more conservative practices, observing the washing of feet and the shunning of excommunicated members.

---

[44] Horsch, *Mennonites in Europe*, 72–73.
[45] Hiebert, *Holdeman People*, 18.
[46] Krahn, *Dutch Anabaptism*, 253.
[47] Grimsrud, "Anabaptism," 371–90.
[48] Driedger and Kauffman, "Urbanization," 285.
[49] Krahn, *Dutch Anabaptism*, 258–59.

There were, of course, significant theological differences which will be left to other scholars to explore.[50] We turn now to Menno Simons, the former Dutch priest who became an evangelist and dedicated his life to the creation of a new religion.

---

[50]For example, one major theological difference dealt with how Christ received his flesh through Mary. The Swiss and South German Anabaptists did not accept the celestial-flesh Christology held by Menno Simons and Dirk Philips. See Weaver, *Becoming Anabaptist*, 155.

CHAPTER TWO

Menno Simons — The Former Priest

S ANABAPTISM SPREAD from Germany into the Netherlands, the hope for a reformation of the church was widely entertained by priests and even the regent of the Netherlands, Mary of Burgundy. Menno Simons[1] (Figure 3) was one of the priests who began to have serious doubts about the daily Mass. Although he confessed the doubts to another priest, Menno found that these troubling thoughts persisted.

Menno Simons was instrumental not only in the establishment of the early church, but also in the formation of the Mennonite religion. His early years are interesting and perhaps not known to all readers. Menno was born in 1496 to a Dutch family living in Witmarsum, a province in Friesland in the far northwest part of the European continent (Map 1). Quite early, his parents decided to consecrate Menno to the service of the Catholic Church. Menno devoted long years to the excercises required of a monk and the theological study to become a priest. Through this work, he was able to read and write Latin and read Greek. The fact that Menno spent many years educating himself in preparation for the priesthood suggests that his family was financially well off.[2]

Like the typical village priest, Menno did not take his office or his life very seriously. He had an easy going life, as he later confessed, indulging regularly in "card playing, drinking, and all manner of frivolous diversions".[3] After he was ordained, it was several years before he began to seriously read the Bible. His first jolt came after reading about how the bread and wine were actually transformed into the body and blood of Christ. He rejected this interpretation, having convinced himself that the sacrament had only symbolic meaning. Upon further study, he could not find any scriptural

---

[1] The image is in the public domain and available for commercial use. See https://commons.wikimedia.org/wiki/Menno_Simons.

[2] Horsch, *Mennonites in Europe*, 186–87.

[3] Horsch, *Mennonites in Europe*, 185.

support for infant baptism.⁴ It was this self-education that led him to lay down his office in 1536 as a priest and join a small group of evangelical brethren known as the Anabaptists.⁵

Menno was well aware that deviation from Roman Catholic religious practices would result in swift punishment from the government and religious authorities. In following this new movement aligned with the Dutch Anabaptists, Menno became a hunted man in 1542 when Emperor Charles V (Figure 4) issued an imperial edict, offering one hundred guilders — a priest's annual salary, for Menno's apprehension.⁶ Thus, Menno began his new life as an outlaw and fugitive, taking refuge in homes and congregating in wilderness areas. Gradually, a small dedicated group of peaceful Anabaptists emerged under Menno's direction and soon became known as Menists or later as Mennonites.

Figure 3: Menno Simons

As an Anabaptist leader, Menno had a difficult life. Although he was apparently married to a woman named Gertrude, he did not have a permanent residence and referred to himself as homeless. He was relentlessly pursued by the Catholic authorities as is evident in a letter dated May 19, 1541 from provincial authorities to Mary, the regent of the Netherlands regarding Menno's activities in Friesland:

> . . . this sect would doubtless remain extirpated, were it not that a former priest Menno Symonsz who is one of the principal leaders of aforesaid sect and about three or four years ago became fugitive, has roved about since that time . . . and has misled many simple and innocent people. To seize and apprehend this man, we have offered a large sum of money, but until now with no success.⁷

The letter continues by suggesting that they might offer a pardon if those who have been misled would assist in bringing about the imprisonment of Menno.

In these formative years, Menno gradually turned to the Sacramentist view which holds that the Lord's Supper is symbolic. He found help in this view from the writings of Luther and took solace in Luther's view that

---

⁴Krahn, *Dutch Anabaptism*, 171–72.
⁵Bender, *Menno Simons*, 1–2.
⁶Epp, *Mennonites in Canada*, 34.
⁷As quoted in Bender, *Menno Simons*, 26.

Map 1: The Sketch of the Netherlands shows Witmarsum in Friesland, the birthplace of Menno Simons, and Groningen, the home of the Groningen Old Flemish Society in the Seventeenth Century (map by the author).

violations of Catholic tradition cannot lead to eternal death if founded on a Biblical basis.[8] Melchior Hofmann, another religious sojourner and lay preacher, also espoused the Sacramentist view of the Lord's Supper.[9,10] Hofmann traveled extensively and came into contact with the Anabaptists in Strasbourg where he was baptized by one of the Swiss Brethren. Hofmann and his followers helped transfer Anabaptism from Switzerland to Dutch lands. Thus, Menno Simons became the intellectual beneficiary of the Swiss Anabaptist movement[11]

Dirk Philips was a leading Dutch theologian and one who worked closely with Menno Simons in helping guide the church in the early years and establish faith communities in Prussia. Menno and Dirk landed in Danzig in 1548 and had to take up lodging in nearby Schottland because Mennonites were still not tolerated in the city.[12] Dirk was a tireless worker, preaching and baptizing in Danzig and strongly advocating for two doctrines that remain popular for conservative Mennonites today — avoidance[13] and foot washing.[14,15]

Figure 4: Holy Roman Emperor Charles V

After seven years in Holland, Menno left for northwest Germany where the edicts of the Holy Roman Emperor were not in force. During his last years, Menno was crippled and some portraits show him with crutches. He had at least two daughters and one son named Jan. Menno's wife, Gertrude, preceded him in death. In 1554, the nobleman Bartholomew von Ahlefeldt offered Menno permanent residence in a village near Oldesloe which is a few miles southwest of Lubeck, Germany. It was here that Menno finally enjoyed a measure of physical safety and stability, passing away on January 31, 1561.

---

[8] Krahn, "Menno Simons," 577–78.

[9] Through his evangelistic mission from 1530 to his imprisonment in May, 1533, Hofmann had an overwhelming influence on Dutch Anabaptism and the views of Menno Simons. See Snyder, *Anabaptist History*, 209.

[10] Sacramentist was a designation used in the Netherlands for those who did not believe in the efficacy of the sacraments of the Roman Catholic Church. See Zijpp, "Sacramentists," 398–99.

[11] Weaver, *Becoming Anabaptist*, 111.

[12] Horsch, *Mennonites in Europe*, 229.

[13] The term "avoidance" refers to the practice of having no fellowship with excommunicated members. See 1 Cor. 5:11 which instructs Christians "not to eat" and "not to keep company" with the sinners. See also Wenger, "Avoidance," 200.

[14] Zijpp, "Dirk Philips," 65.

[15] Smith, *Story*, 102–03.

Menno was buried in his own garden however, due to the destruction of the Thirty Years' War, the exact location of the grave is not known.[16,17]

In the late sixteenth and early seventeenth centuries, the Dutch Anabaptists and their compatriots in Prussia established more formal congregations based on different theological and doctrinal perspectives. From these efforts, a most conservative group known as the Groningen Old Flemish originated in the northeast provinces of the Netherlands.

The Groningen Old Flemish

As Emperor of the Holy Roman Empire (1519-1556), Charles V had the responsibility to protect the Catholic Church and his influence extended over much of Europe including the Netherlands and Germany.[18] The shaded area of Map 3 illustrates the vast geographic extent of the Holy Roman Empire.[19] In the Netherlands of the sixteenth century, Mennonite refugees were forced from their homes by Catholic persecution, war, and citizen intolerance and they began to look for homes where they could practice their faith openly. Royal Poland and the city-state of Danzig offered communities of relative tolerance and Mennonites established settlements along the Vistula river, lands that were, at the time, part of Royal Prussia and under the jurisdiction of the Polish crown.[20]

The early Dutch Mennonites were actively involved in their church and communities. There was much Mennonite activity during the sixteenth century in and around the city of Groningen in the northeastern part of the Netherlands (Map 1). In the late sixteenth century, the churches in Holland had organized into three groups — the Waterlanders, Frisians, and Flemish. Of the three groups, the Waterlanders were most liberal, accepting those banned by other Mennonite groups and not requiring re-baptism when transferring from one of these groups.[21]

There was much discord among these groups, frequently having more to do with minor issues of human conduct rather than the more substantive

---

[16] Weaver, *Becoming Anabaptist*, 150.

[17] Krahn, "Menno Simons," 582.

[18] The image is in the public domain and available for commercial use. See https://commons.wikimedia.org/wiki/File:Emperor_charles_v.png.

[19] Permission to use this map image has been granted by the Brigham Young University Copyright Licensing Office. See https://contentdm.lib.byu.edu/digital/collection/Civilization/id/537/.

[20] Royal Prussia remained a part of the Kingdom of Poland until the first partition of Poland in 1772. West Prussia was established as a province of the Kingdom of Prussia in 1773 and was noted for its ethnic and religious diversity due to immigration and the presence of many different cultures. See Wikipedia at https://en.wikipedia.org/wiki/West_Prussia.

[21] Weaver, *Becoming Anabaptist*, 154–55.

theological differences. These internal divisions having to do with dress, customs, and the ban[22] lead to what has been called the Anabaptist sickness (German: *Täuferkrankheit*).[23] In the turmoil of persecution and migration of the early seventeenth century, these Mennonites of different perspectives began forming diverse congregational communities.[24] About 1630, when most of the Flemish and Old Flemish congregations united, the Mennonite churches in Groningen, the Netherlands did not join this union, forming the Groningen Old Flemish Society.[25,26]

The Groningen Old Flemish Society of northern Holland was the most determined of the Dutch Mennonites to hold on to the Anabaptist principles and the doctrines articulated by Menno Simons and Dirk Philips. This group insisted on plain living, applied the ban rigorously to fallen-away members, and kept their meeting houses simple with no religious symbols or organs. Any member of another Mennonite congregation wishing to join the Old Flemish had to be re-baptized.[27] The twentieth century descendants of the Groningen Old Flemish, many of whom are Holdeman Mennonites, found these doctrines expressed clearly in the writings of John Holdeman.

After 1632, the Groningen Old Flemish existed as an independent group and Dutch ministers began making forays into the Mennonite communities of the Vistula delta.[28] These visits resulted in three of the Prussian congregations joining the Groningen Old Flemish Society — Jeziorka (*Kleinsee*), Schönsee, and Przechowka (*Wintersdorf*).[29] The Groningen Old Flemish congregations had excellent leaders such as Arent Jans, Derk Alles, and his son Alle Derks.[30]

---

[22]The ban was an instrument of church discipline which was used to exclude a member from the congregation and is derived from Matt: 18:15-17. The ban or excommunication is considered one of the most important doctrines in the Gospel in order to insure the purity of the church and is still actively used by the Church of God in Christ, Mennonite. See Holdeman, *Mirror of Truth*, 476.
[23]Epp, *Mennonites in Canada*, 38–39.
[24]Urry, *Mennonites*, 28.
[25]Zijpp, "Groningen," 590.
[26]The term "Flemish" originated with Mennonites fleeing persecution in Belgium and Flanders and taking up refuge in northern Holland. However, the term evolved to not have any geographic meaning but rather was associated with those Mennonites typically living in Groningen whereas the term "Frisian" referred to those who had a majority in Friesland. See Neff, "Flemish Mennonites," 337–38.
[27]Zijpp, "Groningen Old Flemish Mennonites," 595–96.
[28]Hiebert, *Holdeman People*, 40.
[29]Boese, "The Andre Kant," (part of Introduction, no page number.)
[30]Zijpp, "Groningen," 593.

The Life and People of Przechowka

Przechowka (German: *Wintersdorf*) was a royal village which originated in the year 1540. It is located about 65 miles south of Danzig which today is the modern port city of Gdańsk in Poland (Map 2). The estate of Przechowka was originally sold to five Mennonites from the Netherlands by the heirs of a Polish nobleman. The Przechowka community is a very important one for many of the Mennonites who later emigrated to Russia and then to America.

Three Mennonite congregations, Przechowka, Jeziorka, and Schönsee, became the only Prussian churches to join with the Old Flemish Mennonite Society of Groningen.[31,32] The land leases of 1727 and 1767 granted freedom of religion, however these Mennonite groups were frequently at odds with the Bishop of Kulm and other Catholic authorities. In 1727, thirteen Mennonites of Dutch origin moved from Przechowka to Jeziorka (German: *Kleinsee*) and began to cultivate the land that had been destroyed by soldiers.[33] The 1776 census for Jeziorka lists nineteen Mennonite families with the following surnames: Becker, Buller, Jantzen, Koehn, Nachtigal, Ratzlaff, Schmidt, Unrau, and Voht.[34,35]

The Groningen Old Flemish communities in Prussia — Przechowka, Jeziorka, and Schönsee — were most conservative and followed the basic principles set forth by the founders of Anabaptism in the sixteenth century. In their journeys across Europe, the Groningen Old Flemish separated themselves from society and worked primarily as farmers or day laborers. The religious roots of the Church of God in Christ, Mennonite are founded in the Groningen Old Flemish Society and many of their beliefs are very similar to those of the Old Flemish. In their practices, the Old Flemish Mennonites performed foot washing, rejected offerings during sermons, did not offer salaries to their ministers, banned organs from their churches and, in general, stood for plain living and simplicity in clothes.

The industrious Mennonites were welcome in Prussia where much help was needed to drain the swampy lands along the Vistula river (German: *Weichsel*). However, the Dutch Mennonites who emigrated to Prussia struggled with land reclamation and with the religious authorities, both Lutheran and Catholic.

---

[31] Hiebert, *Holdeman People*, 40–44.

[32] In note no.77, Hiebert identifies a handwritten 185 year-old church record book that identifies the ancestral families of the Gröningen Old Flemish group: "Die Erste stamm Nahmen Unserer Bisher so genannte Oude Vlamingen oder Groningersche Mennonitisten Societaets alhier in Preusen." See Hiebert, *Holdeman People*, 53.

[33] Zijpp, "Jeziorka," 110.

[34] Zijpp and Thiessen, "Jeziorka," para. 3.

[35] Readers might want to glance at Table 1 in Appendix Two to view the frequency of surnames in twentieth century Holdeman communities, showing a strong correlation with the surnames of eighteenth century Mennonite communities.

Map 2: The Congregations of the Groningen Old Flemish in Prussia (Przechowka, Jeziorka, and Schönsee) Superimposed on Modern State Boundaries (map by the author.)

Although they had escaped the persecution of the Spanish government in Holland, they did not achieve the full religious freedom they were seeking in Prussia. King Frederick William II (1786-1797) of Prussia was a benevolent ruler who was generally supportive of the Mennonite population, recognizing that they were hard working and contributed much to the economy. However he was also concerned about too much land passing into Mennonite hands and complaints from non-Mennonite citizens that the Mennonites were becoming too prosperous. To control this situation, he ordered the Prussian churches to record the statistics of their congregations, certainly not realizing at the time that his mandate would prove beneficial to future historians and genealogists. The census revealed a Mennonite population of 13,069 and land holdings of 2038 Hufen, about 83,000 acres.[36] In order to comply, Jacob Wedel, an elder of the Przechowka Mennonite Church, wrote the Przechowka Kirchen Buch. The translated version of this book *Church Records of the Old Flemish or Groeningen Mennonisten Societaet in Przechowko, West Prussia* is a tremendously beneficial record since it identifies almost all the common surnames that were found in these Dutch-Prussian settlements.[37]

Schönsee, a Mennonite village on the right bank of the Vistula (Map 2), was the home of two congregations — one associated with the Flemish and the other with the Frisians. Sometimes for many weeks, members of the Schönsee congregations could not cross the river to worship in the Przechowka church because of floods.[38] To solve this problem, a little church was built early in the eighteenth century on the right bank of the Vistula river. The drawing (Figure 5) depicts the church in Schönsee in which the settlers worshiped. The drawing is by Sylvia Duerksen based on a photograph by H. Wiebe.[39] The following Mennonite names were listed as residents in the Schönsee land leases of 1695 — Buller, Jantz, Koehn, Nachtigal, Nichol, Penner, Unruh, and Voth.[40]

Figure 5: Schönsee Old Flemish Church

In Przechowka and neighboring villages, the land was not good for cultivating, being frequently flooded by the Vistula river. The Mennonite settlers raised some rye and barley, however much of their efforts were spent in dairy

---

[36] Jantzen, *Mennonite German Soldiers*, 32.
[37] Pankratz and Unruh, *Church History*, 1–60.
[38] Duerksen, "Przechowka and Alexanderwohl," 78.
[39] Duerksen, "Przechowka and Alexanderwohl," 82.
[40] Zijpp, "Schönsee," 475.

farming and producing dairy products such as cheese and butter. They also had their hands full trying to fight back the periodic floods from the Vistula. In spite of these hardships, they continued to prosper and became the targets of their not-so-friendly non-Mennonite neighbors. These residents, wary of immigrants speaking Dutch and practicing a strange religion, became jealous of their prosperity and frequently lodged complaints with local officials.[41]

Dutch Origins and Ethnic Bonds

In the eighteenth century of Prussia, conservative religious practices, persecution from government authorities, and the rural, agrarian farm life produced a close-knit group of Dutch settlers. The Dutch-Prussian Mennonites of the Przechowka communities were tied together by both ethnic and family bonds.

In these early years, Plattdeutsch was the language of conversation for the Mennonites and the Dutch language was used in church services.[42] After the emigration to Prussia, the high German language began to gradually replace Dutch in church services. However remnants of the Dutch language remained well into the nineteenth century, with some Dutch bibles being carried to Russia and even to America in the great migration of the 1870s.

In the sixteenth and seventeenth century, the most common Dutch naming convention was based on the father's name, referred to as patronymics. Typically, the patronymic was formed by adding -sz, -szoon, or -szen to the father's first name. These customs are evident in the communities of conservative Mennonites. Dirksz (sometimes spelled Dirks) is a typical Mennonite name meaning son of Dirk. Also we can see this pattern in the name of the founder of the Mennonite religion. Menno Simons or Simonsz is the "son of Simon".

A quote from Clarence Hiebert's book *The Holdeman People* illustrates how closely Holdeman family names are tied to the Dutch.[43] Hiebert states:

> Sixty-five to 75 percent of those who ultimately became a part of the Holdeman faction came predominantly from the two originally Dutch groups – the Ostroger Mennonites who migrated to Kansas in 1874 from Volhynia in central (Polish) Russia, and the Kleine Gemeinde Mennonites who migrated to Manitoba from south Russia in 1874 and 1875.

---

[41]Unruh, *Helpless Poles*, 33.

[42]The generic term "Low German" refers to several dialects used by the Prussian and Russian Mennonites. The Plattdeutsch spoken by the Ostrogers was known as the "Polish" type in contrast to the dialect of the south Russian Mennonites (see Hiebert, *Holdeman People*, 149). These dialects are not to be confused with those of the Swiss and Pennsylvania Germans that are spoken by the Amish. See Nolt and Meyers, *Plain Diversity*, 58–60.

[43]Hiebert, *Holdeman People*, 36.

Tracing Family Names

Kinship and marriage relatioships demonstrate how a few family names have remained clustered together over a period of several centuries.[44] Although the Groningen Old Flemish followed many divergent paths in seeking religious freedom, this small set of surnames can be found in Przechowka, in the Russian settlements of Karolswalde, and in Holdeman communities of the Great Plains (see Table 1 in Appendix Two - page 160). The family names of Koehn (Köhn, Koen, Kuehn), Jantz (Jansz, Janz, Johnson), Schmidt (Schmid, Smit, Smith) and Unruh (Unrau, Onrouw) were widespread in the Prussian Mennonite settlements, appearing in the Danzig church records of 1568 and in the Church Records of the Old Flemish Society. These family names are found in the Prussian and Russian settlements and in groups traveling together on ships bound for the United States. In some cases, specific unbroken genealogical lineages over some three hundred years can be demonstrated (See Appendix One). The following vignettes introduce a sampling of these early settlers with explanations of how surnames were formed.

In July, 1719 elder Hendrik Berents Hulshof of the Groningen Old Flemish visited the Przechowka congregations, providing both spiritual and practical advice. He cautioned against the wiles of authorities by preaching from Eph. 6:11–13: *For our struggle is not against enemies of blood and flesh, but against the rulers, against the authorities, against the cosmic powers of this present darkness, against the spiritual forces of evil in the heavenly places.* Hulshoff also officiated over baptisms and recorded in his extant diary that there were fifty-seven adult members of the congregation in Przechowka.[45] In these emerging communities, there were a small number of family names that were dominant. The frequency and diversity of surnames provide insight into village life and an understanding of group cohesion in the Prussian settlements while also enabling us to trace migrations of these groups from Prussia to Russia and then to America. Francis reports that there are only about two hundred and seventy family names found among the Russian Mennonites and at one point forty names accounted for 60 percent of the whole group.[46]

The Jantz name was one of the most widespread Mennonite family names of Dutch-Prussian background.[47] The many variations of the name Jantz can all be traced to a common origin. Jan was a very popular Dutch name

---

[44] The database of some 6200 people has been developed by consulting many genealogies that have been published by members of the Holdeman church. In addition, the Holdeman publication *Messenger of Truth* has been used to further develop the database with more recent demographic data.

[45] Crous, "Przechovka," 225.

[46] Francis, "Russian Mennonites," 105.

[47] Krahn, "Janzen," 95.

similar to John or to the German Johann. To this name an ending such as -sz or -szoon was added to indicate that the person was the son of Jan. This convention is evident in the story of Jan Claesz who wrote a poignant letter to his children, Claes Jansz and Geertge Jansz, prior to his beheading in 1544 (see page 23).

Arent Jansz was born in Groningen, the Netherlands on May 28, 1610 and he was appointed an elder in the Groningen Old Flemish congregation. Arent was a wealthy merchant, active in religious affairs, and one of the founders of the Groningen Old Flemish congregation. In its early days, Jansz' community was referred to as *Arent Jansgemeente* (the Arent Jantz congregation). His father, Jan Arents was a preacher in the Flemish congregation and he attended the debate at Middlestum in 1628 on whether the Old Flemish Mennonites should be united with other Mennonite communities.[48]

Less frequently, we find names that are based on occupations. Smit (Schmidt, Smith) is named after one who creates useful items such as tableware and jewelry out of various metals. In 1572, Jan Smit was martyred for his Mennonite beliefs in Amsterdam (Figure 2). The first records of the Schmidt (Schmid, Smit) name can be dated back to 1586 in Prussia. Because of severe persecution in Moravia, now part of the Czech Republic, the Schmidt and Schellenberger families emigrated in 1640 to Przechowka in Prussia.[49] It is thought that the first bearer of the Schmidt name, likely a master smith, fled Moravia to Hungary and then to Przechowka.[50] The Przechowka Kirchen Buch lists 107 Schmidts with the earliest birth date being that of Ehrenst Schmidt (*prz790*), born 21 May 1699.

Of course there are oddities that we don't yet fully understand. One of the most popular conservative Mennonite names is Koehn which has many variants (Köhn, Könn, Koen, Kuehn, Kien, Kane, Kahn) and was first recorded in Danzig church records in 1681.[51] One possibility is that this name was derived from the Hebrew word kohen, which means priest. There are 45 Koehns listed in the Przechowka Kirchen Buch. Willem Köhn is the earliest of this family for which there are dates, born in 1702 and identified as *prz589* in the Kirchen Buch.

Similarly, there are many variants of the family name Unruh including Unrau and Onrouw. There is some speculation that the origin of the name is based on the German *unruhig*, meaning restless and may have been first used as a nickname. Herbert Wiebe found the Unruh name recorded first in 1568 in the communities of Przechowka, Jeziorka, and Schönsee. Abram Unruh was a minister in the Przechowka congregation of the early eighteenth

---

[48]Zijpp, "Jans(z), Arent," 93.
[49]Duerksen. "Przechowka and Alexanderwohl," 80.
[50]Schmidt, "Schmidt," 465.
[51]Krahn, "Koehn," 211.

century and Heinrich Unruh (likely *prz968* in the Przechowka Kirchen Buch) served the Brenkenhoffswalde congregation from 1782–88.[52]

Not all family names in the Przechowka community are of Dutch origin. Goertz notes that Mennonite surnames ending in "er" or "el" are likely of non-Dutch origin. The bearers of these names settled in Holland after fleeing religious persecution in Switzerland and Bavaria.[53] Swiss family names including Becker, Buller, Penner, and Wedel began appearing in Prussian Mennonite communities in the late seventeenth century.[54] The Swiss Anabaptists were persecuted as relentlessly as the Mennonites in Holland. The councils of Bern and Zurich developed instructions for how to exterminate the Anabaptists. In 1641, information about this persecution reached the Netherlands and prominent Dutch Mennonites attempted to intercede with authorities in Switzerland. In 1710, Frederick I (1701-1713) of Prussia also interceded on behalf of the Swiss Mennonites. These intercessions resulted in an extensive migration of Swiss Mennonites to Holland and Prussia in the early eighteenth century where many joined their brethren in the Groningen Old Flemish congregations.

Schrag provides more detail on how the Swiss and Dutch family names came to co-exist in the same communities. He traces a group of Swiss Mennonites from Switzerland to south Germany, France, and Russia, noting that a Swiss group joined the Dutch Prussians in Michalin on the eastern edge of Volhynia.[55] The Michalin community is important for this history since this group, dissatisfied with their land grants, moved from Michalin to Ostrog, Volhynia.[56] Many of this group emigrated to America on the *S.S. Nederland* on November 27, 1874 and ultimately joined the Holdeman Church. Family names included Dirks, Nickel, Penner, Schmidt, and Voth.[57]

---

[52] Unruh, "Unruh," 784–85.
[53] Goertz, "Marriage Records," 240–50.
[54] Horsch, *Mennonites in Europe*, 109–12.
[55] Schrag, "Swiss Volhynian Mennonite Background," 159.
[56] Hiebert, *Holdeman People*, 44, 95.
[57] Unruh, *Helpless Poles*, 63–64.

PART ONE   CHAPTER TWO   Menno Simons

A Short Stay in Prussia

Bound together by conservative Anabaptist principles, an agrarian lifestyle, and a few Dutch-Prussian surnames, the Groningen Old Flemish spread out through the lowlands of the Vistula delta in Royal Poland. To avoid persecution and government intrusion, they abandoned many of the skilled craftsman and artisan occupations found in urban areas and turned increasingly to agricultural pursuits. Life as Dutch non-citizens with an odd religion would last for only a hundred years or so in Prussia before pressures from government, religious authorities, and citizenry forced yet another migration.

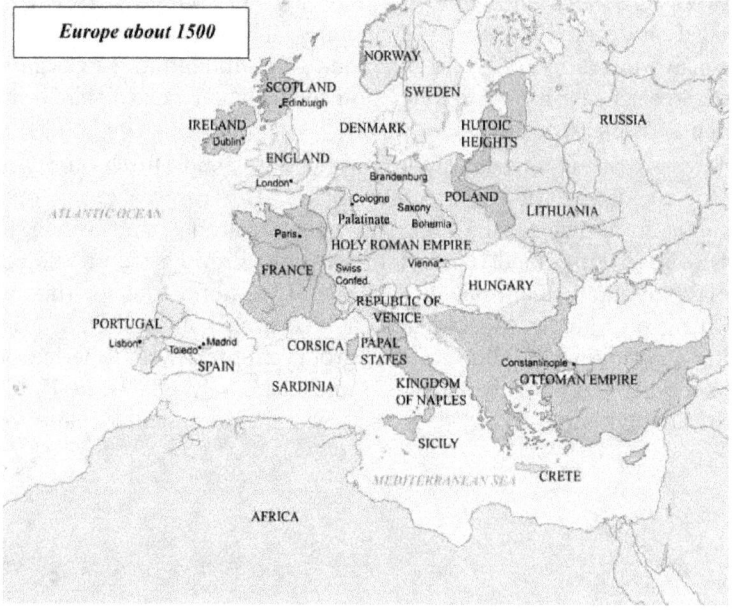

Map 3: *A Map of Central Europe ca. 1500 Showing the Holy Roman Empire*

CHAPTER THREE

The World of the Dutch Mennonites

O ESCAPE THE PERSECUTIONS and antagonistic political attitudes in the Netherlands, the Dutch Mennonites emigrated to Danzig (today, the port city of Gdańsk, Poland) and to the Vistula delta in Prussia. Trade between Danzig and Amsterdam was thriving in the sixteenth century, a commercial environment that created opportunities for merchants, artisans, and farmers in the nearby Polish lowlands. It is likely that many of the Dutch-Prussians gradually moved to more rural and agricultural pursuits, in part to avoid persecution and bias that was more prominent in urban areas.[1]

The political environment in Poland that surrounded the early Mennonite communities was established at the beginning of the sixteenth century. In 1505, the King of Poland granted the Bishop of Kulm extensive rights to the city of Danzig and surrounding lands.[2] This royal decree set the stage for succeeding bishops to either favor or oppose the Mennonites, depending on the political and religious circumstances of the time. In 1608, the Bishop of Kulm recommended taking action to stop the coming of Mennonites.[3] Later, in West Prussia, the Catholic bishops threatened to expel Mennonites for accepting Catholics into their communities. To avoid these possible actions, converts were encouraged to take a ship back to the Netherlands, be baptized there and then return to Prussia as a Mennonite.[4] A contemporary Dutch chronicle recorded numerous instances of this practice.[5] Those seeking Mennonite baptism were joined by many refugees in that almost every ship which sailed from Holland to Danzig after 1534 brought persecuted Anabaptists from the low countries to the shores of Prussia.[6] For many years, Danzig and Royal

---

[1] Klassen, *Mennonites in Early Modern Poland*, 83–84.
[2] Klassen, *Mennonites in Early Modern Poland*, 88.
[3] Klassen, *Mennonites in Early Modern Poland*, 45.
[4] Barrett. "PART II: Anabaptist Europe," para. 14.
[5] Klassen, *Mennonites in Early Modern Poland*, 149.
[6] Penner, "West Prussian Mennonites," 233.

Poland became a safe haven for fleeing Mennonites. In 1764, Stanislaus II Augustus, the last monarch of the Polish–Lithuanian Commonwealth, issued a strong defense of Mennonite religious and economic rights.[7]

For much of the seventeenth and eighteenth centuries, Prussia was under the sovereignty of the kings of Royal Poland. In 1737, King August II published a manifesto indicating that Mennonites had been called into the country to clear the swampy wastelands along the Vistula River. The manifesto also granted the Mennonites the privilege of freely practicing their religion and establishing their own schools.[8] The landowners of the Prussian regions included the Polish king, the Catholic Church and various Polish barons. Religious differences notwithstanding, the Mennonites were welcomed and valued for their work ethic and their skills to drain the swampy lands.[9]

Royal Poland and the Vistula Delta

Royal Poland offered refuge to the Dutch immigrants who were fleeing religious persecution in the Netherlands during the sixteenth and seventeenth centuries. Klassen writes that it was in this region that Mennonite refugees found a surprisingly large measure of freedom. For almost two and one half centuries, Mennonites lived under the Polish crown. Incredibly, the Polish parliament was able to establish a policy of toleration while most of Europe was decidedly intolerant. In 1573, the Polish Sejm (parliament) approved a declaration known as the Confederation of Warsaw, an inspirational commitment to toleration rarely seen in those days. No Polish monarch ever expelled Mennonites from his realm. Mennonites found champions and homes in the domains of various jurisdictions — royal, noble, and church.[10]

Horst Penner describes the incredible accomplishment of the Dutch Mennonites to drain the swampy lands in Prussia. This great enterprise in the Vistula delta began in 1547 and covered an area forty miles in width and included the two great delta areas east of Danzig, an undertaking which was to require three to four generations. About one hundred years after the beginning, the basic work in the drainage of the three werders (deltas) had been completed, with windmills, dikes, sluices, and countless drainage ditches. In the polders (lowlands reclaimed from the swamps), fat cattle pastured on the fertile meadows.[11]

The flood on the Vistula that occurred in the spring of 1698 was especially devastating. As Unruh recounts, water began spilling over the banks on

---

[7]Klassen, "Faith and Culture," 199.
[8]Horsch, *Mennonites in Europe*, 229–30.
[9]Klassen, *Mennonites in Early Modern Poland*, 9–11.
[10]Klassen, *Mennonites in Early Modern Poland*, 12–15.
[11]Penner, *West Prussia*, para. 18.

March 26 in the vicinity of Montau. Later, on April 2, a large break developed in the dike, flooding the whole Vistula valley. The water rose higher than anyone could remember and a large number of dairy cattle were swept away in the flood waters. All the settlers in the community, Mennonites, Lutherans, and Catholics, worked together to stem these floods.[12]

It is worth looking more closely at this incredible feat of clearing the marshlands in the Vistula delta. The projects to drain the flood waters were of great magnitude and extended for about one hundred miles on both sides of the Vistula, reaching to where the river empties into the Baltic Sea.[13] The Dutch Mennonites in Prussia brought with them the skills and knowledge to drain the swamps. In this process, the workers erected a windmill at the lowest place for each tract of land to be drained. The windmill and the prevailing winds worked to lower the water level of the polder (a tract of lowland). Much manual labor was also required to remove bushes and shrubs, exposing the workers to the deadly swamp fever.[14] This tremendous achievement was accomplished at a very high cost in human life, resulting in many settlers dying of the marsh fever.

In her painting of the Prussian landscape, Marie Birkholtz-Bestvater celebrates her Mennonite heritage and the determination and perseverance of her Dutch forefathers to settle the marshlands of the Vistula river valley.[15] The reproduction in Figure 6 captures these thoughts and the importance of Dutch windmills in establishing a homeland in Prussia.[16,17]

---

[12] Unruh, *Helpless Poles*, 32–33.

[13] Unruh and Unruh, *Tobias A. Unruh Biography*, 16.

[14] Driedger, "Farming among the Mennonites," 16–17.

[15] The Bestvater family name was found in the Frisian congregations of West Prussia in the early 1600s. See Reimer, "Bestvater", 301 and Birckholtz-Bestvater, "Mission," 53–55.

[16] Marie Birckholtz-Bestvater, "Mennonite Farm and Windmill". Oil painting: Original held in the Mennonite Library and Archives Art Collection, North Newton, KS.

[17] Permission to use this image was granted by John D. Thiesen, Archivist, Co-director of Libraries, Mennonite Library and Archives, Bethel College, North Newton, KS.

Figure 6: Mennonite Farm and Windmill in Prussia

In spite of the difficult work and reoccurring swamp fever, the Mennonites of Prussia were able to master the landscape for their benefit.[18] Their initial efforts yielded meadows and pastures with excellent grass. However as Urry notes, there were also problems in the Mennonite communities.

> Their success, combined with their continued visibility as a people easily distinguished by their beliefs, dress, endogamous marriage practices, use of Dutch, and links with brethren in the Dutch republic, made them easy targets for political cliques and disaffected citizens.[19]

In spite of the inconsistent policies of the kings, royals, and religious authorities, the Mennonites prospered in Prussia. By the middle of the eighteenth century, Mennonites were involved in virtually every occupation, business, and profession in Danzig.[20]

---

[18] Driedger, "Farming among the Mennonites," 16–21.
[19] Urry, *Mennonites, Politics*, 47.
[20] Klassen, "Faith and Culture," 199–200.

Living with the Fredericks

For over 150 years, the Mennonites had a contentious relationship with the Fredericks of Prussia. The first Frederick (Frederick William I, 1713-1740) was initially benevolent toward the Mennonites. In the early eighteenth century, he brought in thousands of religious refugees — mostly Mennonites, to settle in the wastelands of Prussia, what he called *wüste Stellen* (wastelands or desolate places).[21] However, this benevolence soon turned to conflict and confrontation as Frederick William sought to build up his military forces. On the night of September 14, 1723, his agents dragged a number of Mennonites off to Königsberg and tried to force them into military service by starvation. The prisoners refused and Frederick William harbored a grudge against the Mennonites for the remainder of his reign.[22] Harassment also continued from the religious authorities throughout the seventeenth and much of the eighteenth centuries with the Bishop of Kulm stating that "The whole valley is run over by Mennonites."[23]

Much changed for the Mennonite settlers in 1772. Generally, the Fredericks (Frederick II, Frederick William II, Frederick William III) were benevolent toward the Mennonites. However, on September 13, 1772 Frederick the Great (1740-1786) declared himself King of Prussia and Royal Poland ceased to exist. In this act, Frederick II became the ruler of all the Mennonites who had previously been subjects of the King of Poland.[24] Under the administration of Frederick II, the government imposed a collective tax on all Mennonites in exchange for their freedom from military service. The amount was set at 5,000 Reichstaler annually, a significant sum, at a time when one hundred Reichstaler was a good annual salary for a skilled workman.[25] This assessment was to be paid to the Kulm military academy in order to avoid military service. and amounted to about one thaler for every Mennonite male adult.[26]

Frederick II (Figure 7)[27] had a rather secular view of religion as evidenced in this quote: *It is no concern of politics whether a ruler has a religion or whether he has none. All religions, if one examines them, are founded on superstitious systems, more or less absurd.*[28] Based on this somewhat jaundiced view, Frederick established the principle that civil rights should

---

[21] Asprey, *Frederick the Great*, 12.
[22] Mannhardt, "Frederick William I," 386.
[23] Unruh, *Helpless Poles*, 34.
[24] Mannhardt, "Frederick II," 383.
[25] Jantzen, "Seeking," para. 14.
[26] Durant's note indicates that the thaler of 1789 was approximately equal to $5.25 in the U.S. currency of 1970. See Durant, *Age of Napoleon*, x.
[27] The image of Frederick the Great is in the public domain. See https://commons.wikimedia.org/wiki/File:Friedrich_Zweite_Alt.jpg.
[28] Urry, *Mennonites*, 50.

not depend on a religious creed.²⁹ In this more tolerant atmosphere, all Mennonites became subjects of Frederick II and much of the territory became known as West Prussia. However, given the militarization by the House of Hohenzollern,³⁰ relations between the nonresistant Mennonites and the Hohenzollern rulers were often problematic.³¹

Restrictions became even more harsh under Frederick's successor, Frederick William II (1786-1797). Under his dominion, Mennonites were forbidden to purchase more land and were forced to pay regular taxes to the state Lutheran church.³² With these more onerous regulations, the Mennonites began in earnest to look for better opportunities in Russia, hoping to take advantage of a generous offer from the Czaress of Russia, Catherine II.

Exodus from Prussia

Przechowka, the Prussian home of the Groningen Old Flemish, originated in 1540. Over the next several hundred years, the Dutch pioneers created productive meadows and farmlands through the building of canals and dikes.³³ However, continuing floods and disagreements with the Catholic authorities in Kulm made life difficult for the Mennonites. Also, the non-Mennonite population voiced strong feelings against the more prosperous Mennonite communities. Growing dissatisfaction among the Przechowka Mennonites led many settlers to begin looking elsewhere for opportunities. In the late eighteenth century, the Przechowka congregation numbered only about 300 members, having experienced significant losses as various groups migrated west to German provinces or to south Russia. By 1830, the Prussian Old Flemish congregation was extinct.³⁴

Figure 7: Frederick II, King of Prussia

With declining prospects in Prussia, it became increasingly difficult for a Mennonite to purchase land and the Napoleonic wars had wreaked havoc on the economy. Napoleon also rescinded the exemption of Mennonites

---

²⁹Mannhardt, "Frederick II," 383.

³⁰The House of Hohenzollern was a German royal dynasty whose members were variously princes, electors, kings and emperors of Hohenzollern, Brandenburg, Prussia, the German Empire, and Romania. See https://en.wikipedia.org/wiki/House_of_Hohenzollern

³¹Urry, *Mennonites*, 48–49.

³²Klassen, *Faith and Culture*, 201.

³³Unruh, *Helpless Poles*, 37.

³⁴Crous, "Przechovka," 225–26.

from military service.³⁵ 812. With these worsening conditions, the Prussian Mennonites once again began an arduous journey to a new and foreign land, hoping to take advantage of Catherine II's, generous offers to German farmers to settle the vast expanses of the Ukraine.

Klassen writes about the barriers the Mennonites encountered in trying to emigrate from Prussia. The emigrants were anxious to take advantage of Catherine II's manifesto that invited foreigners to settle in Russia. Yet these hopeful and hapless souls encountered many obstructionist tactics designed to prevent farmers and laborers from leaving Prussia.³⁶ The flight from Prussia began in the late eighteenth and early nineteenth centuries. There appear to be many paths that the migrants traveled, embarking with high hopes on a risky journeys from Brenkenhoffswalde, Danzig, and the Przechowka communities. Several vignettes demonstrate the complexity of cross-country migrations in the eighteenth century while also revealing the ingenuity and persistence of the Mennonites.

Brenkenhoffswalde

One such group of Mennonite families from the Jeziorka congregation decided to accept an offer from King Frederick's counselor, a person by the name of Von Brenkenhoff.³⁷ In exchange for land and religious freedom, they were to settle and clear the swampy areas in the Netze River valley. In 1764, these Mennonite families received settlement rights and special privileges including exemption from military service and the swearing of oaths. They were also granted permission to establish and maintain their own schools. In the spring of 1765, they established the Mennonite Brenkenhoffswalde congregation, named after King Frederick's counselor.³⁸

In the Brenkenhoffswalde community, Wilhelm Lange, a Lutheran teacher, emerged as a leader. Lange had grown up and was educated among Mennonites and he felt closely attached to the group. He asked permission of the authorities to transfer to the Mennonite faith. On October 24, 1788 he received permission to join the Mennonites, on condition that his obligations to the state and his duties as a citizen would not suffer. Lange became a respected and influential member of the Mennonite congregation. In 1802, he was chosen preacher and in 1810 elder, an office he held when the congregation emigrated to Russia in 1834.

Because of difficulties to purchase more land, the Brenkenhoffswalde community only remained in the Netze River valley for about seventy years. In

---

³⁵Neff, "Napoleon I,"
³⁶Klassen, "Barriers," 84–95.
³⁷Hiebert, *Holdeman People*, 43.
³⁸Klassen, *Mennonites in Early Modern Poland*, 86–87.

1833 Lange sent a petition to the Czar Nicholas I in the name of forty families of Brenkenhoffswalde and Franztal requesting permission to emigrate to Russia. Lange and his group received information on 10 January 1834 through the Russian consulate in Danzig, that the Czar would permit immigration on the following conditions: (1) presentation of a permit from the Prussian government to emigrate; (2) only families having at least five members would be permitted to emigrate; (3) a sum of eight hundred rubles was to be deposited, which would be returned when they arrived. In that year the forty families emigrated and found a welcome reception in south Russia. The Mennonite church at Brenkenhoffswalde was thereby dissolved. This Wilhelm Lange is listed as *alx345* in the *Church Book of the Alexanderwohl Mennonite Church of the Molotschna Colony of South Russia*.[39] In the turmoil of these migrations, the few remaining members of the Brenkenhoffswalde community joined the Lutheran state church, including Peter Janz, who later became a Protestant preacher.[40,41]

Danzig

The free city of Danzig became a major point of departure for Mennonites emigrating to Russia. In 1788 around the time of Easter, some 228 families gathered in Danzig to prepare for their journey to south Russia. Their unique route must have been quite adventuresome, crossing the Baltic Sea, traveling by way of Riga, today the captial of Latvia, and then downstream on the Dnieper River. This group settled shortly after Easter, 1789 along the Chortitz River, joining the already established Flemish and Frisian communities.[42,43]

---

[39] Duerksen and Duerksen, *Church Book*, 50.
[40] Mannhardt, "Brenkenhoffswalde," 416–17.
[41] Mannhardt, "Brenkenhoffswalde and Franztal," para. 3.
[42] Unruh, *Helpless Poles*, 38–39.
[43] Klassen, *Mennonites in Early Modern Poland*, 193.

Map 4: The map sketch shows the trek of the Mennonites from the Przechowka communities to South Russia (map by the author).

PART ONE   CHAPTER THREE   Dutch Mennonites

Molotschna

The Molotschna settelement of Alexanderwohl was one of the most prominent villages in south Russia. At some time during the period of 1820-21, elder Peter Wedel led his Przechowka group to south Russia, establishing the village of Alexanderwohl. As shown on Map 4, the Wedel group traveled past Warsaw and near the city of Ostrog, finally terminating at Alexanderwohl.[44] During their travels to south Russia, it is said that they encountered Czar Alexander I who was enroute to Warsaw. The Czar wished them well and later presented the travelers with a gift of six thousand rubles for a church building. Alexander's benevolence is remembered by the Mennonites in the naming of many villages in south Russia and the United States — Alexanderwohl, Alexandertal and Alexanderfeld to name a few. The Alexanderwohl group established a village and church in the Mololotschna colony and emigrated to Kansas in 1874, crossing the Atlantic on the *S.S. Cimbria* and *S.S. Teutonia*.[45,46]. In Kansas, they established the Alexanderwohl Church in Goessel, joining with the General Conference Mennonite Church in 1876.[47] In 1903, the Alexanderwohl population of 630 people owned a little over 6000 acres of land. Today, the Alexanderwohl community in Kansas extends from Newton 30 miles north to Hillsboro and more than 15 miles east to west.[48]

---

[44]The map is an adaptation of the map shown in the *Church Book of the Alexanderwohl Mennonite Church in the Molotschna Colony of South Russia*, 19.
[45]Neff, "Alexander I," 44.
[46]Duerksen and Duerksen, *Church Book* 50.
[47]Bender and Smith, *Mennonites and Their Heritage*, 123.
[48]Krahn, "Alexanderwohl," 48–50.

Map 5: Ostrog, Chortitza and Molotschna Located in Modern Ukraine (map by the author)

Jeziorka

Eight Mennonites from Jeziorka met with the Prussian authorities of the district Schwetz in West Prussia on September 15, 1803 and gave notice that they and their families wished to emigrate to Russia. This group ultimately settled in the community of Molotschna near the town of Ekaterinoslaw. Family names included Ratzlaff, Krahn, Schmidt, Buller, and Foth. In addition, the petitioners provided detailed information on their land holdings which they intended to sell prior to going to Russia. In 1804 permission to emigrate was granted, resulting in a 10 percent tax on all property taken out of Prussia.[49]

---

[49] Goertz, *From Jeziorka*, para. 4, no. 8.

The Ostrogers

The group that was to become the Ostrogers did not follow their co-religionists to south Russia. This smaller close-knit group settled near Ostrog, Poland, Russia and helped establish the villages of Antonofka and Leeleva, part of the Karolswalde circuit (Map 5). Hiebert speculates that this group of Mennonites was too poor to travel another five hundred miles to the south Russian settlements of Chortitza and Molotschna.[50,51] After these migrations, the Prussian Mennonite communities around Przechowka rapidly drifted into oblivion.

Our narrative now takes us to Russia and what is today the modern state of Ukraine. It is here that the Ostrogers settled for most of the nineteenth century, hoping to make a life in the land of the Czars.

---

[50] Hiebert, *Holdeman People*, 95.
[51] The names Karlswalde and Karolswalde have been used in different contexts. This text standardizes on Karolswalde since most of the research indicates that the community was established on the estate of Count Karol Jablonovsky.

CHAPTER FOUR

The Russian Mennonites - Living with the Czars

HILE LIVING UNDER the reign of tolerant Polish kings, the Mennonies had built prosperous communities along the Vistula river. However the autocratic rule of the Fredericks and the dismemberment of Poland in the late eighteenth century brought an end to what had promised at first to be a more permanent homeland. Emigration to Russia must have surely raised a sense of foreboding within the Mennonite communities of Przechowka. In the early nineteenth century, Prussia, Russia, and France were at war and the Dutch Mennonites were certainly wary at the thought of moving yet again to a strange land.

Catherine and the Alexanders

As with the Fredericks in Prussia, the Czars of Russia were generally favorable toward the Mennonites, seeing many benefits from their work ethic and economic production. Czarina Catherine's ukase of March 17, 1764 granted German immigrant farmers an allotment of eighty-one acres, of which forty were to be of arable land, fourteen acres each of meadow and woodland, and also including pasture land and a house. This generous allotment was doubled in Alexander I's (1801-1825) ukase of February 20, 1804.[1] Alexander I was a great benefactor of the Mennonites, having also presented a gift to the south Russian Molotschna colony to help them build a church.[2] Similarly, Alexander II (1855-1881) confirmed the Mennonite charter of privileges and thanked the Mennonites of the Chortitza colony for their nonmilitary service during the Ukrainian war (1854) and the Turkish

---

[1] Belk, *Great Trek*, 44.
[2] Neff, "Alexander I," 44.

war (1877).³,⁴ Alexander II (Figure 8) also expressed his good wishes for the Mennonites of the Molotschna colony for the quartering and feeding of six thousand Bulgarian immigrants.⁵ These more prosperous colonies in south Russia — Chortitza and Molotschna — benefited greatly from the actions of the Russian Czars.

However, the lesser known Mennonite settlements in the region of Ostrog did not receive any of these government benefits and they struggled to make ends meet. Smith notes that the Ostrogers were influenced by an unwholesome environment and, strictly speaking, were not colonists since they were not located on Russian frontier territory. Thus, they did not benefit from the special inducements offered by the Russian government.⁶

Figure 8: Czar Alexander II of Russia

Why did this small group of Prussian Mennonites end their journey in the Ostrog area (about 125 miles southwest of Kiev) while many of the other Mennonite groups continued on to the more fertile farming areas of south Russia? Some have speculated that the Ostrogers lacked the economic means to complete the longer journey to south Russia. However, other factors such as warring armies, inclement weather, and poor health might have forced a decision to homestead in the Volhynia region.

When did the Mennonites leave the villages of West Prussia? We know that a sizable group settled first in Brenkenhoffswalde. After some give and take with Frederick the Great, the king worked out a plan to give the Brenkehoffswalde Mennonites complete religious freedom in a special charter, assuming they provide financial support for the Kulm Military Academy. However, a new edict of 1787 prevented the Mennonites from acquiring additional land. Confronted with this prohibition and the intolerant attitude of the local Catholic bishop and various priests, the settlers began again to look for opportunities elsewhere. Many from Brenkenhoffswalde relocated to south Russia while a smaller group settled initially in Michalin, some 90 miles

---

³The czar's thank you is likely in reference to the Crimean War of 1854-55 in which Russia fought against the alliance of England, France, Sardinia, and the Ottoman Empire. The Ukrainian provinces functioned as the primary source of supplies for the Russian imperial armies.

⁴Subtelny, *Ukraine*, 252.

⁵The image of Czar Alexander II is in the public domain. See https://commons.wikimedia.org/wiki/File:Alexander_II_of_Russia_photo.jpg.

⁶Smith, *Story of the Mennonites*, 400.

southeast of Ostrog. Disagreements with the government again resulted in many of the Michalin group joining the Karolswalde communities in 1801.[7]

Although it is difficult to discern the exact migration paths, some settlers emigrated directly from Jeziorka on the right bank of the Vistula to the Karolswalde communities.[8] The family of Cornels and Trincke (Ratzlaff) Jantz resided in Jeziorka in the late nineteenth century. Cornels youngest son, David, was born on April 2, 1794 in Jeziorka whereas David's son, Benjamin, was born on April 24, 1824 in one of the Ostrog communities. Birth records for Cornels and David from the Przechowka Kirchen Buch provide evidence of these movements between the years 1794 and 1807.[9] Census records of the year 1819 for the Ostrog communities indicate that the families of Heinrich, Tobias, Andrew, and Bernth (all older brothers of David) were living in the communities of Karolwalde and Antonofka in the early nineteenth century. These brothers were all born in Jeziorka.[10]

The Mennonite migrations to Russia were not under the best of conditions and likely encountered considerable military activity. The Napoleonic wars were disrupting much of Europe at the time, creating pressure on the Mennonites to join the military. In the fall of 1806, Frederick William III led Prussia into war with Napoleon's forces. After a major defeat on October 14, 1806, the Prussian state collapsed and Frederick's court fled Berlin. In this journey, the court stopped in Graudenz, only a few miles distant from the Dutch-Prussian villages of Przechowka, Jeziorka, and Schönsee. In this setting, deacon Abraham Nickel encountered one of Frederick's generals, indicating that the Mennonites were collecting money to donate for the soldiers' widows and orphans. After meeting with the royal couple, Abraham Nickel arranged to transfer thirty thousand thaler to the Prussian state. This event marked a turning point in which the Prussian Mennonites began to develop a bond with the German fatherland, ultimately embracing German identity.[11] However, the Ostrogers of Volhynia settled amongst the Polish and Russian peasants, maintaining much of their Dutch heritage and identifying less with either the German or Russian nationalities.

---

[7] Unruh, *Helpless Poles*, 57–60.

[8] The Jacob B. Janz working paper indicates that the first group left West Prussia in 1802 and traveled to Volhynia. See Janz, *Mennonite Life*, 1–3.

[9] Pankratz and Unruh, *Church Records*, 19. Note that there are several variant reports of different dates for the birth of David Jantz, *prz1136*.

[10] See Census of Mennonites located in Ostrog: 1819 Russian State Historical Archives (RGIA) Fond 383, Opis 29, Dielo 528 Translated by Sergei Chaiderman, August 1997. http://www.mennonitegenealogy.com/russia/Census_of_Mennonites_located_in_Ostrog_1819.pdf.

[11] Jantzen, *Mennonite German Soldiers*, 80–83.

PART ONE   CHAPTER FOUR   Leaving Prussia

Photo 1: A Mennonite Home in Karolswalde (photo courtesy of Dale Schrag)

The Ostrog Mennonite Villages of Volhynia

Having spent over one hundred years adapting to the cultures of Royal Poland and Frederick's Prussia, the Dutch Mennonites would now enter the domain of the Czars. Living in the Russian provinces would be equally tumultuous, contending with Napoleon's armies and the efforts of Alexander II to remake Russian society.

The Ostroger Mennonites settled in a part of Poland that had been annexed by Russia and these people were later to be identified by Abe Unruh as "the helpless Poles".[12] Unfortunately, the Ostrogers had settled in an area where the land was heavily forested and not very fertile. The settlers struggled with agricultural pursuits and did not have time for a lot of education or social activities. In the late eighteenth and early nineteenth centuries, the conservative Mennonites established four main communities — Michalin, Karolswalde, Antonofka, and Heinrichsdorf. These communities congregated together and even made the trip to America on the same ships. Although the Russian czars accepted the Mennonites as non-citizens, they continued to demand participation in the military. This tension created uncertainty in the Ostrog Mennonite communities, resulting in a stay of only about seventy years before many of the settlers undertook the journey to America.

---

[12]Unruh, *Helpless Poles*, 42–43.

Michalin

The Michalin community was established by emigrants from the villages of the province of Brandenberg, Germany, most notably Brenkenhoffswalde and Franzthal. In a few short years, these communities again experienced problems with government demands to participate in the military. Many Mennonites left these villages and traveled to south Russia, however those associated most closely with the Groningen Old Flemish settled in Michalin which was located on the eastern edge of Volhynia. The Michalin group did not formally organize as a congregation until 1811 when David Siebrandt was elected elder.[13,14] Unruh indicates that the Michalin group was the first Mennonite settlement in Russia, established some time in the early 1780s.[15,16] In the second partition of Poland in 1793, the Michalin area passed under Russian control. A short time later, many of the Michaliners moved to the Ostrog area and joined the Karolswalde settlement.

Karolswalde

The Karolswalde community was organized with the permission of Crown Prince Karol Jablonovsky and was located near Ostrog, Volhynia, Russia. Karolswalde was established in 1801 when Michaliners, dissatisfed with government mandates, relocated to the region. Although we do not have accurate records, it appears that the community of Karolswalde was established in Volhynia in the early nineteenth century. Abe Unruh states that Karolswalde originated in 1802, translating from the cover of the Karolswalde Church Record Book as follows:[17]

> Mennonites who previously lived in the Kingdom of Prussia, near Driesen and Swetz, who migrated and settled in the Wohlynien government, near the city of Ostrog, in the year 1802 and later, with the permission and written agreement of his sovereign Majesty, the Russian Crown Prince, Karl Jablonovsky.

Benjamin Dirks was ordained elder of the Karolswalde group in 1817. Tobias A.Unruh also became an elder of the Karolswalde congregation in 1853.[18,19] C.H. Smith notes that this small group did not prosper and

---

[13] Schmidt, "Michalin," 667.
[14] Schmidt, "Siebrandt, David," 523.
[15] Unruh, *Helpless Poles*, 56–58.
[16] Hiebert, *Holdeman People*, 43–44.
[17] Unruh, *Helpless Poles*, 60.
[18] Crous, "Karolswalde," 152.
[19] Unruh, *Helpless Poles*, 59–60.

remained poor throughout their stay in Russia.[20] There was too little land available for everyone to farm so many worked as day laborers. Abe Unruh writes that they worked in all kinds of trades — linen weavers, stone masons, bricklayers, cabinet builders, blacksmiths, lumbermen, and others.[21] Toews describes the life of Benjamin T. Jantz in Karolswalde, noting that the family farmed 2.7 acres that provided essential foodstuffs. Benjamin produced some income from his weaving and day labor. These long hours barely provided the most basic diet which consisted mostly of bread and potatoes. Because of worsening economic conditions in Karolswalde, Benjamin T. Jantz relocated to south Russia in 1875, joining the much larger body of Mennonites who settled in the two major colonies — Chortitza and Molotschna.[22]

Antonofka

Antonofka was located about fifteen miles to the southwest of Karolswalde and was the second-oldest Mennonite village in the Ostrog area after Karolswalde. Antonofka was situated on the southern bank of the Vilna River. The settlement and church parish were established in 1816. Life in Antonofka and the nineteenth century Karolswalde communities was difficult, bordering on poverty and lack of basic foodstuffs. Many supplemented their income as day laborers, doing hand sawing in the nearby forests or weaving linen in the homes. The villages of Waldheim and Fürstendorf affiliated with Antonofka. Common family names in the village included Becker, Buller, Eck, Jantz, Koehn, Nachtigal, Ratzlaff/Ratzloff, Schmidt, Unruh, Voth, and Wedel. Many of the Antonofka Mennonites traveled on the *S.S. Vaderland* to America and settled in the Lone Tree community of McPherson, Kansas.[23]

In 1821, Karolswalde and Antonofka were the two primary Ostroger villages consisting of thirty-eight families with surnames such as Dirks, Jantz, Koehn, Schartner, and Unruh. From Jacob Janz's notes, we know that living conditions deteriorated in the Karolswalde communities and parents started sending their sons to Molotschna where they worked as hired hands.[24] In 1836, some of these families left Volhynia and settled in Mototschna, south Russia. These migrants frequently ended up as *Anwohner*, ones who "lived adjacent" and were forced to become artisans or farm hands because land was not available for purchase.[25] Some families moved back and forth between south Russia and Karolswalde. The Alexanderwohl church record identifies several individuals who "returned to Karolswalde". For example,

---

[20]Smith. *Story of the Mennonites*, 400.
[21]Unruh, *Helpless Poles*, 51.
[22]Toews, *Courage*, 2.
[23]Unruh, *Helpless Poles*, 62–63.
[24]Janz, *Mennonite Life in Volhynia*, 11.
[25]Krahn, "Anwohner," 135–36.

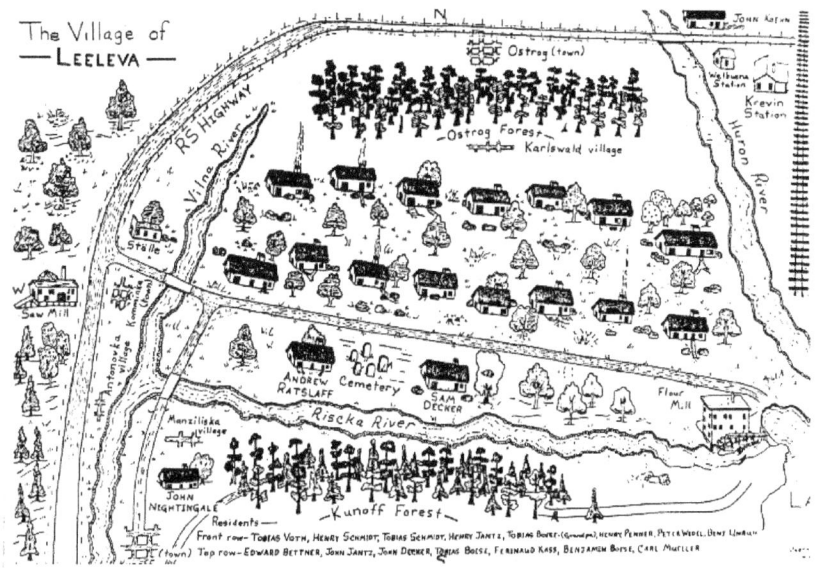

Map 6: The Village of Leeleva (Lileva)
Front Row: Tobias Voth, Henry Schmidt, Tobias Schmidt, Henry Jantz, Tobias Boese, Henry Penner, Peter Wedel, Henry Unruh
Top Row: Edward Bettner, John Jantz, John Dekker, Tobias Boese, Ferinaud Kass, Benjamin Boese, Carl Mueller

Jacob Jantz's $(alx468)$[26] birthplace is shown as Karolswalde but additional comments from the Church record indicate that he returned to Karolswalde "with transfer" on 10 November 1863. Others in this church record are also shown as returning on the same date, perhaps resulting in an organized group that returned to Karolswalde.[27]

---

[26] The designation ALX will help the reader locate the individual in the Church Book of the Alexanderwohl Mennonite Church in the Molotschna Colony of South Russia.

[27] Duerksen and Duerksen, *Church Book*, 57–57a.

PART ONE CHAPTER FOUR Leaving Prussia

Leeleva

Lileva, or Leeleva, is a smaller village of the Karolswalde group that has been documented in several Mennonite genealogies. A popular sketch, reprinted in many genealogies, shows the members of the village and the proximity to Karolswalde and Antonofka (Map 6).[28] Johann Jantz was the leading minister in the village with Johann Nachtigal as co-minister and Johann Dekkert as deacon.[29] In the map, we can see these elders listed in the top row as John Jantz[30] and John Decker. John Nightingale is associated with the home in the lower left corner of the figure. The John Koehn residence is in the upper right corner of the figure. A saw mill, flour mill, and cemetery are located in the center of the map.

Heinrichsdorf

The village of Heinrichsdorf was established in 1848 by a group coming from Waldheim in south Russia. Because of continued concerns about being forced into military service, some seventy-three families migrated in the 1830s from the Volhynia region to the Molotschna colony in south Russia. This group experienced issues of conscience and decided to move back to Volhynia in 1848, establishing the village of Heinrichsdorf some sixty miles east of Ostrog.[31]

The origins of the village of Heinrichsdorf suggest that the movement of people among the communities of the Volhynia region was perhaps more frequent than one might expect. Although Heinrichsdorf was sixty miles east of Ostrog, the group maintained close ties with the Karolswalde people and there were occasional social interactions and marriages between the young people. Ministers also worked closely together throughout the stay in Russia. Common family names in this group included Buller, Boese, Ewert, Nachtigal, Penner, Schmidt, and Wedel. Most of the group traveled on the *S.S. Colina*, arriving in New York on September 2, 1874. Ministers at the time of migration included Benjamin Schmidt and Tobias Ratzlaff. The group left New York immediately and traveled by rail to Yankton, Dakota Territory and homesteaded in an area that is seven to twelve miles south of what is now Avon, South Dakota. Once settled in this area, they established

---

[28]The map of Leeleva was produced by Jake Unruh who lived in the Volhynia region until 1907. See Ratzlaff Family Blog, "Location of Leeleva," para. 12.

[29]Krahn, "Lileva," 345.

[30]The John Jantz shown in Map 6 can be tracked down to two possibilities. He was either Johann Jantz (b 6 Oct 1825) and the grandson of Peter Jantz *prz532* or Johann Jantz (b 26 July 1825) and the grandson of Cornels Jantz *prz528*.

[31]Unruh, *Helpless Poles*, 63–64.

the Friedensberg congregation which is today associated with the General Conference Mennonite Church..[32]

Life and Culture of the Ostrogers

The Mennonite villages in the region of Volhynia were the last home for the Ostrogers in Europe before they emigrated to America. In two of the main villages, Karolswalde and Antonofka, there were thirty-eight families in the year 1821.[33] As non-citizens, these Mennonite communities enjoyed complete administrative, religious, and educational freedom from the Russian authorities.

The church elders exercised strict discipline and the ban was used to maintain order and control. "Drinking, card playing, swearing and stealing, as well as all manner of excesses, were taboo."[34] Abram Jantz, a preacher, was relieved of his speaking privileges because he played a folk song on his flute.[35] School and education ended when an individual was old enough to work. When one could read fluently from the Bible, his education was considered sufficient and his schooling was over.[36] The settlements in the Ostrog area continued to grow even though the land was marshy and insufficient for a family to earn an adequate living. Many supplemented their income with odd jobs such as hand sawing in the nearby forests or weaving linen in the home.[37] These additional pursuits did little to allay the considerable poverty in these communities. Many families were landless, either living in the forest or considered "Anwohner" – those who lived along side or in the back yards of the lucky families who owned land. In this environment, there was considerable cultural and educational isolation, not only from the Russian population but also from the more well to do Mennonites who were settling in south Russia. Life was hard, basic and uncomplicated and the settlers learned to get contentment from small joys and routine tasks.

The Ostrogers worked hard to establish themselves in the Russia of the 1800s. They generally lived in their own communities, continued to converse in Plattdeutsch and had little interaction with the Russian peasants. Jacob B. Janz[38] has provided a detailed account of what life was like in Karolswalde:

---

[32] Boese, "Story of the Mennonites," 29–43.
[33] Schrag, "Volhynia," 844–47.
[34] Toews, *Mennonite Life*, 9.
[35] Toews, *Mennonite Life*, 10.
[36] Unruh, *Helpless Poles*, 66.
[37] Hiebert, *Holdeman People*, 95–96.
[38] Janz, *Mennonite Life*, 10–12.

In spring, according to Janz's account, a single share plow drawn by two horses turned the soil. Crops were sewn by hand. In fall the grain was cut with a sickle, bound into sheaves and threshed with flail.[39] Crop yields barely met basic needs. Food stuffs were simple: brown bread, soup, and potatoes. Everyday clothes were home spun and hand sewn. Benjamin Tobias Janz to whom the manuscript refers, could only send his children to school for one year. At best they might learn to read. Culturally and intellectually life in Karolswalde centered on a small, self-contained community, which developed its own folkways.

The Karolswalde people continued to experience the disruptive forces that plagued the Russian Mennonite communities including quarrels between those who owned land and the landless and the policies of the czars. The relatively small and impoverished villages of the Karolswalde circuit apparently did not benefit from all the good will coming from the czars of Russia. Nevertheless, the Karolswalde residents probably thought they had found a more permanent home in Russia. Unfortunately, the privileges granted to the original settlers by Catherine II were not to last. In the 1860s, Czar Alexander II (Figure 8) began his Great Reforms which significantly altered the structure of Russian society and included the plan to introduce compulsory, universal military service.[40,41] The most troubling aspect of this edict was the termination of the military exemption. To have to enter into military service would severely compromise the basic religious principles of this close-knit Mennonite community.

The imperial *ukase*, a proclamation of Czar Alexander II regarding universal conscription, caused the Mennonites to mobilize, sending delegations to St. Petersburg in an attempt to seek a compromise with the Russian government. When this approach did not work, a delegation of twelve men was sent to America where they toured southern Manitoba, Minnesota, the Dakotas, Nebraska, and Kansas, observing the agricultural possibilities and opportunities for religious freedom.[42]

The Ostrogers lived for a period in Russia without leadership and in considerable religious uncertainty. The remnants of the Groningen Old Flemish had disappeared in Prussia by 1835 and the isolation from their co-religionists in south Russia resulted in a cultural schism that would never be healed. For the Ostrogers, the lack of leadership and isolation created an

---

[39]The term "flail" is defined as "a hand threshing implement consisting of a wooden handle at the end of which a stouter and shorter stick is so hung as to swing freely." See the Merriam-Webster dictionary at https://www.merriam-webster.com/dictionary/flail.

[40]Hiebert, *Holdeman People*, 102–105.

[41]Urry, *Mennonites*, 95–96.

[42]Hiebert, *Holdeman People*, 116.

unimaginative and routinized religious life.

Today in Karolswalde

Today there is not much evidence in the Ukraine of the villages of the Ostrogers. The ravages of time, two world wars and the policies of the now defunct Soviet government have combined to make it very difficult for any researcher to find actual remnants of the Mennonite villages of the 1870s. From correspondence with Dale Schrag, a current view of the Karolswalde area is possible.[43] Mr. Schrag wrote that there are three or four homes in the Karolswalde community that were probably of Mennonite origin. The photograph (Photo 1) taken during a visit by Mr. Schrag in 1992 is one of those homes. The Schrag group also visited Jadwaninne which was a Mennonite village affiliated with the Karolswalde congregation and was located just a few miles southeast of Karolswalde. In the area, tourists can see a Russian bunker from World War II and visit an old cemetery. Someone interested in preserving history has erected a fence around the cemetery. Many of the headstones are unreadable. Mr. Schrag has taken a picture of one of the Mennonite headstones (Figure 9) with the following inscription: "Hier ruhet (given name unreadable) Boese geboren in Jahre 1891 den 5 April, gesterben den 9 April 1891" (Here lies Boese, born on 5 April 1891, died on 9 April 1891). Today, the towns in the area bear Russian and Ukrainian names and few citizens can recall any of the German Mennonites of the late 1800s. German Lutherans acquired many of the Mennonite homes in the 1870s and most of the German population left on their own during World War I or were deported by the Stalinists in the 1920s.

Who of the Ostroger descendants live in Russia and the Ukraine today? Although Russian archives are much more accessible, significant research will be required to unearth credible documents. There is considerable research that has produced records for the nineteenth century but much less for the twentieth century.[44] A firsthand account is offered by Raleigh Koehn who had the opportunity to travel through Ostrog in 1999. He re-

Figure 9: A Mennonite Headstone

---

[43] Correspondence with Dale E. Schrag of Newton, Kansas.

[44] See the research by Tim Janzen, Richard Thiessen, Glen Penner, Michael Penner. *Russian Mennonite Genealogical Resources.* http://www.mennonitegenealogy.com/russia/.

ports that *there has been little change for many years in the style of living in the rural areas such as Antonokfa. The hay meadows are dotted with man-made stacks of hay 6 to 8 feet in size and height. These are loaded onto horse-drawn wagons in the fall and winter and taken to the yard for livestock.* Koehn continues, indicating that Antonofka remains a single street village. Raleigh was able to make the acquaintance of the last man of German descent in the area — a Leonid Koehn.

Raleigh Koehn and his wife became acquainted with Leonid Koehn whose house was at the far end of the village of Antonofka, overlooking fertile fields and the Vilna River which is depicted in Map 6. Of Leonid Koehn, Raleigh notes:

> He couldn't speak English or German so we communicated through our interpreter in Russian. He said that all he knew of his ancestry was that they had come from the lowlands of Holland! His father Ernest had returned to the Ukraine in 1946 after his grandfather Andrew had died while living in Siberia.[45]

Stepping Back

In making the transition from Prussia to Russia, the Mennonites engaged in much introspection and reflection on beliefs and practices. As the migrants from the conservative Groningen Old Flemish began to settle in Prussia, government policies, war, poverty, and internal disagreements about their faith led to diverse groups forming. In following the trek of the Groningen Old Flemish, we find that most of these people ultimately dispersed into four different churches - the Church of God in Christ, Mennonite (CGCM); the Kleine Gemeinde; the Mennonite Brethren; and the Alexanderwohl group. The Kleine Gemeinde, the Mennonite Brethren, and Alexanderwohl were established in Russia whereas the CGCM, informally the Holdeman Church, originated in the United States. A brief synopsis will help put these various groups in context.

In 1858, John Holdeman, a member of the Old Mennonite Church in Wayne County, Ohio, began preaching and holding meetings in his home, claiming to be inspired by visions and dreams. He believed that the old church had departed from the truth.[46] Membership in Holdeman's church grew slowly until 1878 when he started meeting with and baptizing the Ostrogers, most of whom had journeyed from Antonofka, crossing the Atlantic on the *S.S. Vaderland*. A few years later, a significant number of the Kleine Gemeinde who had settled in Manitoba also joined the Holdeman Church.

---

[45]Schmidt and Caldwell, *Schmidt Family*, 682–83.
[46]Smith, *Story*, 602–03.

The Kleine Gemeinde congregation orignated in the early nineteenth century in the Russian Mennonite colony of Molotschna. Klaas Reimer was installed as the first minister of a small group of believers who decided to separate from the larger church (die Grosse Gemeinde).[47] The Kleine Gemeinde community held similar beliefs to those of the Holdeman Church. Their beliefs cautioned against modern life styles, becoming too involved in education and politics, and they forbid the use of tobacco. As their religious beliefs took shape and the community grew, the Kleine Gemeinde separated physically from the other south Russian Mennonites. The emigration to America found these people settling in Nebraska and in Manitoba, Canada. Popular surnames included Reimer, Friesen, Toews, Janzen, Esau, Fast, Heidebrecht and Giesbrecht. Many of the Kleine Gemeinde people who settled in Manitoba joined the Holdeman Church in 1881.[48]

The Mennonite Brethren originated in south Russia in 1860. Migrants from both Prussia and Brenkenhoffswalde formed the nucleus of the group that initially settled in Chortitza. In a bold and revolutionary step, a group of eighteen men created a document that stated the reasons for wanting to withdraw from the main body of Mennonites, protesting primarily of the religious decay and frivolous life that was rampant. In spite of opposition from the (old) Mennonite Church, the Mennonite Brethren grew and prospered in the ensuing years. Among the early leaders were Jacob Jantz, Abraham Schmidt, Johan Fast, and Abraham Schellenberg.[49,50]

The Alexanderwohl village originated in 1821 when twenty-one Mennonite families, led by Peter Wedel, departed Przechowka to settle in Molotschna, south Russia. It appears that this group was initially associated with the Groningen Old Flemish and also had close ties to the Brenkenhoffswalde community. Before World War II, about one-third of the Alexanderwohl village belonged to the Mennonite Brethren Church. Almost the entire village emigrated as a unit to Kansas. After arriving in Kansas, leaders purchased thirty-four sections of land north of Newton in Marion and McPherson counties where today the bulk of the group have formed a compact settlement.[51]

Seeking an Ethnic and Religious Identity

Having arrived at the decision to emigrate to the United States, the descendants of the Groningen Old Flemish Mennonites might have wondered about their culture and who they were. C.H. Smith offers a description of

---

[47]Janz, *Profile*, 88.
[48]Hiebert, *Holdeman People*, 40.
[49]Smith, *Story*, 429–30.
[50]Lark, "Mennonite Brethren Church," 595–602.
[51]Krahn, "Alexanderwohl," 48–50.

these people — *They were Dutch racially, German culturally, and Russian nationally.*[52] This Mennonite group also lived in pervasive and crippling poverty. John Schmidt writes that the Karolswalde group which emigrated to America in December, 1874 on the *S.S. Vaderland* became a special burden on agencies who were helping them get started in the new land.[53] As they embarked on the journey to America, these immigrants surely hoped that they would at last be able to live their lives as Mennonites in a more prosperous community. When the migration began in 1874, the colony of Mennonites in Volhynia consisted of about 450 families, living in eight villages. There were five villages in the Karolswalde settlement and three villages in the community of Antonofka. Of the 450 families, about 300 joined the emigration to America.[54]

It is useful to draw a contrast between the Ostrogers and the more well-to-do Mennonites who settled on Russia's southern steppes. In general, the more liberal minded and propertied Mennonites found it possible to reconcile themselves to the Czasrist government's policies.[55] Urry writes that the Mennonites of south Russia grew prosperous, wealthy, and even worldly from the benefits of their agricultural endeavors.[56] However, the Ostrogers remained an inward looking group, living off of subsistence farming, and demanding total obedience from their members. This environment combined with severe poverty and lack of education led to the Ostrogers being open to a new form of leadership in America. John Holdeman stepped into this void with a message that appealed to this impoverished group. The majority of the Karolswalde group settled in Canton, Kansas, many becoming members of the Church of God in Christ, Mennonite.[57]

The Mennonites who decided to continue their lives in Russia were able to extract concessions from the Czarist government, fulfilling their state obligations in forestry service rather than serving in the military.[58] Given their prosperity and relative autonomy from the government, many felt that the future looked promising. However, the Russian revolution and the establishment of Communism brought the nationalization of property, state mandated starvation, and total confusion for the settlers. Some of the Ostrogers did move to the Molotschna and Chortitza colonies and were caught up in the chaos of the early twentieth century. How the Russian Mennonites survived Lenin and Stalin is part of our story before proceeding with the Ostroger's journey to America.

---

[52] Smith, *Story*, 631.
[53] Schmidt, "Three Years," 35–39.
[54] Unruh, "Pawnee Rock Mennonites," 131–32.
[55] Sawatsky, *Sought a Country*, 7.
[56] Urry, *None but Saints*, 21–22.
[57] Crous, "Karolswalde," 152.
[58] Krahn, "Russia," 390.

CHAPTER FIVE

Surviving Lenin and Stalin

HOSE OF THE RUSSIAN MENNONITES who emigrated to America in the 1870s, in hindsight, must have been very thankful for the decision they made. Immigrants always face a decision fraught with peril — to stay or to leave. Although the Mennonites who remained were experiencing increased prosperity and enjoying special privileges from the Russian Czars, it was not to last. The twentieth century brought prosperity to American Mennonites and misfortune to those who remained in Russia. Russian Mennonites had to deal with Lenin and Stalin, enduring much hardship and frequent banishment to Siberia. The decision to remain in Russia also represented a theological split in that many of the south Russians aligned with the more progressive Mennonite Brethren whereas the Ostogers ultimately joined with John Holdeman's church in America.

Chaos in the Early Twentieth Century

World War I and the Russian revolution resulted in the prohibition of the German language, of German preaching, the closing of the German press, and the russification of German schools. Plett writes that this period amounted to the "Mennonite holocaust" in which 35,000 perished.[1] The vision of becoming prosperous Russian citizens never materialized. Rather the Mennonites suffered evacuations, deportations, confusion and terror.[2] Livelihoods and farming were threatened as the Russian military and the Bolsheviks requisitioned materials and livestock so that not a single draft animal was left on the farms.

---

[1] Plett, *Saints and Sinners*, 104.
[2] Unruh, "Background," 267–81.

Bread was lacking, clothing was lacking, fuel was lacking — in other words, there was a catastrophic economic decline, a decay in all phases of economic life of the colonies.[3]

In the Spring of 1917, an all-Russian Mennonite Convention was held to deal with the economic and cultural problems facing the German colonists. A few short months later in the revolution of October 1917, Lenin (Figure 10) established the dictatorship of the proletariat and anarchy reigned in south Russia.[4] David Rempel, who personally experienced the ensuing chaos, has written about the early stages of the Russian civil war in 1918. Bolsheviks, Ukrainian peasants, German troops, and the counter-revolutionary White Army all fought for control of the strategically important region that was home to many Mennonites. However, the Makhnovite bandits were most feared, wreaking havoc through their intense hatred of the colonists, plundering settlements, and slaughtering innocent victims.[5] Patterson describes one such event in which the Makhnovist calvary surrounded the Mennonite village of Eichenfeld on the night of November 8, 1919 and proceeded to massacre the inhabitants, resulting in the death of 136 people. Survivors were typically Anwohner[6] living on the outskirts of the village, returning several days later to bury the dead in a series of twelve unmarked graves. In a reaction to these terrorist incursions, young Mennonites began to question their forefathers' pacifism, many accepting training from their Austro-German occupiers with the hope of protecting their communities.[7]

Figure 10: Vladimir Lenin - Russian Communist Leader

With the defeat of the White armies and the withdrawal of the German troops from the Ukraine, the Mennonite colonists were left to deal with the godless Soviet government. The colonists' religion, prosperity, private ownership, self-defense (German: *Selbstschutz*) units, and administrative autonomy all clashed with the vision of a Communist utopia. The Mennonites

---

[3] Unruh, "Background," 269.

[4] The image of Lenin is in the public domain and available for commercial use. See https://commons.wikimedia.org/wiki/File:Lenin_dibujo_1901.jpg.

[5] Rempel and Carlson, *Mennonite Family*, 183–86.

[6] The German term "Anwohner" was used to designate Mennonites in south Russia who lived in shacks on the outskirts of prosperous villages barely eking out a living. This condition was largely due to surplus land not being available for purchase. In 1860, nearly two-thirds of the Molotschna Mennonites were considered Anwohner, sometimes translated as "living adjacent". See Krahn, "Anwohner," 135.

[7] Patterson, "Eichenfeld Massacre," 151–74.

were faced with an existential dilemma — emigrate or assist the Soviets in rebuilding the economy of a war-torn country.[8]

A few years after the Makhnovite incursions, the drought of 1921 destroyed the harvest and famine soon became a reality. Many families fed themselves on field mice, crows, carcasses, and wild plants. To cope with the impendiing disaster, many villages divided their small grain crops among all the people in the village. Conditions were made worse by the influx of thousands of refugees from outlying villages. Beggars trudged from house to house, knocking on doors and windows, and asking for bread.[9]

But for the assistance of American and Dutch Mennonites, tens of thousands would have starved in the years between 1921 and 1923.[10] By 1924, total Mennonite relief from the Mennonite Central Committee and the American Relief Administration totaled about $1,200,000 including tractors, horses, and food.[11] In these worsening conditions, many Mennonites emigrated to Canada and were able to rebuild their lives and flourish in America. Those who decided to stay in Russia were at best exiled. At worst, they either starved in the famine of 1932 or perished in the Russian Gulag.[12]

Four Hundred Years The years between the world wars were chaotic for the Dutch-Russian Mennonites. Much has been written about the work of a man named B. B. Janz and his efforts to help Mennonites emigrate from the Soviet Union in the 1920s (see family picture, Photo 2).[13] Janz's story is illustrative of the different paths the Russian Mennonites followed through life. His grandparents and parents, the Benjamin T. Jantz and Benjamin B. Jantz families, had settled in Karolswalde but relocated to Molotschna in south Russia in search of better living conditions. In the south Russian community, B.B. risked the disapproval of his parents and joined the Mennonite Brethren Church in 1897 and only a few years later in September, 1909 he was elected leader of the Brethren in Tiege, south Russia.[14,15] Given all the Benjamin's in his lineage, it appears that the community decided that "B. B." was the best nickname. [16]

---

[8] Toews, *Lost Fatherland*, 43–45.
[9] Nickel and Nickel, *Nikkel-Nickel Family*, 6.
[10] Klassen,"Mennonites of Russia," 69–80.
[11] Juhnke, "Mennonite Benevolence," 23.
[12] Rempel and Carlson, *Mennonite Family*, 255.
[13] Photo from the book Toews, *Courage*, 25.
[14] Toews, *Courage*, 20–21.
[15] Janz experienced a crisis of faith which led to much searching and reading of scriptures. Ultimately, he decided to abandon the traditional Mennonite Church and join the Mennonite Brethren, in part based on his belief that baptism should be performed by immersion. His mother and sister were very disappointed, his sister responding "I will not hurt my parents by allowing myself to be in the river." Toews, *Courage*, 16.
[16] It should be noted that B.B. changed his last name from "Jantz" to "Janz" sometime in the early 1920s. See Toews, *Courage*, 1.

Photo 2: The Family of B. B. Janz in 1914

In 1922, Janz became the chairman of a group called the *Verband der Bürger Holländischer Herkunft, VBHH* (Union of Citizens of Dutch Lineage), an organization that carried on a persistent dialogue with the Bolsheviks regarding nonresistance and the military question.[17] Janz, a little known teacher from Tiege, was eminently qualified for this new role in his quiet dignity, courage, and ability to penetrate into the heart of complex issues.[18] In this role, he represented some 70,000 Mennonites in the Ukraine. In the early 1920s, the Mennonites in the Ukraine were confronted with Soviet policies that might involve them in the Red Army medical service. Although this was a non-combatant role, B.B. Janz worried that Mennonites associating with the Red Army would cause problems and lobbied for alternatives in medical and forestry units.[19] These negotiations continued throughout the mid-1920s. However, the Soviets adopted a new policy in 1926 in which "all hope for a special legal recognition of the Mennonite attitude towards war and the bearing of arms was shattered." Exemption from military service was virtually unheard of after 1926 and emigration was reduced to a trickle in the following years.[20] Life became increasingly perilous for Janz and he escaped from the Soviet Union in June, 1926.[21] Elder Johann Nikkel served with Janz

---

[17] Toews, *Lost Fatherland*, 55.
[18] Toews, *Czars, Soviets*, 96–98.
[19] Martin, "Revolution," 20.
[20] Toews, *Czars, Soviets*, 102–03.
[21] Toews, *Courage*, 56.

in the Tiege Mennonite Brethren Church. In 1929, Nikkel was arrested and starved to death in prison. The church building was taken over by the Soviets and converted to a club.[22] The complete story of Janz's efforts to defend the Mennonites' nonresistance beliefs and assist his people in emigrating to Canada is available in a biography by John B. Toews entitled *With Courage to Spare: The Life of B. B. Jantz, 1877 - 1964*.[23]

Beginning in 1926, Soviet policy began a more terroristic approach. Stalin's five-year plan was intended to create the Communist state, transforming the peasant farmer into a factory worker. These poor peasants were given the authority to decide which of the kulaks — the well-to-do farmers — were to be deported. Anne Applebaum quotes an American journalist's description of a kulak.[24]

> When therefore a man came into possession of two or three horses, as many or a few more cows, about half a dozen pigs, and when he raised three or four hundred poods of rye or wheat, he fell into the category of a kulak.

In 1929, Stalin ordered an intensification of the war on kulaks, ultimately demanding the liquidation of the kulaks as a class, a practice that came to be called "de-kulakization".[25,26] In contrast to Soviet propaganda, the famine of 1932-1933 was caused by a state mandated policy to starve the Ukrainians, driven by Stalin's fear of the Ukrainian nationalists.

Anne Konrad writes of her experiences to uncover prison interrogation records in her pursuit of information regarding her Mennonite relatives who disappeared in the USSR during the Stalinist purges. She explains that a "kulak" was anyone who employed more than three workers, had an annual income of more than 15 roubles, or was a registered church member, priest or preacher. Thousands of kulaks, many of them Mennonites, were deported to the barren regions of Siberia. Mennonite farmers were convicted of counter-revolutionary activity during the purges of the 1930s. In 1937, the Soviets were frantic about Hitler's anti-Bolshevism, targeting ethnic Germans in the Ukraine for counter-revolutionary activity. Konrad has uncovered interviews in the NKVD[27] files of Mennonites by the Ukrainian Security Service. In one such interview, a Mennonite farmer, Ivan I. Braun, was interrogated. After days of interrogation, Mr. Braun was accused of "shallow ploughing of

---

[22]Lohrenz, "Tiege," 721.
[23]See https://archive.org/details/WithCourageToSpareOCRopt.
[24]Applebaum, *Red Famine*, 86–87.
[25]Klassen, "Mennonites of Russia," 79.
[26]Konrad, *Red Quarter Moon*, 41.
[27]The NKVD was the leading Soviet secret police organization from 1934 to 1946. It is known for its role in political repression and for carrying out the Great Purge under Joseph Stalin. https://en.wikipedia.org/wiki/NKVD

land" and thus reducing the productivity of farm fields. He was convicted of sabotage and sentenced to death by shooting.[28]

Many of the Russian Mennonites chose to stay behind, hoping to preserve their way of life under the Czars. In fact, about two-thirds of the Mennonites decided to stay in Russia rather than emigrate in the early 1870s. The exact reasons for this are unknown and probably differed widely with each family. Some were perhaps too old to emigrate and withstand the rigors of travel by train, ship and wagon. Others perhaps felt that they could find ways of living with the Russian government and not compromise their faith. Koop argues that economic conditions were a significant factor, resulting in the more affluent Mennonites remaining in Russia whereas the less well off emigrated to America.[29,30]

All of those who stayed behind could not have anticipated the chaos and human tragedy that would descend upon them during the next seventy years. In rapid succession, they became the victims of what appeared to be a world gone mad. World War I, the Russian Revolution, the Stalinist purges and World War II all eventually destroyed the Mennonite way of life in Russia. Perhaps the most vicious and deadly era was that of Stalin's forced collectivization of Russian farms. In 1929, Stalin felt the collectivization process was not progressing rapidly enough and he ordered the army, police, and political extremists into the countryside. The resulting chaos is hard to comprehend for those of us who have lived with peace and prosperity in the United States. According to John Toews[31]:

> Families were simply loaded on sleighs in mid-winter and sent into wilderness areas with no provision for their survival. Many of the small children froze to death. A Mennonite minister, Wilhelm W. Janzen, was exiled to the far north soon after his return from Moscow in 1929. Janzen's children survived the journey only to die of starvation. Not long after that, both parents likewise succumbed to famine.

Life became pretty chaotic in 1945 after the German surrender since Russian agents were trying to prevent Mennonites from leaving the Soviet Union. Peter and Elfrieda Dyck tell the epic story of the rescue of Mennonites from the Soviet Union. The Soviets considered German-speaking people as "undesirable" and possible spies. These Mennonites made it clear that their heritage was actually Dutch and their ancestors had immigrated from

---

[28] Konrad, *Red Quarter Moon*, 289–290.
[29] Koop, "Economic Aspects," 143–56.
[30] In fact, it can be plausibly stated that the migration from Prussia to Russia was primarily based on economic rather than religious issues. Rempel states "economic necessity took our people to Russia." See Urry, *None but Saints*, 13.
[31] Toews, *Czars, Soviets*, 154.

the Netherlands. Incredibly, as late as 1949, some 5,500 West Prussian Mennonites were still living as refugees in the British Zone of Germany and the number in the Russian zone was about 1000.[32] Through the Mennonite Central Committee, the Dycks worked to relocate the Russian Mennonites to the Netherlands where they could emigrate to Canada or the United States.[33] Mennonites who remained and survived the Stalinist purges and World War II ultimately became citizens and began to live a normal life in the Soviet Union.

Exile to Siberia

Siberia is a huge almost unimaginable vast territory consisting of about one-third of the Asian continent and is one of the most sparsely populated regions on earth, containing only a small fraction of the world's population. Exile from what is now the Ukraine has resulted in Mennonites occupying almost all of the regions and territories of Siberia. In the last decades of the nineteenth century, Slavgorod in the Kulundian Steppes of Siberia offered Mennonites opportunities to purchase land. The czarist government was anxious to settle the vast, unpopulated Siberian regions and offered inducements including reductions in railroad fare, exemptions from taxes for five years, and a loan of 160 rubles.

After able leaders such as Franz Buller, Abraham Dück, and Isaac Friesen had reviewed the findings from earlier exploratory ventures, fifty-nine villages were established in 1911 as the Slavgorod settlement. Buller, Dück, and Friesen became respected elders and ministers of several churches in this settlement. Some Mennonites voluntarily migrated to Siberia from the Ukraine, encouraged in their decision by government loans and exemption from government service for three years. Peter Wiens was one of the first Mennonites to settle in Siberia. Peter emigrated from Schönau, Molotschna and established a business in agricultural machinery. As others joined, the settlement became known as Slavgorod and a Mennonite Brethren Church was established in 1914. The first minister was Dietrich Friesen who was followed by P. P. Friesen. Oberschulze Jacob A. Reimer was an outstanding leader during these formative years.[34] Later, the Soviet government closed the Brethren church and Mennonites began attending the Baptist Church of Slavgorod.[35]

The early pioneer days in Siberia were difficult with harsh winters and a very short growing season, resulting in settlers planting summer wheat.

---

[32] Penner. "West Prussian Mennonites," 245.
[33] Dyck and Dyck, *Up from the Rubble*, 15–33.
[34] Krahn, "Slavgorod," 537.
[35] Krahn, "Slavgorod Mennonite Settlement," 540–42.

Although the Mennonites might have expected to improve their plight in Siberia, they encountered many difficulties in this frontier land. There were no railroads or water transportation and harvested products had to be delivered over long distances by horse-drawn wagons. In addition, the colonists were subject to diseases such as typhus, small pox, and scarlet fever. Drought, prairie fires, roving wolves, and long, severe winters presented many hardships. In spite of these hazards, the Mennonite settlements were very productive in the early years, raising wheat, feed, wool, and eggs. However, this good fortune was not too last as the Siberian settlements and those in south Russia suffered severe economic and cultural decline in the wake of the World War I and the Russian Revolution.[36]

Unfortunately, most of the Mennonite emigration to Siberia was forced, beginning in 1931-1932 and continuing for the years 1937-1938 and in 1941. After World War II, Mennonites were repatriated from Germany to the Soviet Union, many thought to be spies and sent to Siberia.[37] In the 1950s, it was estimated that approximately 25,000 Mennonites were living in Siberia, most in the settlements of Slavgorod, Omsk, and Pavlodar. Today, these Mennonites are a mixture of Stalinist exiles and those repatriated by the Red army in 1945-1947.[38] In a village west of Omsk, one can still hear Plattdeutsch spoken and encounter Mennonite names such as Klassen, Wiebe, and Wiens. However, the borders between the Mennonite and Baptist communities are becoming blurred although surnames such as Tissen (Thiessen) and Vins (Wiens) still reveal Mennonite origins.[39]

In their decision to emigrate to America, the Ostrogers avoided the chaos created by Lenin and Stalin. Although their travels to America and the early settlements brought many challenges, these pioneers rarely encountered the human tragedy of their co-religionists in Russia. We return now to the Ostrogers journey to America and their pioneering efforts in the Great Plains. It was in these vast expanses where they encountered the dust bowl days of the 1930s while also holding onto their nonresistant beliefs during the tragedy of World War II.

---

[36] Toews, "Visit," 86–90.
[37] Krahn, "Siberia," 517–21.
[38] Yoder, "Mennonites are Strongest," para. 1.
[39] Juhnke, *People*, 287.

CHAPTER SIX

From Ostrog to Lone Tree, Kansas

EADERS SHOULD TRY to put themselves in the frame of mind to understand what life was like in the early 1870's to force another emigration to a foreign land with strange customs and a different language. Many of the elderly residents of the Ostrog villages could certainly remember the upheaval of their lives and the arduous journey from West Prussia in the early 1800's, less than fifty or sixty years earlier. The people of the Karolswalde communities had toiled hard in a land where the soil and weather conditions did not support the growing of grain crops yet they must have begun to call their villages home. America was often painted as a utopia and the threat of the Russian government to enforce the military draft and the use of the Russian language would have been strong inducements to emigrate. Yet we all know how the security of a home and established way of life can affect our desires to move to strange new environments.

The Journey to America

The Mennonite communities in the Ostrog area were barely seventy years old when Czar Alexander II issued an edict in 1870 ending the special privileges of the German Mennonites. The Russian language was to become the official language and within the decade the German residents were to become citizens of Russia. Military exemption would be abolished. Once the decision was made to emigrate, it was almost unanimous. In a letter[1] written by Tobias Unruh to the *Herold der Wahrheit* (Herald of Truth) on December 9, 1873, he states:

---

[1] Unruh, *Diary*, 1–12.

Here in Wolhynien nearly all Mennonites have decided to immigrate. Wherever possible people are disposing of property for a small proportion of what it is ordinarily worth; they take whatever they can get for it.

Tobias A. Unruh (Photo 3) was the district manager of the Mennonites in the Ostrog area, having oversight of eight villages with two church parishes, Karolswalde and Antonofka. Tobias was born in Karolswalde on 28 May 1819 and was married to Helena Thomas born in 1821. Unruh was sent to St. Petersburg in 1871 to ascertain facts about rumors that reached the villages regarding the Mennonites being placed in the military ranks of Russia.[2] In 1873 he was chosen as one of twelve delegates from Russia, Prussia, and Poland and sent to locate favorable territory for settling in America. Faced with compulsory military draft and a dire economic situation, the Karolswalde Mennonites were overjoyed to hear Tobias' glowing reports of life in America. After touring America, Tobias worked diligently through many trials and difficulties to insure that those who desired were able to come to America.[3] Tobias emigrated from Russia in 1875, crossing the Atlantic on the *S. S. Illinois* and arriving in Philadelphia on January 28, 1875. The following spring he settled in Turner County, South Dakota.[4]

Apparently, the Ostrogers sold their homes to Lutheran and Baptist Germans who were moving into the area.[5] In the face of economic loss, difficulties with the Russian authorities, a dangerous Atlantic voyage and an uncertain future in America, they pressed on with the decision to leave and follow the course of action that they believed to be right. Although most of these hardy souls left Russia in 1874 and 1875, many Mennonites continued to emigrate in small groups for the remainder of the nineteenth century. In the late nineteenth century, the main villages in the Ostrog area, Karolswalde and Antonofka, were practically abandoned. In 1910 there were only some twenty families gathering in a private home in Waldheim to conduct church services. Waldheim was one of two villages settled by Swiss Mennonites in 1837 and was served by elders Joseph and Johann Schrag.[6]

In preparation for the journey to America, each family packed all their belongings into a single crate that measured eight feet long, 2 1/2 feet wide and two feet deep. The most valuable and prized possessions were packed into this crate including cooking utensils, farm implements, bedding and clothes.[7] Each adult paid between $35 and $45 for the passage across the Atlantic

---

[2]Unruh and Thiessen, "Unruh, Tobias A." para. 3."
[3]Hiebert, *Holdeman People*, 97–99.
[4]Unruh, "Unruh, Tobias A." 786.
[5]Wuschke, "German Settlements," 52.
[6]Schrag, "Waldheim," 876.
[7]Unruh, *Helpless Poles*, 103–04.

Photo 3: Tobias A. Unruh

and children from one to fifteen traveled for one-half the adult fare. Infants traveled free of charge. The Ostrogers crossed the Atlantic on the ships of the Red Star Line. There were six ships that carried most of the Volhynia Mennonites from Europe to America.[8,9] In tracing families who made the arduous journey from Prussia to Russia and finally to America, we are able to identify shipboard passengers whose grandparents and great-grandparents were born in Prussia.

S.S. City of London - This ship left Liverpool on October 24, 1874 and arrived in New York City on November 18, 1874. There were 40 families from the Karolswalde area on this ship including ten Unruh families, five Schmidt families and six families who had the surname Jantz or Yantz. Jacob B. Johnson (Jantzen) *(id=1421434)* is listed as Jacob Yantz with his wife Helena Unruh and children Heinrich and Susan. Interestingly, Jacob's occupation is listed as "joiner" which some have defined as a skilled carpenter. As can be seen by his ID (i.e. a "4" in the seventh

---

[8] Haury, *Index*, 217–224.
[9] Schmidt, "Passenger Ship Lists," 7.

digit), Jacob is a grandson of Heinrich Jantz whose ID is 14214. The reader should consult Appendix Two (page 161) for a detailed description of this methodology for identifying people.

S.S. City of Montreal - This ship left Liverpool on November 16, 1874 and arrived in New York City on November 27, 1874. There were 27 families from the Karolswalde area on this ship including eight Unruh families, three Schmidt families and three Jantz families. It is highly likely that Caroline Jantz *(id=142191A)*, a descendant of David C. Jantz and wife of Henry C. Koehn, was one of these individuals. She was twelve years old at the time and listed as a "spinster".

S.S. Vaderland - The largest single group of emigrants embarked on this ship from Antwerp on December 4, 1874 and arrived in Philadelphia on December 26, 1874.[10] There were 115 families in this group from the village of Antonofka with the following tallies: Koehn (Köhn) - 20; Unruh - 14; Jantz - 13 and Schmidt - 11. Cornelius Jacob Koehn with his first wife Maria Becker and family traveled on the *S.S. Vaderland*. Cornelius' grandfather Heinrich *(prz604)* and wife Ancke Ratzlaff *(prz148)* can be found listed in the Przechowka Kirchen Buch. This fabled ship (Photo 4),[11] part of the Ostroger ancestral history, was sold to France in 1879 and renamed the Geographique. It was renamed the Southland in 1915 and sunk by a torpedo in 1917 off the Irish coast.[12]

S.S. Abbotsford - This ship left Antwerp on November 24, 1874 and experienced numerous difficulties including an outbreak of small pox and serious mechanical problems. The Abbottsford actually never made it to the shores of America and its passengers were picked up by the *S.S. Kenilworth* and the *S.S. Illinois*.

S.S. Kenilworth - This ship departed Liverpool with 284 passengers and arrived in Philadelphia on January 9, 1875. There were ten Jantz families, two Koehn families, six Schmidt families, and seven Unruh families on this ship. Benjamin D. Jantz *(id=142191)*, son of David C. Jantz, and wife Anna Nichols are listed on this ship.

---

[10] Although the German word for father is "Vater", most of the Mennonite literature lists this ship as S.S. Vaderland. This convention will be retained in this text.

[11] Photo 4 is from the George Grantham Bain Collection (Library of Congress). See https://www.loc.gov/resource/ggbain.19973/. There are no known restrictions on publication. For more information, see George Grantham Bain Collection - Rights and Restrictions Information https://www.loc.gov/rr/print/res/274_bain.html.

[12] See *The Red Star Line*, https://en.wikipedia.org/wiki/Red_Star_Line.

S.S. Illinois - Many of the original Abbottsford passengers, some 93 people, arrived in Philadelphia on the *S.S. Illinois* on January 28, 1875. There were five Jantz families and four Unruh families on this ship.

Photo 4: The S.S. Vaderland landed in Philadelphia on December 26, 1874.

Typically, these Mennonite emigrants held third-class tickets. For them, the passage to America was no pleasure trip: they were kept at the bottom of the ship, packed tightly together in large dormitories with hundreds of beds. If the weather obliged, they would be allowed on deck to escape the stuffy conditions. One can imagine the confusion on arriving in America and trying to locate friends and relatives who took different paths in their journey to America. Excerpts from Abe Unruh's book are revealing:[13]

> They had a stormy voyage but all arrived safely. One family had to remain in New York on account of a sick child . . .
>
> Sunday morning January 10 1875, a number of emigrants arrived and came to this county from the station, Bird-in-Hand, they received a hearty reception from our brethren and the Amish. . . four Jantz families, two Dirks familes, two Schultz families, one Unruh family, one Schmidt family.
>
> . . . they are all scattered abroad and many of them will not see each other here in America any more . . . Adam Jantz would like to know the address of Henry Schmidt, both parties are from the village of Karolswalde.

---

[13] Unruh, *Helpless Poles*, 131.

Generally speaking, the Mennonites from the Ostrog area quickly traveled from the East coast to Kansas with a few staying behind in Pennsylvania. Later moves occurred to Oklahoma, the Dakotas and Canada. Although many of the Ostrogers came to America on the *S.S Vaderland*, other groups traveled separately and settled in different communities. J.A. Boese writes about the Mennonites of Avon, South Dakota who came to the United States on the *S.S. Colina*, arriving in New York on September 2, 1874, settling initially in Yankton, Dakota Territory.[14] Many of the Kleine Gemeinde group traveled on different ships including the *S.S. Cimbria*, *S.S. Hammonia*, and the *S.S. Teutonia.*, settling initially in Manitoba, Canada.[15]

Arrival in America and Early Years in Kansas

Abe Unruh has written that 1275 Mennonite families arrived in America during the years of the greatest emigration.[16] Of these almost half eventually traveled to Kansas and settled on the vast, desolate prairies. Although the Ostrogers knew that they were settling in an area where the land was fertile and the climate good for raising grain crops, they were probably not ready for the bitter winters and the difficulties they would encounter in those first few years. Although much had been made of the fierce Indians that roamed the Plains, the Indians had been largely subdued and relocated to reservations by the time the Mennonites settled in Kansas.[17] The last attack on white settlements in Kansas occurred in 1878, four years after the Mennonite settlements began in Kansas. The settlers would encounter other more serious natural and man-made calamities before they had successfully homesteaded in Kansas. A quote from Christian Krehbiel's autobiography[18] indicates what it was like in the fall of 1873, shortly before the Mennonites arrived in America.

---

[14]Boese, "Story," 29–43.
[15]Plett, *Saints*, 324–29.
[16]Unruh, *Helpless Poles*, 137.
[17]The Mennonite settlers benefited from government actions that have since been roundly condemned. Soon after the Civil War, nomadic Plains tribes were forced by government treaties to accept reservation confinement. The U.S. government reservation policy was adopted for the benefit of white farmers, railroad builders, miners, and others who were anxious to move onto Indian hunting lands in Kansas, Colorado, Nebraska, and the Dakotas. See Kroeker, "Natives," para. 3.
[18]Krehbiel, *Steppes*, 38.

That fall grasshoppers in dense swarms descended on Kansas and ate everything that was green or soft. Christian Hirschler, who had his first stand of corn in the fields, tried to save something by cutting and shocking some of the corn; but the grasshoppers ate even the shocks. The insects lay so thick on the railroad tracks that the engines slipped and stalled. Throughout that part of Kansas ..., the pest left everything bare and black. It was terrifying.

The Ostrogers arrived in America in the winter of 1874–75. The Mennonite communities in America were severely taxed to accommodate such a large influx of people and help them get settled. During the first winter many stayed on the East coast with friends or relatives in the Mennonite and Amish communities of Lancaster, Pennsylvania. Some traveled to Ohio to stay in the Mennonite settlements of that state. The group of immigrants arriving on the *S.S. Vaderland* almost met with tragedy when they decided to go on to Kansas that first winter. These people were penniless and had to depend completely on the welfare of the American Mennonite community. Some ninety families were put on trains and transported to Florence, Kansas where they were finally accommodated in one large store about thirty feet wide by eighty feet long. Through the efforts of the Mennonite Board of Guardians and the Kansas Relief Committee, these people were helped through that first terrible winter in Kansas. David Holdeman, the uncle of John Holdeman, was a member of the Kansas Relief Committee and he worked closely with these immigrants to help get them settled and begin investments in land so they could become self-sufficient.

Figure 11: A Mennonite Residence in Oklahoma Territory

By June of 1875, many of the immigrants were beginning settlements on a seven section plot of land near Canton, Kansas. This land had been dispersed in forty acre plots to each family and had been purchased through the assistance of the Kansas Relief Committee. In the fall of 1878, John Holdeman made his first visit to this community to preach and become acquainted with the people.[19] Many worshippers believed that Holdeman preached the truth and seventy souls were converted and received baptism into the Holdeman Church, the beginning of the Lone Tree congregation.[20,21] By

---

[19] Hiebert, *Holdeman People*, 116.
[20] Gospel Publishers, *Histories*, 297.
[21] Hiebert, *Holdeman People*, 92–93.

1882, there were 218 members in the Lone Tree congregation. These Kansas pioneers were beginning to prosper in their new land and the original forty acres per family was not sufficient. About this time, some of the Lone Tree congregation began to look for land in Oklahoma, taking advantage of the land rush that began in 1893. A small Holdeman group established a church in the vicinity of what today is the community of Fairview, Oklahoma.[22,23]

Homesteading in Lone Tree

Lone Tree Township was named after a large, lone, cottonwood tree, the tallest in the community for many years and, in fond memories, sometimes thought to be the only tree in the township when the Ostrogers first arrived. One hundred families, a total of 662 persons, immigrated from Antonofka and settled in Lone Tree on a seven section block of land near Canton, Kansas.[24] From the Canton Church Book, 22 Jantz families, 46 Koehn families, 22 Schmidt families, and 27 Unruh families are listed.[25] The Lone Tree congregation of the Church of God in Christ, Mennonite holds much symbolic meaning for the Holdeman people with resonant connections to the sister village, Antonofka, in Ostrog and the journey to America on the *S. S. Vaderland*. Today, the Lone Tree congregation continues to be one of the largest among the Holdeman groups.

In Lone Tree, the original homes were situated along a middle road with farmland extending out on both sides, similar to the arrangement in the Russian communities. The first church was a sod structure which was built in 1879 and where the settlers said their first prayers while kneeling on a dirt floor.[26] This church served the Holdeman Mennonite community for two years before a frame structure was built in 1880. The original sod church was located seven miles north of Moundridge, Kansas.

Henry B. Koehn, born 5 December 1846 in Antonofka, was one of the first ordained ministers at Lone Tree. Henry and his family made the journey across the Atlantic on the *S. S. Vaterland*, settling in a sod home on section 23, Lone Tree Township, McPherson County, Kansas.[27] An excerpt from the *The Helpless Poles*[28] describes the experiences of a son of Henry B. Koehn and gives us some idea of how difficult it was to get started in the new world:

---

[22] Kroeker, "Mennonites," 114–120.
[23] The image in Figure 11 is from the article by Kroeker, "Mennonites," 120.
[24] Hiebert, *Holdeman People*, 111.
[25] Mueller, *Church*, 1–4.
[26] Unruh, *Helpless Poles*, 175–76.
[27] Koehn, *Compilation*, 1–3.
[28] Unruh, *Helpless Poles*, 151.

Figure 12: A Residence on the Treeless Plains of Kansas

In April when spring was well on its way, father took his family and belongings to Newton, Kansas, from there they were taken by wagon to their farmstead on section 23, in Lone Tree Township, McPherson County. They camped on the open prairies the first night, no protection or shelter over their heads, nothing in sight but barren prairies in every direction. The next morning he dug a trench six feet wide and twelve feet long in the banks of Sand Creek, laid up a side with sod and built a roof over it with long slough grass and moved into their dwelling. But their first home was only of a short duration, since it was built near the stream along the banks of Sand Creek. The first rain overflowed its banks and the family had to abandon their new home. The next home was built a little larger, and although, also out of sod, it was built more durable and far enough away from the creek that overflowing waters could not molest it. When the home was completed, a small plot was dug for a garden, and father went looking for work.

The Lone Tree congregation grew rapidly and some of the Holdeman people began to look for land in Oklahoma. Mennonite migrations to Oklahoma began as soon as the Indian Territory was opened for white settlement on April 22, 1892.[29] The Cherokee Strip Land Run began at noon on September 16, 1893, with an estimated 100,000 participants hoping to stake claim to part of the six million acres and 40,000 homesteads on what had formerly been Cherokee grazing land.[30] Over the next several years and into the early twentieth century, several Holdeman congregations were established

---

[29] Krahn, "Oklahoma," 33.
[30] See https://en.wikipedia.org/wiki/Land_Run_of_1893.

in Oklahoma at Fairview and Pauls Valley near Chickasha in 1902.[31] The Oklahoma settlers faced a harsh and unfriendly environment where there were no graded roads and no bridges to cross the Cimarron River. Rattlesnakes were an ever present danger. The families of Benjamin T. Nightingale, Henry Nichols, and Henry W. Koehn were the first of the CGCM congregations to leave central Kansas and establish the Fairview congregation in March, 1895.[32] Benjamin H. Schmidt, his wife Helena and her father Benjamin D. Jantz, all passed away in Chickasha and Pauls Valley.

A reproduction of an image (Figure 12) from Clarence Hiebert's scrapbook about Russian Mennonite immigrants provides the reader with a visual experience of what life might have been like on the treeless plains of Kansas.[33] The early settlers faced many hardships and were unprepared to deal with Kansas pioneer life. Lack of doctors and medical aid resulted in much sickness and early death. Drought, the relentless southwest winds, grasshopper plagues, and intense heat were frequent companions of the early settlers. In the mid-twentieth century, an editor writing in the *Messenger of Truth* aptly describes the challenges of Kansas weather:[34]

> The farmer may sow and never reap a harvest. In our great plains, the winds may blow away both seed and earth. Late hard frosts will destroy growing grain, and drought will turn fertile fields into a parched wasteland. The tremendous forces of nature may bless and prosper the plant, and may also utterly destroy it. Sometimes it also is true that a farmer reaps where he has not sown. Nature has a wonderful power of carrying out its ways, and it may be to man's advantage, or he may be crushed by its resistance.

Citizens of America

Today, the Holdeman people are citizens and have spread all over the United States and Canada. In the 1930s, many of these people found themselves struggling for a living in the dust bowls of the prairie states. Their home towns provide an odd mixture of names reflecting the Indian presence in the Plains, early explorers, and the impact of political leaders. We are often informed about these towns through publlished genealogies: Chickasha, Montezuma, Ulysses.

Halstead, a small town along the Santa Fe railroad in Harvey County, became the administrative and cultural center of the Kansas Mennonite

---

[31] Hiebert, *Holdeman People*, 119, 243.
[32] History read by Jerry Koehn, Fairview Congregation: April 1895–1995, Central Worship Services and Recollections (Printed in the U.S.A - no date).
[33] Hiebert, *Brothers*, 9.
[34] no author, "Sin and Grace", para. 8.

Photo 5: The Halstead Milling Company

immigration movement. Bernard Warkentin established a milling business in Halstead and also introduced the hard red winter wheat. The Halstead Mill (Photo 5), situated along the Little Arkansas River, was operated by water power. The mill was opened by Bernhard Warkentin in 1874. In 1877, the mill was converted to steam power and moved near the railroad tracks.[35] In this early photograph, one can see the railroad crossing and the beginnings of what was to become Main Street in Halstead.[36] In Photo 6, the Halstead Co-op of 2019, previously the Mill, is pictured from the same vantage point along Main Street. The first school of Mennonite higher education was also founded in Halstead — the Halstead Seminary. Situated in a new building on the corner of 4th and College Street, the seminary was the only post-primary educational institution in America at the time. The building was dedicated on September 16, 1883 and 545 students studied in the seminary over the next decade.[37]

It is interesting to look at the birth places of the Ostroger descendants who were born in the twentieth century. A sample from the author's database shows that 132 people were born in Moundridge, Kansas; 103 in Montezuma, Kansas; 93 in Halstead, Kansas; and 55 in Chickasha, Oklahoma. Each community had its uniqueness that has provided a lasting treasure of memories. Halstead was actually known as Black Kettle in the early 1870s before it was incorporated in 1877.[38] Chief Black Kettle was one of the most eloquent speakers for the Cheyenne Indians and an advocate for peace. Today, Chief Black Kettle has only a small creek flowing behind the mill in Halstead to

---

[35] Haury, "Bernhard Warkentin," 74.
[36] Smith, *Story*, 651.
[37] Juhnke, "Lord Build," 4–7.
[38] Mayfield, *Halstead*, 5.

PART ONE   CHAPTER SIX   Lone Tree

Photo 6: The Halstead Co-op in 2019, Viewed from the Same Vantage Point as the Halstead Mill in 1877 (photgraph by the author).

honor his memory.[39,40]

In the 1930s, farming practices and soil conservation methods had not matured significantly to counteract the wind, drought, and dust in the prairie states. Many struggled to make a living during the dust bowl days where the unanchored soil and the prevailing southerly winds created huge clouds that sometimes blackened the sky — referred to as Black Blizzards.[41] Western Kansas, Oklahoma, and the Texas Panhandle were in the heart of the dust bowl. A farm in Dalhart, Texas provides a visual clue of these dust bowl days where a solitary windmill suggests that there was once a thriving family (Figure 13).[42]

Figure 13: Abandoned Farm Dalhart, Texas. 1938

In addition to the dust, hot weather, and insects, the settlers lived with tornadoes since all of the prairie states lie in what has been called "tornado alley." Probably each community has its tales to tell of tornadoes. Halstead was hit hard on May 1, 1895. In a letter published by the Halstead Independent from J.W. Smith to his wife, the tornado was described as being forty to eighty rods wide and visible for an hour.[43] There was considerable injury and loss of life.

---

[39] Rydford, *Indian Place Names*, 300–09.

[40] As a youth, the author was able to use the Black Kettle as a pleasant summer swimming hole. However, the history of the Black Kettle is painful and raises questions about the white settlements in the Plains states. Cheyenne Peace Chief Black Kettle was murdered in the massacre on the Washita River (Oklahoma) on November 27, 1868 by George Custer and the Seventh Calvary. See Kroeker, "Natives," para. 4.

[41] See https://en.wikipedia.org/wiki/Dust_Bowl.

[42] Dorothea Lange, "Abandoned Farm North of Dalhart, Texas. 1938," The Library of Congress, Prints and Photographs Division.

[43] A rod is equivalent to 16.5 feet. So, the tornado at eighty rods wide would be approximately a quarter mile wide.

PART ONE CHAPTER SIX Lone Tree

Building the Church

We have, figuratively speaking, traveled from Groningen in the Netherlands, through Prussia and Russia and finally to America. We also have an understanding of the hardships and challenges that the conservative Mennonites encountered. We have seen how the folkways and religion have been passed down through the centuries in specific families as they moved from Przechowka to Antonofka and then to Lone Tree.

Across the span of 400 years, the people and their religion have coalesced into an ethnic group and a conservative Mennonite religion. In the early days of the sixteenth century, small but passionate and disorganized groups of Anabaptists worked to establish a more coherent institution. In this mix of cultures and beliefs, Menno Simons stepped forward to build a church, laying the foundation for John Holdeman to establish the Church of God in Christ, Mennonite.

PART TWO

Nonresistance and a People Apart

HE EXPERIENCE OF LEONID KOEHN in the village Antonofka of modern Ukraine tells us what life might have been like if the so called "helpless Poles" had remained in Russia — most certainly starvation or exile to Siberia. Although the Ostrogers faced a hazardous journey, the decision to emigrate can be seen in hindsight as one that ultimately led to a prosperous and peaceful life in America.

In their migrations across the countries of Europe, the conservative Mennonites affiliated with different congregations, however they never abandoned the core beliefs that had been articulated by Menno Simons in the sixteenth century. In the subsequent 400 years, these families traveled together, worshiped together, worked and lived together while also holding on to the basic tenets expressed by the Anabaptists, among them nonresistance and separation from the world. In their travels, they sometimes lost contact with established congregations as when the Groningen Old Flemish Society dissolved in 1815, resulting in considerable uncertainty about their formal faith community. Upon arriving in America, they found in John Holdeman and his convictions, a leader and religion that was compatible with their way of life and view of the world. In contrast to the chaos of Russia, the Holdeman Mennonites confronted more subtle challenges in a society focused on material goods and the rapid advancement of technology, offering benefits while also making it difficult to retain their commitment to live apart from worldly society.

In Part Two, we look first at the gradual emergence of the Mennonite faith and the early church. Menno Simons and Dirk Philips worked to build the church in the Netherlands and northern Germany. Through these leaders' commitment and tireless efforts, the Anabaptist doctrine was spread throughout conservative Mennonite communities. In the early sixteenth century, the basic tenets were readily observable in the practices of the Groningen Old Flemish Society and in the related congregations in northeastern Netherlands and Prussia. Tracing these groups through Prussia, Russia and America leads us to the modern day Church of God in Christ, Mennonite and the members have embraced Anabaptism in daily life. What one sees in these four hundred years is an unbroken chain connection people, faith, and practice. Now, in the modern world, we examine how the Holdeman people are challenged to maintain their adherence to the core principles of Anabaptism — separation from the world and nonresistance.

As they now embrace many of the modern conveniences of a secular world and accept new members from diverse communities, the people of the Church of God in Christ, Mennonite are likely to face even more serious challenges than the ones their forbears encountered in the Europe of earlier centuries. Computers, technology, the Internet, higher education, and even mission outreach are stressing the Church and its members in unexpected ways.

Through their beliefs and Dutch-Prussian heritage, the Holdemans have forged a group identity that is evident in many of their local communities. However, some scholars have suggested that a crisis of group identity exists within the various Mennonite groups. Identity can take on many forms and, in Part Two, we use the writings from the *Messenger of Truth* and family relationships as a method to better understand group cohesion and adherence to the Anabaptist principles among the Holdeman people. In their candid reports about the difficulties of living in modern society, we are able to understand how they view their responsibilities to society and citizenship. We are left with one question. Will the world let the Holdemans retain their unique Mennonite identity or are they facing an existential threat from the press of a modern, pluralistic society?

CHAPTER SEVEN

Building the Church

S THE MENNONITES ESTABLISHED COMMUNITIES in Russia, various social, economic, and political pressures led to the emergence of diverse communities. This divergence in belief resulted in what scholars have called the "Anabaptist sickness" (German: *Täuferkrankheit*) — a tendency for the settlers to form new groups based on relatively minor differences. As Epp writes, these bifurcations became almost endless.[1] The internal fragmentation was largely the result of the Anabaptist rejection of external authority such as the Catholic pope while also insisting that each Mennonite could interpret the Bible for himself. This freedom obviously led to many different perspectives and, in south Russia alone, to the founding of the Mennonite Brethren, the Krimmer Mennonite Brethren, and the Kleine Gemeinde.[2,3] This trend persisted in Manitoba, Canada where three groups quickly diverged into eight churches in the early twentieth century.[4] These break-away groups tended to be critical of secular society, reacting to what they saw as godless living within their own ranks. In the transition to America, these sojourners found their religious homes in many different congregations. Driedger describes the turbulent environment that the Mennonites faced in America, a situation that led to the emergence of talented and courageous leaders.[5]

> The world is a changing mass of individuals, groups, communities, nations struggling for selfhood, for stable environments, for meaningful arenas which make sense, and for important ideals and goals.

---

[1] Epp, *Mennonites in Canada*, 37–40.
[2] Bender and Smith, *Mennonites and Their Heritage*, 122–28.
[3] Toews, *Mennonites in American Society*, 28.
[4] Epp, *Mennonites in Canada*, 283–84.
[5] Driedger, *Mennonite Identity*, 24.

PART TWO   CHAPTER SEVEN   Building the Church

The rulings of emperors, czars, and kings shaped much of the life and behavior of the early Mennonites in the Netherlands, Prussia, and Russia. Out of this chaos, leaders emerged who organized the congregations and sustained the church membership throughout the tumultuous years in Europe and the early settlements in America.

Menno and Dirk Build a Church

Initially, Menno Simons was ambivalent about assuming leadership of the Dutch Anabpatists, savoring for a time his position of parish priest and the associated income, ease of life, and prestige. However, in the autumn of 1533, the militant Münterites became active in the Netherlands, a situation which moved Menno to actively counteract the grievous errors of this radical sect. Given his reticence about leaving the Catholic Church, it wasn't until January 30, 1536 that Menno publicly renounced his priesthood and shortly thereafter he was baptized by Obbe Philips.[6] About a year after leaving the priesthood, a group of Anabaptist Brethren urged Menno to become a minister. He consented to assume this new role, being fully aware that he would now bear the "heavy cross of persecution".[7]

The early Anabaptists debated the need for a physical church, some believing that one could serve God without preachers, elders, and a visible church. Menno Simons and his close compatriot, Dirk Philips, believed that there were both practical and faith-based reasons for a physical church and they proceeded to build this church.[8] Building the church became very difficult when anyone who gave food or shelter to Menno was to be punished by death. Organizing and preaching to groups encountered great risk. Several meetings of the emerging Mennonite church in Amsterdam were held in the home of minister Jan Claes for which Claes suffered death on January 19, 1544.

After he left the priesthood, Menno traveled extensively, spending most of his time in the Dutch province of Groningen (Map 1). In January 1537, Menno was ordained bishop of the Groningen Anabaptists by Obbe Philips. His writings and presence in the province of Groningen clearly had an impact on the formation of the group known as the Groningen Old Flemish Society

---

[6] Obbe Philips was a leader of the Anabaptists in the Netherlands and a brother of Dirk Philips. He was the illegitimate son of a Catholic priest at Leeuwarden. Obbe applied himself to the study of medicine and, in his contacts with learned men, he soon began to question Catholic doctrine. See Zijpp, "Obbe Philips," 9–10.

[7] Horsch, *Mennonites in Europe*, 189–93.

[8] Dirk Philips, perhaps the greatest Dutch Anabaptist theologian, opposed the spiritualist movement, believing that Christ had commanded the founding of the visible church with apostles organizing congregations of elders, ministers, and deacons. See Zijpp, "The Early Dutch Anabaptists," 77–78.

and the related Przechowka churches in Prussia. In part due to the dangers he encountered in the Netherlands, Menno moved his labors to northwest Germany and Poland, out of the reach of Emperor Charles V, and where many of the free cites such as Danzig were more tolerant of the Anabaptists.[9]

Perhaps Menno's greatest legacy lies in his preservation of Anabaptist principles in the Netherlands at a time when there were serious trials and challenges. Notably, his *Foundation Book* did much to restore the original Anabaptist concepts where his writings revealed a man who sincerely wanted to give all for the Christian church. One of the most significant theological controversies that has relevance for the Holdeman people today was Menno's stance on church discipline. This issue was discussed in a major conference in 1557 where some fifty representatives appealed to Menno to not take an extreme position related to the ban and avoidance. In the end, Menno and Dirk responded in writing and defended the more rigid position.[10] These more conservative stances were readily embraced by the Groningen Old Flemish and their congregations in the Przechowka communities. In the sixteenth century, there were fifteen Old Flemish congregations in the province of Groningen and three in Prussia that adhered to these more conservative practices.[11,12]

The Przechowka Churches

The Groningen Old Flemish congregations insisted on the strict maintenance of both doctrine and practice, holding fast to Anabaptist principles endorsed by Menno and Dirk such as footwashing and the ban. Simply put, they stood for plain living and plain clothing. Although the Groningen Old Flemish did not form until some seventy years after Menno's death, it is clear that his ministry had a deep impact on the practices of the Old Flemish churches.

Early in the eighteenth century, several Old Flemish Dutch ministers traveled to the Przechowka communities, preaching and providing support to assist the fledgling Prussian congregations. In July, 1719 elder Hendrik Berents Hulshof visited and based his sermon on Eph. 6:11–13 — *Put on the whole armor of God, so that you may be able to stand against the wiles of the devil.* The Prussian brethren also requested the Dutch visitors to bring them Biestkens Bibles[13], hymnals and the works of Menno Simons

---

[9]Horsch, *Mennonites in Europe*, 196–98.
[10]Krahn, "Menno Simons," 579–82.
[11]Zijpp, "Groningen Old Flemish Mennonites," 595.
[12]Zijpp, "Groningen", 593.
[13]The Bible known as the "Biestkens Bible" was printed in 1560 in Emden by Nikolaes Biestkens. Biestkens was a member of the Mennonite congregation in Emden. Prior to 1560, the Mennonites used a Low German Bible. The use of the Biestkens Bible was continued longest by the Old Flemish churches. See Neff, "Biestkens Bible," 340-41.

and Dirk Philips. This moral support was greatly appreciated and the Dutch Mennonites continued monetary assistance to the Prussian churches throughout much of the eighteenth century.[14]

Like their mother church in Przechowka, the Jeziorka Mennonites belonged to the Groningen Old Flemish and they also received financial aid from the Dutch Mennonite Committee in Amsterdam.[15] In 1727, thirteen Mennonites of Dutch origin established the congregation just west of the Vistula river and were joined a few years later by twelve families who were fleeing persecution from the Catholics in Kulm (Map 2). At some later point, the meadering Vistula changed course and the Jeziorka community found themselves on the right bank of the river.[16] This group was closely affiliated with Przechowka and they routinely crossed the Vistula river to attend church services.

The Russian Mennonite Churches

The seeds of religious controversy and diversity were sown in the Prussian congregations. Among the growing divisions within the Mennonite communities, several leaders stepped forward to carry the faith to Russia and lead the migration to America. Their efforts shaped new congregations, stemming from earlier cultural and religious differences. The nineteenth century in Russia was a time of great religious debate and ferment for the Mennonites, leading to various splinter groups — the Kleine Gemeinde (*De Kleen-gemeenta* in Low German), the Mennonite Brethren, and the Krimmer Mennonite Brethren.

The Kleine Gemeinde

Klaas Reimer and other like-minded members of his group were concerned about lapses in the Mennonite communities of Prussia. Reimer and his group left Danzig in 1801 and settled initially in the Chortitza colony of south Russia and later moved to Molotschna. In 1812, Klaas Reimer, Cornelius Janzen, and supporters began their own worship services. Reimer was elected elder of this group in 1814 in the presence of elder Heinrich Janzen.[17]

Reimer felt that the principles that initially united the Anabaptists were becoming less relevant in the traditional congregations. The core principle of separation from the world had disappeared. Frivolous behavior was becoming part of everyday life and proper nonresistant behavior was less evident. Reimer stirred up a lot of dissension and he questioned the right of the local

---

[14]Crous, "Przechovka," 225–26.
[15]Zijpp, "Jeziorka," 110.
[16]Klassen, *Mennonites in Early Modern Poland*, 86–87.
[17]Friesen, *Mennonite Brotherhood*, 127–35.

police authority, the Gebietsamt, to silence him.[18] He ignored these threats and joined with eighteen others to organize their own church which was to become known as the Kleine Gemeinde (Little Church or Congregation).[19]

The entire Kleine Gemeinde (KG) group emigrated to North America in 1874, maintaining all the while an ultra-conservative heritage based on the teachings of Klaas Reimer. A smaller group led by Peter Jansen settled in Nebraska and two larger groups established communities in Manitoba.[20] It is in Canada and the province of Manitoba that we see the connection to the Holdeman group. Elder Peter P. Toews had become concerned with the spiritual condition of the KG church and initiated correspondence with John Holdeman who visited the Kleine Gemeinde group in 1879. Holdeman advised Toews that he needed to be rebaptized and reordained in order to be in the apostolic succession of truth.[21] In 1881, elder Peter Toews, three other ministers, and 165 members of the Kleine Gemeinde Manitoba group were re-baptized and joined the Holdeman church. Toews became a leader in the church, co-founding in 1897 the *Botschafter der Wahrheit* (Ambassador of Truth) of the Church of God in Christ, Mennonite — the first denominational paper among the Russian Mennonites.[22] However, the schism between the Kleine Gemeinde and the Church of God in Christ, Mennonite continued, dividing families with children joining the Holdeman church while parents remained with the Kleine Gemeinde. For example, the Giesbrecht children Wilhelm and Margaretha joined the Holdemans while their mother, Margaretha, stayed with the Kleine Gemeinde.[23]

---

[18] The Gebietsamt was the authority established by the Mennonites in Russia to govern a settlement consisting of a number of villages. See Krahn, "Gebietsamt," 441.
[19] Smith, *Story*, 422–25.
[20] Miller, "Jansen Nebraska," 173–75.
[21] Epp, *Mennonites in Canada*, 290.
[22] Plett, *Saints and Sinners*, 307.
[23] Plett, *Saints and Sinners*, 230.

The Mennonite Brethren

The Mennonite Brethren was another break-away group in the turbulent environment of nineteenth century Russia, protesting specific types of moral decadence that they found in the Mennonite Church — drinking, dancing, and card playing. In 1860, the founders of this group delivered the Document of Secession to the elders of the Molotschna Mennonite Church as a means of recapturing *wie es im Anfang war* (how it was in the beginning).[24] The Mennonite Brethren Church continued to grow in the years from 1865 to 1872 with able leaders such as Jacob Jantz, Christian Schmidt, and Johan Fast.[25] This group thrived in Russia until the Communist Revolution, many emigrating to Canada in the 1920s.

The Holdeman Church in America

The dissolution of the Groningen Old Flemish in 1815 left the Ostrogers without a stable religious framework in contrast to the Mennonites in south Russia. The south Russian congregations were separated both geographically and theologically from the more conservative Ostrogers. When they arrived in America, these hapless souls turned to John Holdeman for succor and spiritual guidance.

John Holdeman was the founder of the Church of God in Christ, Mennonite, commonly referred to as the Holdeman Church. Holdeman was married to Elizabeth Ritter on November 18, 1852. As a young adult, John studied the Bible, church history, and the historic Mennonite confessions, concluding that his Old Mennonite Church was corrupt.[26] Holdeman established the Church of God in Christ, Mennonite in 1858 hoping to restore the teachings of the early Christian fathers that he felt had been abandoned by most Mennonite churches. All questions were to be decided on a Scriptural basis after much prayer and careful study.[27] Holdeman studied and wrote extensively and major publications included *Eine Geschichte der Gemeinde Gottes* (History of the Church of God) and *Ein Spiegel der Wahrheit* (Mirror of Truth). In the preface to his book, the *Mirror of Truth*, we can see Holdeman's commitment that resulted in the creation of the Church of God in Christ, Mennonite.[28]

---

[24] Kauffman and Leland, *Anabaptists*, 39–40.
[25] Lohrenz, "Mennonite Brethren Church," 497.
[26] Hiebert, *Holdeman People*, 61.
[27] Bender and Smith, *Mennonites and Their Heritage*, 107.
[28] Holdeman, *Mirror*, 12–13.

> With a sorrowing heart one finds that in recent years, especially with the passing of the eighteenth and the beginning of the nineteenth centuries, the Church has slackened in its labor to maintain the whole truth. An apostasy has set in on account of the laxity and drowsiness of the ministry, caused by the love of this world. . . . Because of such apostasy and erroneous opinions among so-called Mennonites and others, I have been persuaded to take up my pen, that the reader may better differentiate between truth and falsehood, light and darkness, the sweet and the sour, righteousness and iniquity, the true doctrine and unclean or false teachings.

This passage demonstrates Holdeman's rhetorical skills and his desire to establish the true church. However, John Holdeman was to experience many trials and tribulations before the Church of God in Christ, Mennonite was to become a reality.

In his early years, John lived in Ohio and, as a young man of twenty-five years, he struggled to remain a member of the established Mennonite Church. He soon realized that he could not remain faithful to the church and inner voices were calling him to become a minister. Holdeman stated publicly that the old church should be split into two parts and cited the works of Menno Simons and Dirk Philips to support his position. In April, 1859 Holdeman separated from the old Mennonite Church, explaining at a conference that those who do not practice avoidance should be excommunicated.[29] In addition to his doctrine on avoidance, Holdeman weathered other theological storms including the form of baptism — by immersion or pouring. In fact, he dedicated an entire chapter to the form of baptism in his book *The Mirror of Truth*, stating in his conclusion:[30]

> Thanks be to God that He has to this hour by His unfailing providence preserved baptism by pouring, which is appropriate to all places, times, and circumstances.

Given the controversies, the church grew slowly with a few converts from the Amish and Lutheran churches. In 1878, the Lone Tree Church near Moundridge, Kansas was established where John Holdeman baptized seventy members.[31] With the influx of these impoverished Ostrogers from Russia, the Holdeman Church grew rapidly to about 500 members in 1883.[32] In addition to the Ostrogers from Antonofka, many members of the Kleine Gemeinde, the little church that had originated in an 1812 schism in Russia, also joined

---

[29] Hiebert, *Holdeman People*, 185–189.
[30] Holdeman, *Mirror*, 107.
[31] Johnson, "Lone Tree", 388.
[32] Hiebert, *Holdeman People*, 202.

with Holdeman.³³ John Holdeman died on March 10, 1900 and is buried in the Lone Tree Church cemetery (Photo 7).

Photo 7: *John Holdeman Gravestone (photograph by the author).*

Surviving in the Twentieth Century

How was the Church going to survive after the passing of John Holdeman? The Church of God in Christ, Mennonite turned to Frederick C. Fricke, a German-born minister who converted from Lutheranism to assume Holdeman's responsibilities. Fricke was ordained to the ministry by John Holdeman on October 31, 1893. He was an able evangelist and wise counselor who successfully introduced Sunday school to many congregations.³⁴ Given the tensions in the Church that existed between the Ostrogers and the Kleine Gemeinde, Fricke was a logical choice, having not been associated with either

---

³³Juhnke, *Vision*, 51–52.
³⁴Fricke, "Fricke," 398.

faction.³⁵ After Fricke's passing in 1947, leadership in the church became much more diverse with many individuals assuming responsibilities.

Fricke had an abiding interest in evangelizing, evident in his tract and *Messenger of Truth* publications. With this growing support, missionary work was initiated in the 1921 General Conference with the appointment of five evangelists. Missionary work began in earnest a few years later with pioneering efforts in Mexico.³⁶ In the fall of 1927, several Koehn families prepared for a long journey to Cuauhtémoc, Chihuahua, Mexico with plans to establish new homes and begin mission work. In addition to sharing their faith with groups in Mexico, these pioneers were concerned about looser trends in the Church and activities in the public schools such as saluting the flag. Brother John Koehn was instrumental in sharing the Gospel with the Mexican people. The Koehn families experienced much hardship but their efforts ultimately led to the establishment of missions in Mexico.³⁷

Membership

Excommunication, avoidance, and re-acceptance are the procedures used by the Holdeman Church to discipline wayward members. This practice is based largely on Matt. 18:15–18 and, in part, suggests the member should be treated as an outsider if they refuse to correct their ways: *If the member refuses to listen to them, tell it to the church; and if the offender refuses to listen even to the church, let such as one be to you as a Gentile and tax collector.* According to John Holdeman, excommunication was one of the most important church doctrines in order to keep the church pure and "to chastise the wicked flesh of the offenders".³⁸

There is no other Mennonite group that disciplines members as severely as the Church of God in Christ, Mennonite. Avoidance, shunning or the practice of the ban begins once the congregation has decided to expel the erring member. At this point, members begin a period of spiritual and social ostracism in which they are forbidden to shake hands or eat at the same table with the expelled person.³⁹

In the 1970s, an exceptionally large number of church members were disciplined and many were excommunicated. The level of bitterness felt by those who had been disciplined, as well as a general emotional depression, was noted by non-Mennonite neighbors who lived close to the congregations.⁴⁰

---

³⁵Hiebert, *Holdeman People*, 234–35.
³⁶Hiebert, *Holdeman People*, 342–43.
³⁷Gospel Publsishers, *Histories*, 165–67.
³⁸Holdeman, *Mirror*, 476.
³⁹Hiebert, *Holdeman People*, 401.
⁴⁰Hiebert and Hiebert. "Church of God," para. 15.

In spite of the turmoil and emotional stress caused by excommunication, the Church continued to grow modestly in the twentieth century. Members have been added to the faith from diverse backgrounds and nationalities including Mexico, Haiti, Belize, Philippines, Domincan Republic, India, Nigeria, and other African nations.[41]

Congregations

Active CGCM congregations in the continental United States as of the year 1999 are displayed in the maps of Appendix Three. Typical sizes of these congregations range from 100 to 200 members although many have less than 100 members. The formation of new congregations frequently occurs when the size of a church becomes too large. As one example, the Gospel Congregation of Moundridge, Kansas was formed in 1971 when the Lone Tree congregation approached 700 members.[42] The CGCM had membership of 14,804 in the United States for 2010, a growth of 22 percent from 12,144 in the year 2000. Total membership worldwide in 2010 was 22,779. A geographical accounting in 2010 reveals that the state of Kansas had, by far, the largest group of CGCM members at 16 percent of the total United States membership or a little over 4400 people.[43] Map 7 displays the twenty CGCM congregations in Kansas with a key for locations.[44]

The Holdeman Church authorities — bishops, deacons, and ministers, have worked throughout the twentieth century, creating the modern Church of God in Christ, Mennonite and establishing religious life in a peaceful America. Today, the Church of God in Christ, Mennonite remains a relatively small institution in comparison to its Anabaptist cousins — the Amish and Hutterites. Nolt and Meyers estimate that there are approximately 170,000 Amish in North America, albeit of many diverse congregations.[45] The Hutterite communities have about 45,000 members, living primarily in Western Canada and the upper Great Plains of the United States.[46] In contrast to these groups, the Holdeman Church maintains a high degree of uniformity throughout their some 200 congregations. This uniformity is promulgated via the annual General Conference meetings. Each congregation is a separate unit within the general conference structure. Keeping the congregations together in doctrine and practice is promoted through a series

---

[41] Gospel Publishers, *Histories*, 10.
[42] Gospel Publishers, *Histories*, 301.
[43] Data is from the Association of Religion Data Archives. See www.thearda.com.
[44] The congregations are current as reported in *Histories of the Congregations*. Moundridge, KS: Gospel Publishers, 1999. The maps have been produced by the author using open source QGIS.
[45] Nolt and Meyers, *Plain Diversity*, 4.
[46] See "Hutterites" at https://en.wikipedia.org/wiki/Hutterites.

of revival and evangelistic meetings that are held by each congregation. Some four centuries after the beginning of the Anabaptist movement, this small group of committed Christians has gone forth "with much fear and trepidation," admitting some failures but also acknowledging many spiritual and material benefits.[47]

As acknowledged earlier, there were many varieties of Anabaptism in which the congregations differed in both doctrine and practice. As Clasen writes, there was never an institutional hierarchy and the Anabaptists themselves "encouraged an almost unbridled individualism by rejecting all human authority."[48] The premise to be explored further in Part Two of this narrative is that the Holdeman people are the spiritual descendants of the Anabaptists in the sense that they practice today the principles that were first articulated in the *Schleitheim Confession* of the sixteenth century. Certainly, the Church of God in Christ, Mennonite can claim to participate in the basic convictions of Anabaptism as defined by Harold Bender's vision: 1) Christianity as disciplehsip, 2) voluntary church membership based upon true conversion, and 3) the ethic of love and nonresistance applied to all human relationships.[49,50] We turn now to how the Holdeman people practice the specific tenets expressed by the founders of Anabaptism in the sixteenth century.

---

[47] Gospel Publishers, *Histories*, 9–14.
[48] Clasen, *Anabaptism*, 36.
[49] Bender, "Anabaptist Vision," 76-85.
[50] Grimsrud, "Anabaptism," 371-90.

PART TWO   CHAPTER SEVEN   Building the Church

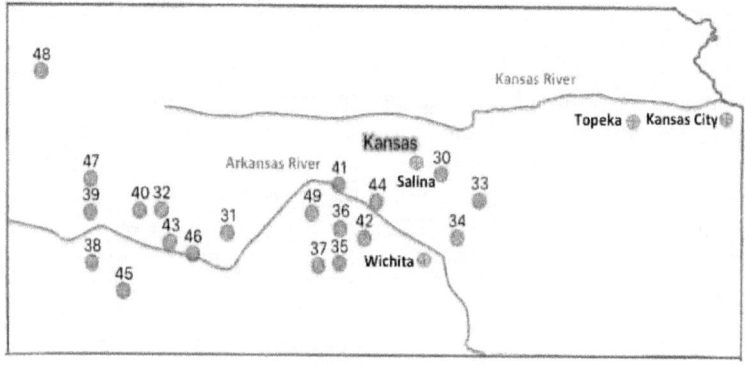

Key to Locations:
32. Cimarron, 33. Eden-Burns, 34. Emmanuel-Fredonia, 35. Garden View-Halstead, 36. Gospel-Moundridge, 37. Grace-Halstead, 38. Grant-Ulysses, 39. Lakin, 40. Living Hope-Ingalls, 41. Lone Tree-Galva, 42. Meridian-Hesston, 43. Montezuma, 44. Morning Star-Durham, 45. Plains, 46. Salem-Copeland, 47. Scott City, 48. Sharon Springs, 49. Zion-Inman.

Map 7: Congregations of the Church of God in Christ, Mennonite in Kansas (map by the author).

CHAPTER EIGHT

The Holdemans and Schleitheim

VER THE PAST SEVERAL CENTURIES, the deeply held values, beliefs, and practices of the conservative Mennonites have been challenged by an increasingly secular society and nationalistic governments that were caught up in wars and many military adventures. However, the seven principles of Anabaptism are still readily observable in the practices of the Church of God in Christ, Mennonite. The Holdeman people will not present themselves as Anabaptists nor will they take an activist role in confronting the ills of society. Their non-verbal message to contemporary American culture is one about living peacefully while also offering a defiant act of resistance to the predominant way of being Christian in America.

The two world wars created social and institutional challenges for the Holdeman people. The aftermath of these cataclysmic events left the Holdemans with many new and sometimes painful experiences resulting from military demands and integrating with a non-Mennonite world. As Hiebert writes, confronting new places and people was both threatening and exciting.[1] Today's conservative Mennonite communities find themselves struggling to bolster the nonresistant faith of their young people, a faith that was tested in the world wars more than at any time since the sixteenth century. In the following brief sketches, we trace four core principles of Anabaptism from the origins in the 1520s to how the Holdeman Church expresses these principles today.

Adult Baptism

The Anabaptists regarded infant baptism with nothing but revulsion and contempt, believing that infant baptism originated with the devil. Their derogatory phrases reveal the depth of their contempt – "a simple water

---

[1] Hiebert, *Holdeman People*, 318.

bath", "a filthy ablution" and "an act of idolatry".[2] For the early Anabaptists, the view that teaching must precede baptism was based on Erasmus' interpretation of Matt. 28:19, suggesting that this order was taught by Jesus and put into practice by the apostles.[3] Based on this understanding, they created persuasive arguments grounded in common sense and justice that convinced peasants, laborers, and craftsmen while embarrassing religious authorities. Perhaps the most cogent of these arguments is the reference to Matt. 28:19 and Mk. 16:16 indicating that baptism should be restricted to believing people.[4] In the ancient world, adult baptism was common and was administered with appropriate questions such as "Do you believe in Jesus Christ, the Son of God, . . .who was crucified under Pontius Pilate . . .?".[5] Only after several hundred years in early Church history was infant baptism instituted, appearing to be a ruse to keep everyone in the church.[6]

In the sixteenth century, the commitment to adult baptism of believers was a threat to the established religious order, resulting in many Anabaptists and early Mennonites being branded as heretics and subject to the death penalty. In the early 1500s, Zurich, Switzerland was the seat of much protest against the established church. On January 17, 1525, a public debate took place in Zurich in which the unstated purpose was to silence opposition to infant baptism. Shortly after the meeting, the Council of Zurich issued a decree that all children must be baptized within eight days of birth. Four leaders of the early Anabaptist movement – Conrad Grebel, Felix Manz, Georg Blaurock, and Wilhelm Reublin – were soon to take the next step in rejecting infant baptism. After the debate, these radical reformers met in a private meeting in which Grebel baptized Blaurock. Blaurock then baptized a number of the others in the meeting. This radical departure from current religious practices mobilized the Zurich Council to implement even more stringent penalties, soon resulting in the imprisonment of Grebel, Manz, and Blaurock.[7]

---

[2] Clasen, *Anabaptism*, 95.
[3] Weaver, *Becoming Anabaptist*, 42–43.
[4] See, for example, Mark 16:16 — *The one who believes and is baptized will be saved; but the one who does not believe will be condemned.*
[5] Grant, *Constatntine*, 211–12.
[6] Clasen, *Anabaptism*, 96–98.
[7] Smith, *Story*, 7–12.

In the conference at Schleitheim on February 27, 1527, Michael Sattler explained the purpose of adult baptism:[8]

> Baptism shall be administered to all who have been instructed and give evidence of repentance and a change of life, and who believe of a truth that their sins have been taken away by Christ, and who desire to walk in the resurrection of Jesus Christ and to be buried with Him into death, that they may also rise with Him, and to all who desire baptism of us by their own decision with this understanding.

A few years later in the Netherlands, Menno Simons joined the debate about infant baptism, stating . . . *we do not find in all Scripture a single word by which Christ has ordained the baptism of infants, or that His apostles taught and practiced it, we say and confess rightly that infant baptism is but a human invention, an opinion of men, a perversion of the ordinance of Christ.* He continues by using common metaphors such as "putting the cart before the horse" and "to sow before plowing" to describe the authorities' confusion about infant baptism.[9]

Some three hundred years after Menno Simons rejected infant baptism, John Holdeman took up the debate. Holdeman has written extensively on issues related to baptism, covering topics such as who was to administer baptism, the forms of baptism (immersion and pouring) and the rationale for infant baptism. In a response to those who defend infant baptism citing both St. Augustine and Luther, Holdeman discusses the reasons that have been put forth for infant baptism and then provides proof that it is baptism upon confession of faith and not infant baptism that is written in the Scriptures. Infants do not have the power to practice faith through hearing the preaching of the word of God.

Holdeman indicates that the foundation of baptism is evident in the commission of Christ and the acts of the Holy Apostles. The apostle Paul and John the Baptist did not baptize infants, baptizing only those who repented and confessed their sins. Paul focused on preaching as is evident in 1 Cor. 1:17: *For Christ sent me not to baptize, but to preach the gospel: not with wisdom of words, lest the cross of Christ should be made of none effect.* Paul baptized only a few of the Corinthians but he converted many, making them believers before their baptism. In building on the examples from the gospels, Holdeman concludes ". . . not one instance can be shown where John the Baptist nor any of the apostles baptized an infant." Further, he cites many passages such as Acts 5:14 that "prove that the apostles were obedient to Christ's commission and baptized only those who received the

---

[8] Horsch, *Mennonites in Europe*, 72.
[9] Bender, *Menno Simons' Life*, 81.

Word gladly and believed through hearing; thus both men and women were added, but no innocent infants".[10]

The question of how the Church of God in Christ, Mennonite (CGCM) viewed baptism was of major importance when members of the Kleine Gemeinde were poised to join the Holdeman Church. In 1881, Minister Peter Toews of the Kleine Gemeinde had much correspondence with John Holdeman and ultimately led some 165 souls to join the Holdeman group.[11] However, foremost on Minister Toews' mind was the rite of baptism. He wondered "whether they would baptize a person the second time if it were found that he had been unconverted at the time of his or her first baptism. They answered in the affirmative . . .".[12]

In the practice of the baptism rite, the Holdeman minister takes a handful of water from a small vessel and pours it upon the head of the applicant,[13] thus carrying out the tradition that was first condemned as heretical in the sixteenth century.[14]

The Ban

The consistent use of the ban can be easily traced from the early Anabaptists, to the Groningen Old Flemish, and finally to the practice of the modern day Holdeman people. As noted above, the early Anabaptists administered the ban towards those who stumble and fall into sin. In the mid-sixteenth century, Menno Simons perhaps most eloquently expressed the need for the ban:[15]

---

[10] Holdeman, *Mirror*, 116.
[11] Hiebert, *Holdeman People*, 143.
[12] Toews, "Report of Investigations," 4.
[13] Hiebert, *Holdeman People*, 396–97.
[14] The form of baptism has caused much controversy within the various Mennonite congregations. John Holdeman dedicated a complete chapter to this issue in the *Mirror of Truth*. Holdeman bases his support for "pouring" on the preposition "with", indicating that one "pours with" while one "immerses in" water. He cites Acts 11:16 in which John baptizes with water. See Holdeman, *Mirror*, 104. However, scholars have mixed views regarding the baptism ritual. Meeks cites Rom. 6:4 that portrays baptism as a symbolic burial requiring complete immersion in water. The early Christian communities may have gradually shifted to "pouring" as a practical accommodation for the lack of water. See Meeks, *Urban Christians*, 150.
[15] Bender, *Menno Simons' Life*, 86.

> Even as a city without wall and gates, or field without inclosure or fence, or a house without walls and doors, so is also a church without the true apostolic exclusion or ban. For it would be open to all deceiving spirits, all godless scorners and haughty despisers, all idolatrous and insolent transgressors, yes to all lewd debauchers and adulterers, as is the case with all the great sects of the world which style themselves, although improperly, churches of Christ.

The Groningen Old Flemish insisted on strict maintenance of both doctrine and practice and rigorously applied the ban.[16] Today, the Church of God in Christ, Mennonite is the most severe among conservative Mennonites in the application of avoidance or shunning of excommunicated members. The practice is based on the writings of apostle Paul in 1 Cor. 5:11 — *But now I am writing to you not to associate with anyone who bears the name of brother or sister who is sexually immoral or greedy, or is an idolater, reviler, drunkard, or robber. Do not even eat with such a one.*

The General Conference minutes itemize some of the inconsistent behavior that is subject to the ban and avoidance including the use of tobacco and intoxicating liquor; the shaving or marring of the beard; dressing contrary to Bible teachings; the use of musical instruments; and the ownership of high priced and flashly cars.[17] An excommunicated member cannot be greeted with the holy kiss or a handshake nor can this member be allowed to eat with the brethren in the Church.[18] In public meetings such as funerals and weddings, members are urged to exercise "conscientious carefulness" in carrying out the practice of avoidance in order to avoid undue offense.[19]

The Oath

The oath is the strongest possible confirmation of the truth of a statement by calling upon God to witness. A few months before the Schleitheim convocation, Hans Denk in his treatise *Von der wahren Liebe* (Of True Love) offers a convincing practical argument for dispensing with the oath.[20]

> . . . since man is unable to keep his vows or covenants, whatever appears as right should be performed without a promise of commitment. Where a man makes a vow concerning something over which he has no power, there is either a presumption without understanding, or else hypocrisy with understanding.

---

[16] Hiebert, *Holdeman People*, 41.
[17] *Conference Reports*, "1946 General Conference," 50.
[18] Barclay, "Plain People," 140–65.
[19] *Conference Reports*, "1959 General Conference," 83.
[20] Klassen, "Oath," 3–8.

As John Holdeman writes, the true Church of God has considered it prohibitive and unlawful to take an oath. In addition to citing multiple passages of the New Testament (e.g Matt. 5:34–37), Holdeman also has some practical advice for government officials. "I feel assured, that if testimonies were accepted without an oath, the government would receive less falsehood in a century, than it now receives in a year from those who swear to their testimonies".[21]

A Shared Ministry

The early Anabaptists believed that the true apostle wandered from place to place, preaching and suffering persecution. The minister was to "read, admonish and teach, to warn, to discipline, to ban in the church, to lead out in prayer . . .".[22] According to the *Schleitheim Confession*, ministers should have the qualifications mentioned by Paul.[23] On the surface, the complexity of choosing a minister might not be obvious to the reader. The Church of God in Christ, Mennonite has debated the possible ways this might be done. A distinction is made between the two aspects of the call to ministry. There might be a direct or inner call which comes from God or an indirect or outward call through the church or congregation.[24] The Holdeman Church debated this issue at the conference of 1884 in McPherson, Kansas, stating a preference for the inner calling and the desire to avoid choosing a minister by lot.[25] A clarification was put forth by the Church in the General Conference of 1946:[26]

> Therefore, in whomsoever the gifts of ministry appear, or are manifest — such brethren are encouraged particularly by the elders to prepare themselves by study and reading and whatever may be in accord with such a call.

This preparation is done in accordance with 1 Tim: 4:12–16:

> *Let no one despise your youth, but set the believers an example in speech, in conduct, in love, in faith and in purity. Until I arrive, give attention to the public reading of Scripture, to exhorting, to teaching. Do not neglect the gift that is in you, which was given you through prophecy with the laying on hands by the council of elders. Put these things into practice, devote yourself to them, so*

---

[21] Holdeman, *Mirror*, 466–67.
[22] Clasen, *Anabaptism*, 54–55.
[23] Horsch, *Mennonites in Europe*, 72–73.
[24] Neff, "Ministry," 704.
[25] Hiebert, *Holdeman People*, 206–07.
[26] *Conference Reports*, "1946 General Conference," 53.

> *that all may see your progress. Pay close attention to yourself and to your teaching; continue in these things, for in doing this you will save both yourself and your hearers.*

John Holdeman has written at length about the ministry, cautioning the church to proceed very carefully in selecting ministers "so that she may lay as little occasion for temptation as possible".[27] He cites many examples of those who were called indirectly and directly. For example, Matthias was chosen by lot (Acts 1:26 — *And they gave forth their lots; and the lot fell upon Matthias; and he was numbered with the eleven apostles*) whereas Paul received his call from heaven.[28] Holdeman cautions that the importance lies not in how ministers are called but in their faithfulness.[29]

A survey in 1967 indicated that Holdeman ministers were dedicated to their role of providing service to the congregation, many spending fifteen to twenty hours per week in preparation including studying, preaching, teaching, and counseling.[30] Popular family names for these ministers included Barkman, Becker, Ensz, Isaac, Jantz, Koehn, Nightengale, Penner, Peters, Schmidt, Wenger, and Wiebe.

In the practices of baptism, the oath, the ban, and shared ministry, we can see the impact of the early Anabaptist principles on the Church of God in Christ, Mennonite. In the following chapters, we turn to perhaps the most challenging and controversial practices, those of nonresistance and separation from the world. These practices are more outward-focused and perhaps create the most difficult challenges for living apart from the world.

---

[27] Holdeman, *Mirror*, 513.
[28] It is noteworthy that Paul was not part of the original twelve apostles. In the Gospel of Luke, the author stresses the importance of adding Matthias to replace Judas so that these apostles could provide continuity for the early church. See Bart Ehrman, *New Testament*, 322.
[29] Holdeman, *Mirror*, 497.
[30] Hiebert, *Holdeman People*, 418.

CHAPTER NINE

Nonresistance

ITH THIS NARRATIVE, we have recorded the events and people who for over four centuries have retained their unique culture and history in spite of persecutions and severe hardships. In this epic journey, the Dutch-Prussian Mennonites have crossed the boundaries of many European countries, experienced the chaos of war, and engaged with the monarchs and rulers who have set the course of history.

Although the accounts of the early church and its leaders imparts a picture of a lived reality, there is a more significant message in this narrative. Our fractured society can learn from the practices of the Groningen Old Flemish Mennonites, the Ostrogers and their modern descendants — the people of the Holdeman Church. These people have lived their lives as nonresisters for over 400 years, pledging never to take up arms or fight in our never-ending wars. The phrase "Die Stillen im Lande" (the Quiet in the Land) is frequently used to describe the withdrawing, peaceful, rural culture of these conservative Mennonites.[1] Our society and certainly the members of the larger Mennonite community will acknowledge this group's steadfast commitment to Anabaptist principles. This heroic commitment in the face of persecution and banishment has forged a culture that is recognizable by all:[2]

> In a world of noise, self-assertion and self-aggrandizement they practice restraint, humility, and quietness. Most Mennonite families do not have a rich tradition of cultivating hyperbole and showmanship. Deference is a more commonly cultivated virtue. Most feel more comfortable in the background, out of the limelight. With little fanfare many Mennonites flavor their communities with acts of service and kindness.

For four centuries, these close-knit families were held together by the core Anabaptist principles and an ethnic identity. Living in America for over one

---
[1] Redekop, "Anabaptists," 133–34.
[2] Toews, "Mennonites," 230.

hundred years has created a situation where few can claim to be of some European ethnicity — Dutch, Russian, or German. Our modern society and the resurgence of nationalism brought about by two world wars and many subsequent skirmishes has caused progressive Mennonites to abandon the long-held principles of the more conservative communities — nonresistance and separation from the world. As Perry Bush writes, the Mennonite landscape has changed dramatically in the twentieth century. While some are still farming in rural communities, many others are found in cities and suburbs, working in factories or offices, or managing privately owned businesses.[3] For many Mennonites, this exposure to the vicissitudes and wiles of human affairs has weakened their hold on two of the most fundamental Anabaptist doctrines.

Foundations of Belief

Nonresistance (German: *Wehrlösigkeit*) is a term little used and little understood by the American public. Nonresistance is frequently confused with pacifism, an opposition to war and militarism that is based on humanitarian and philosophical principles. Christian nonresistance as portrayed by Jesus holds that a believer does not repay evil with evil and does not avenge himself, demonstrating love for enemies and those who persecute him (Matt. 5:39 — *But I say unto you, That ye resist not evil: but whosoever shall smite thee on thy right cheek, turn to him the other also.*).[4] The doctrine of nonresistance has been held almost universally by American Mennonite churches while those who remained in Europe increasingly accepted military service.[5] Most notably, the commitment of the most conservative Mennonite groups in America to nonresistance has been unwavering.

Michael Sattler was one of the most noteworthy leaders of the Swiss Brethren and an active messenger of the gospel.[6,7] His presentation of seven articles to a conference on February 24, 1527 was approved, adopted, and became known as the *Schleitheim Confession*. Looking back to the early Anabaptists and the articles of the *Schleitheim Confession*, we find explicit warnings against the use of deadly weapons — *Separation is needful from all evil and wickedness which Satan has planted in the world. This includes abstinence from all use of the un-Christian, yea, Satanic weapons of violence.*[8] Anabaptists of the sixteenth century spoke eloquently in defense of the

---

[3] Bush, *Two Kingdoms*, 257–58.
[4] See also 1 Thess. 5:15 in which apostle Paul asks the Thessalonians not to repay evil with evil.
[5] Crous, "Nonresistance", 897–906.
[6] Yoder, *Legacy*, 10.
[7] Horsch, *Mennonites in Europe*, 70.
[8] Yoder, *Legacy*, 36–41.

principle of nonresistance. In facing a death sentence on January 5, 1527, Felix Manz, an early Anabaptist, was steadfast in his conviction stating "No Christian smites with the sword nor resists evil".[9]

Menno Simons cast his lot with the Anabaptists of northern Holland and was baptized by Obbe Philips, the leader of the movement.[10] During his seven years of labor in the Netherlands, Menno wrote several books including *The Foundations of Christian Doctrine*, published in 1539. On nonresistance, Menno states that the "regenerated do not go to war nor fight. They are the children of peace . . . Their sword is the word of the Spirit." [11]

Roughly a century later, the Dutch Flemish elder Adriaan Cornelisz produced a draft of eighteen articles, a document that was to become the *Dordrecht Confession of Faith*. The more conservative Mennonite communities in America, including the Church of God in Christ, Mennonite, recognize the *Dordrecht Confession* as their official articles of faith. Article XIV puts forth the nonresistant policy, urging Christians to be *"Biblical nonresistants in suffering and abuse. They shall pray for their enemies, . . . and seek their welfare and salvation"*.[12]

Several hundred years later, John Holdeman followed the leadership of the Anabaptists. He was convinced that the principle of nonresistance stands "as solid as the Gospel itself". Quoting Matt. 26:52, Holdeman states that He (Jesus) does not desire us to defend each other with the sword. If we do we will perish by the sword.[13] In following Christ, we should not lay down our lives on the battlefield. Holdeman offers suggestions for how one can model his behavior, "If we are reviled, let us give a soft answer and revile not again, when mistreated we threaten not . . .".[14]

In the early stages of Anabaptism, the church-state confrontation centered around the issue of re-baptism, a threat to both the established church and the state. However, in the twentieth century, the flashpoint became nonresistance and the refusal to participate in the military. During World War I, the public scorned the Mennonites for speaking the German language and opposing war bond drives.[15] Many Mennonites were physically abused, insulted, and some served time in federal prisons. Amidst the chaos of the world wars, progressive Mennonites began to forge a new doctrine of nonresistance, however the Holdeman Church did not participate in this reformulation.

The General Conference of the Church of God in Christ, Mennonite met in Lone Tree, Kansas on November 23-26, 1896. In this conference, ministers

---

[9] Horsch, *Mennonites in Europe*, 359–66.
[10] Smith, *Story*, 91.
[11] Bender, *Menno Simons' Life*, 89.
[12] Wenger, "Dordrecht," 92–93.
[13] Holdeman, *Mirror*, 380.
[14] Holdeman, *Mirror*, 399.
[15] Juhnke, "Mennonites," 171–78.

clearly stated their commitment to nonresistance indicating that the Gospel prohibits "all fleshly and legal revenge and compulsion". Throughout the next one hundred years, the Holdeman Church remained constant in their adherence to nonresistance. The Deacon's Council of the General Conference met again in Lone Tree on November 26, 1983, reaffirming the nonresistant position of the Church regarding war, violence, and coercion.[16]

Living Nonresistance

The practice of nonresistance is little understood and for those who understand, this way of life is beyond the collective comprehension — considered naive, dangerous and, if embraced more broadly, a threat to our nation. Both modern and sixteenth century Anabaptists separated themselves from societal values that supported violence and war. The practice of nonresistance has implications for all aspects of Christian life — personal, social, political, and economic relationships. Christian nonresistance is more than conscientious objection. As one example of economic relationships, the Christian community does not think in terms of buyer and seller . . . each seeking his own good; it thinks of itself as a brotherhood whose members are laborers together.[17] In today's capitalist economy, this notion of a brotherhood between buyer and seller sounds a bit naive and strange indeed. Turning to the political and social impact, nonresistance implies that others must bear the burden of fighting our country's wars.

Among the Anabaptist doctrines, few have led to more trouble with the governmental authorities than that of nonresistance.[18] Mennonites have always struggled to be good Christians and good citizens, however the nonresistance stance can be very difficult amidst nationalistic fervor. Certainly, it was not easy in Prussia and Russia to resist government demands and withstand the insults of an antagonistic citizenry. The constant pressure from these governments began to weaken the willpower of many Mennonites. Klassen lays out the dilemma of the Prussian Mennonites in trying to hold on to their beliefs in nonresistance throughout the nineteenth century. After much back and forth with the Prussian kings, King William I issued an order on October 3, 1867 terminating the exemption of Mennonites from military service. Although in the minority, this event caused elders Penner, Toews, and Wiebe to begin planning for emigration. Wiebe emigrated to Russia and, after a divisive struggle, Penner left for America in 1877. Klassen concludes:

---

[16]*Conference Reports*, "1983 General Conference," 11, 117.
[17]Crous, "Nonresistance," 898.
[18]Smith, *Story*, 22.

Thus after more than a century of meetings and discussions in churches, debates among church elders, petitions to government officials, and consideration of possible alternatives, the Mennonites of the Vistula Delta concluded that the progressive and enlightened times, far removed from the tyranny and persecution of earlier days, made service to the state, even in the military, an acceptable and conscientious response.[19]

In contrast to the Mennonites who remained in Prussia, those who migrated to Russia and then to America took their nonresistance most seriously. Although there have always been individuals who joined the military, conservative American Mennonites during the wars from the eighteenth to the twenty-first century kept the faith by maintaining a consistent nonresistant position against military service.[20]

The principle of nonresistance has permeated every aspect of Mennonite life. In the seventeenth century, Mennonites on mercantile vessels did not permit ships to carry arms for defense.[21] In 1775 during the American Revolution, Mennonites and Dunkers[22] thanked the Pennsylvania Assembly for its advice and liberal policy in granting freedom of conscience. These people stated their principle of always helping those in need and distress but "we find no freedom in giving, or doing, or assisting in anything by which men's lives are destroyed or hurt".[23] In 1814, the Prussian Cabinet began drafting Mennonites in accordance with a recently implemented military service law. In the Brenkenhoffswalde Mennonite community, minister Peter Jantz spent 24 hours in jail for resisting the draft, an action to be repeated many times against the Mennonites in subsequent years.[24]

The more conservative Mennonites in Russia who emigrated to America in the 1870s continued to hold on to a strong nonresistance belief with few exceptions.[25] On arriving in America, many from the Karolswalde community joined the Holdeman Church. John Holdeman was steadfast in his belief in nonresistance, stating that he found the ground of nonresistance clearly and distinctly recorded in God's Word. He stated "As long as the last member of our body shall move, we will refrain from using carnal weapons to slay our enemies."[26]

---

[19] Klassen, *Mennonites*, 186–91.
[20] Bender and Smith, *Mennonites*, 142–43.
[21] Horsch, *Mennonites in Europe*, 228.
[22] Dunker is a name used for the denomination now more formally referred to as the Church of the Brethren. The origin of the word comes from the German verb tunken, meaning "to dip" and relates to immersion as the form of baptism. See Bender, "Dunker," 109.
[23] Crous, "Nonresistance," 899.
[24] Jantzen, *Mennonite German Soldiers*, 93
[25] Bender, "State," 615.
[26] Holdeman, *Mirror*, 386–90.

Conscientious Objectors

The Selective Service Act of 1917 provided for conscientious objectors who were members of "any well-recognized religious sect ... whose existing creed or principles forbid its members to participate in war in any form" to avoid military conscription.[27] Perry Bush reports that of the 315 Kansas Mennonite draftees from all communities in World War I, 141 (45 percent) remained true to nonresistant principles and refused military service of any type. About an equal number, 151 (48 percent) accepted noncombatant service and 23 (7 percent) entered regular, combatant, military ranks.[28] The men who refused all forms of service — driving munitions trucks, serving in a military hospital, or even writing out paychecks — were court-martialed and about two hundred were sent to imprisonment in Fort Leavenworth.[29]

Those who did agree to serve as non-combatants found relationships with officers and draftees was still difficult. Francis Schmidt recounts the experiences of Nathaniel Schmidt in serving as a conscientious objector in World War I.[30] Nathaniel and several other Halstead, Kansas boys experienced considerable verbal abuse when they signed up for service at Camp Funston in September, 1918.

In the spring of 1941, American Mennonites and the federal government came to an agreement on how to treat conscientious objectors. This agreement resulted in the creation of the Civilian Public Service in which Mennonites could serve in unpaid labor camps.[31] Unfortunately, the hostility toward the pacifist Mennonites continued during World War II. On August 14, 1944, six Mennonites traveled on a bus from McPherson to Leavenworth, Kansas along with thirty-three draftees who would undergo pre-induction physical examinations. Three of the Mennonites were members of the Holdeman Church, a community that required men to wear beards. Arguments broke out during the bus trip and the draftees used a razor and scissors to cut the beards of the Holdeman Mennonites. By the end of the trip, all six Mennonites had suffered cuts and bruises with broken teeth and roughly cut beards. The draftees were tried in civil court and fined ten dollars each, a relatively minor penalty for their unruly behavior.[32,33]

The Mennonites benefited from the Civilian Public Service, however the community lost many of its young men who chose to accept military service.[34]

---

[27] Krehbiel, *World*, para. 2.
[28] Bush, *Two Kingdoms*, 285.
[29] Bender and Smith, *Mennonites*, 143.
[30] Schmidt and Caldwell, *Schmidt Family*, 214–17.
[31] Bush, *Two Kingdoms*, 5.
[32] Juhnke, *People*, 47.
[33] Bush, *Two Kingdoms*, 94.
[34] During World War II, 93.5 percent of eligible Holdeman men were classified as IV-E for

Given the peace and prosperity in twenty-first century United States, it is difficult to imagine the moral dilemma facing many Mennonite men who were of age to be drafted in World War II. Floyd B. Koehn was one who chose to serve and was a member of the 554th Signal Battalion that was actively engaged in the South Pacific. Floyd was a direct descendant of Cornels Jantz (*prz528*, Figure 19) and is shown here in the jungles of a South Pacific island (Figure 14).[35]

Figure 14: Floyd Koehn Serving in the South Pacific - September, 1943

Although the Holdeman Mennonites avoid public debates regarding religious practices, the more progressive Mennonite groups continue to engage the U.S. Government officials regarding nonresistance. In 1969, the Old Mennonite Church adopted a controversial resolution that recognized "total noncooperation" with the Selective Service System as a witness compatible with the historic traditions of the Mennonite church. As a result, Dennis Koehn of North Newton, Kansas decided not to register with the Selective Service. In his trial, Koehn was convicted for refusal to register for the draft and was imprisoned for eighteen months in 1972-73.[36] In another incident shortly after the terrorist attacks of September 11, 2001, the *Topeka Capital-Journal* reported that Hesston College had not flown the American flag since the Vietnam war. As a result, the Kansas state legislature attempted unsuccessfully to eliminate $143,000 of state tuition grants for the college.[37] These relatively recent episodes are evidence that the Mennonite opposition to war remains an essential part of the traditional Mennonite pacifist stance. However, the visible practice of nonresistance raises questions in the public's mind about the responsibilities of citizenship and the proper government policy toward the non-resisters.

The two kingdom concept is foundational for the Mennonite community, suggesting that the doctrine of nonresistance should not become a tool to coerce the state into abandoning the death penalty or not engaging in

---

the Civilian Public Service. Only five percent were in active military service. See Toews, *Mennonites*, 173–74.

[35] The photograph of Floyd Koehn is from the author's private collection.

[36] Juhnke, *People*, 119–21.

[37] This incident is reported by Jantzen in the Introduction to the Kindle version of Wilhelm Mannhardt's book *The Military Service Exemption of the Mennonites of Provincial Russia*.

war. However, once the state declares war, the Mennonite community is confronted with painful moral choices and an antagonistic public. As we have seen in the Prussia of the nineteenth century, German Mennonites ultimately abandoned their nonresistance stance and became willing participants in their government's nationalistic endeavors. American Mennonites in 1917, especially those of German descent in the Great Plains, attempted to remain faithful to their pacifist ideals but were tarred, feathered, smeared with yellow paint, and some even convicted under the Sedition Act.[38]

In the chaos of revolution and civil war in the Ukraine of the early twentieth century, many Mennonites in the Chortitza and Molotschna communities suffered a crises of faith in attempting to protect their families, resorting at times to self-defense units (German: *Selbstschutz*).[39] How were Mennonites in this chaotic period to defend themselves? In the anarchy and revolution that followed the collapse of Czarist Russia, Mennonite communities in south Russia began hiring Cossacks to protect lives and property. Petty theft was a daily occurrence and Russian state control was virtually nonexistent. More serious crimes were testing the ability of the Mennonites to provide their own protection. The self-defense units and the Cossacks raised serious questions about Mennonites being inconsistent in their practice of nonresistance.[40]

Today, the public debate about nonresistance is often couched in terms about how, or if, non-resisters contribute to society. The debate is intensified over policies regarding voting and serving in public office. Members of the Holdeman Church are not permitted to serve in any public office which brings transgressors into judgment by the authority of law. Similarly, members are not permitted to vote for those who hold the authority to govern people.[41] Yet, the Church clearly acknowledges the dilemma and holds a deep appreciation for the generous U.S. Government policies that have been extended to their people. In return, they see their contribution to society in "good works or deeds of charity".[42]

In a changing world, is it possible that Mennonites might rethink their position on nonresistance? In the absence of a government enforced draft policy and the relatively peaceful times in America, Mennonites must be asking about the meaning and practice of nonresistance. In these relatively peaceful times, refusing to join the military can hardly be considered an act of nonresistance. Mast suggests that nonresistance has no relevance when there is nothing to resist. Perhaps nonresistance can take on new meaning in which the practicing Mennonite can engage in a "principled refusal to

---

[38] Bush, "Solidification," para. 5.
[39] Rempel and Carlson, *Mennonite Family*, 250.
[40] Loewen and Urry, "Protecting," 34–35.
[41] *Conference Reports*, "1959 General Conference," 11.
[42] *Conference Reports*, "1959 General Conference," 117.

victimize another."[43]

In suggesting a more active involvement in society, Burkholder states that Mennonites have driven themselves into an unnecessary ideological trap. He claims that there is a place for both nonresistance and nonviolent resistance in the life of a Christian. He explains that Jesus demonstrated nonviolent resistance in his confrontation with Jewish authorities. Jesus' entry into Jerusalem and the cleansing of the temple were audacious, coercive acts (i.e. nonviolent resistance). Burkholder proposes another option for conservative Mennonites, suggesting that nonresistance does not have to mean noninvolvement or uncommitted neutrality. He states that the church, as an institution, could develop an ethic rather than letting each individual make his or her own choice. "The church fulfills its social responsibility by being an example, a witness, a creative minority formed by its obedience to nonresistant love".[44] Burkholder concludes that both nonviolent resistance and nonresistance are genuine alternatives to violence; they belong together in the same life.[45]

Nonresistance and Anabaptism Preserved

Many will not acknowledge the validity or even the social benefit of nonresistance. Most citizens of the United States in today's world would agree that force is necessary to eliminate the violence that seems so persistent and pervasive. The conservative Mennonite nonresistance stance thus appears to be irresponsible and, to some, cowardly. Conservative Mennonites are not likely to engage in social and political causes. Nor, as Kaufman suggests, will they confront their so-called non-Christian neighbors in the wrongness of their convictions.[46]

Is there a compromise between nonresistance and separation from the world? If citizens do not help shape their society beyond what is required by law, then their society will languish.[47] How do conservative Mennonites acknowledge this responsibility while also holding onto their nonresistant commitment? Burkholder believes that those practicing nonresistance can also become involved in a way that does not compromise their commitment to nonviolence. In one interpretation, the practice of nonresistance becomes involvement in the message that is sent to society about the evils of warfare, the death penalty, gun ownership and other violence related policies. The practice of nonresistance becomes a visible behavior that is recognized and

---

[43]Biesecker-Mast, "Towards," 55–58.
[44]Stanley Hauerwas as quoted by Burkholder. See Burkholder, "Nonresistance," 164.
[45]Burkholder, "Nonresistance," 135.
[46]Burkholder, "Perspective," 158.
[47]Audi, "Religious," 64.

honored by the secular world, creating a more tolerant atmosphere in which conservative Mennonites can hold onto their core beliefs.

Historically, this effect was evidenced in the writings of such notables as Leo Tolstoy. Tolstoy believed that the chief deviation of the Christian church from the teaching of Christ was its failure to acknowledge the commandment of nonresistance. In suggesting that church leaders have ignored Mennonite writings, he comments on the Mennonite author Daniel Musser's books which . . . *treat not so much of the theory as of the practical application of the theory of life, of relation of Christianity to military service, which is particularly important and interesting now, in connection with the universal liability to do military service.*[48] Conservative Mennonites may refrain from political involvement but, as is noted in Tolstoy's views, their way of life does become a form of nonviolent resistance, thereby fulfilling a social responsibility by being an example for citizens to ponder and perhaps emulate.

The modern Holdeman Church continues to hold fast to their commitment to nonresistance. However, the related companion doctrine of nonconformity remains a goal that is increasingly difficult to define and achieve. For the Holdemans, their sense of peoplehood and group identity is threatened by the relentless pressure to integrate into the fabric of modern society. As the Holdeman Church peers into the future, the loss of traditional identifiers will make it more difficult to define themselves as a people apart.

---

[48]Gingerich, "Leo Tolstoy," 234–35.

CHAPTER TEN

Separation from the World

HE ANABAPTIST DOCTRINE of nonconformity and separation from the world originated some 500 years ago with the *Schleitheim Confession* of 1527. The Anabaptists were adamant about their commitment to remove themselves from the evil of the world *"Separation is needful from all evil and wickedness which Satan has planted in this world."* Sattler and those who participated at Schleitheim envisioned the withdrawal from social institutions in order to establish a new society based on the pacifist model.[1] Today, some four hundred years later, nonconformity is viewed as a major doctrine for conservative Mennonites. This doctrine is anchored in the Scriptural passage of Rom. 12:2 — *Do not be conformed to this world, but be transformed by the renewing of your minds, so that you may discern what is the will of God — what is good and acceptable and perfect.*[2]

The Holdeman people view themselves as living apart from others. In this practice, they have well-defined markers that symbolize their separation from worldly affairs. Foremost and the most visible are the practices for men to wear the beard and women to wear the devotional head covering.[3] However, there is still a lot of ambivalence about separating from the world. While they are noncommittal about receiving Social Security benefits, the Holdemans prefer to leave service in civil offices to those of the world. The General Conference reiterated the support for separation in 1959 by stating "To maintain our separation from the world, we leave the functions of civil offices to them."[4,5]

---

[1] Weaver, *Becoming Anabaptist*, 62.
[2] See also Bender, "Nonconformity," 890.
[3] In her ethnography, Boyton describes the head covering as circular, black and it covers the hair pinned up on the back of the head. The head covering is worn at all times. See Boynton, *Plain People*, 148.
[4] *Conference Reports*, "1959 General Conference," 85–86.
[5] The General Conference is the highest authority within the Church of God in Christ, Mennonite. It is a conference of the entire church and its decisions apply to all congregations. The objective is to preserve the unity of the Church "so that there will be no schism or

PART TWO   CHAPTER TEN   Separation

Church Doctrine and Compromises

And yet the modern interpretations of Anabaptist principles have created working compromises. From the 2003 General Conference, the Holdeman Church granted permission to conduct necessary business over the Internet, assuming filters are in place to block inappropriate material.[6] Cell phone usage which can infringe on basic Holdeman convictions must also be avoided. Photography for business purposes is permitted while photography for entertainment and self-gratification is prohibited.

As Minister Dale Koehn states "adjusting the wording of our decisions . . . gives us the freedom to operate in a more realistic way."[7] Using technology, participating in civil government, purchasing insurance, and managing a business all represent pitfalls where church members could be drifting into worldly society. The conversations in the *Messenger of Truth* reveal how the church leaders are struggling to resist the drift and preserve their Anabaptist principles.[8]

Using Computers and Technology

The impact of technology represents one of the biggest threats to the Holdeman way of life. The Internet, social media, cell phones, and emerging artificial intelligence innovations are transforming American life. Minister Wilbur Koehn gives numerous examples of how technology "has a tantalizing way of infringing on man's dependence on a higher power" and has brought man to the threshold of believing that he is a god himself.[9] In a letter to the *Messenger of Truth* in 1996, Tony Friesen cautions against the purchase of a computer with sound cards and CD-ROMs, urging members to either buy a computer without a sound card or simply remove the sound card. Sound cards are "out of bounds" for Christians.[10] Today, some twenty years later, sound cards are so ingeniously integrated into modern computer architectures that they are virtually impossible to remove. More recently, Jed Yost uses the metaphor of crocodiles in the Shire River to warn against the perils of the Internet.[11]

---

division within the body." See Giesbrecht, *Enduring Church*, 220–21.

[6] *Conference Reports*, "2003 General Conference," 135.

[7] Huber, "Holdeman Mennonites," para. 13.

[8] Excerpts from the Messenger of Truth are taken form a CD published by Gospel Publishers that provides full text searching of the newsletter for the years 1941 through 2018.

[9] Koehn, "Technology," 1–2.

[10] Friesen, "Computers," 8–9.

[11] Yost, "Filters," 7.

As various technologies became more pervasive, the General Conference of 1993 acknowledged the possible dangers from radio, television, computers, and electronics, suggesting that caution must be exercised in the purchase and use of computers in order to avoid promoting a "computer spirit". The conference resolved that computers can be used for business purposes and not for pleasure and the Church cannot allow "the computer and other electronic technology to violate our Christian doctrines of simplicity, morality, and separation from the world."[12] Even with these cautions, the more recent letters to the *Messenger of Truth* suggest that the Internet and cell phones are becoming part of Holdeman life.

There are 171 references to the word "Internet" in the *Messenger of Truth* with the first occurring in 1996.[13] In these articles, one can see the transition from rejection of the Internet to gradual, grudging acceptance as a tool that is required for many members to be successful in their work and to offer a measure of entertainment. Brandon Becker references Amazon in relating that he never has had a flat screen TV in his cart.[14] Milferd Dirks cites a brother who likes to text a scripture to someone to lighten their load.[15] These comments from members suggest not only a growing awareness of the Internet but also innovative approaches to their religious life. In the space of some twenty years, the view of the Internet has changed significantly.

In 1943, a member writing to the *Messenger of Truth* asks rhetorically "Is photography forbidden in the Scriptures?" He answers definitely "yes", citing Exodus 20:4 — *Thou shalt not make unto thee any graven image*.[16] In 2015, the Church acknowledged that photography can be used for business purposes and such use does not violate the historic conviction against photography.[17] Even with these restrictions, it is not unusual to find members discretely taking photos and uploading them to Facebook.[18]

---

[12] *Conference Reports*, "1993 General Conference," 125.
[13] References are obtained through full text searching of the *Messenger of Truth* CD for the years 1941–2018, published by Gospel Publishers.
[14] Becker, "What is Good," 4.
[15] Dirks, "Dear Readers," 4–5.
[16] Gospel Publishers, "Questions and Answers," para. 3.
[17] *Conference Reports*, "2015 General Conference," 145.
[18] Bradley, "Anti-Fashion," 2.

Yet members continue to struggle with the prohibition as in this poignant admission:[19]

> When our youngest daughter was two, I had her pictures taken for a citizenship paper which we were applying for. When we left the place of business, we had an extra print, and she got it. She was not talking at all yet, as I remember. I distinctly recall her sitting in her car seat holding this print and her looking very attached to it. My conscience smote me, and I traded it for a piece of candy and destroyed the print.

Participating in Government

Civil government has been ordained by God as revealed in Rom. 13:2 — *Therefore whoever resists authority resists what God has appointed, and those who resist will incur judgment.* Although the church acknowledges the authority of government, there are significant prohibitions against actually working for these institutions. John Holdeman gave proof from the New Testament that it is not suitable for Holdeman Mennonite people to serve in the offices of government. Serving in the offices of secular government requires members to put themselves "under the yoke with unbelievers, to govern with them in a spirit in which we dare not govern in the Church of God".[20] The Conference report of 1896 amplifies Holdeman's views, indicating that members of the Church cannot be permitted to serve in any office of the magistracy, *from the highest to the least which require to bring transgressors into judgement by the power and authority of law.*[21] In an editorial for the *Messenger of Truth*, Reuben Koehn provides a modern view for how members should view government and politicians:[22]

> The work of politicians and government parties is selfish and deceitful, betraying the trust of the ones they serve. They wish to make a name for themselves (the pride of life) as well as foster a lust for power. The Apostle says this is not of the Father but of the world. For the Christian to desire or seek offices or help others into such offices is partaking of this evil. Today's political system is not a part of what God ordained as government.

The Holdemans extend the strict separation of church and state to the democratic right to vote with the following statement *It is inconsistent for a*

---

[19] Penner, "Dear Brothers," para. 5.
[20] Holdeman, *Mirror*, 358.
[21] *Conference Reports*, "1896 General Conference," 11.
[22] Koehn, "Love," 1–3.

*nonresistance man to cast his vote for a worldly officer, who is required to use the authority of the law.*²³

In one sense, the Holdeman people represent an adminrable model of separation of church and state in our democracy. They do not use their religious views to affect government policies or political outcomes for fear of becoming involved in Satan's world. Brother Edwin Hughes clearly states the position in a letter to the *Messenger of Truth*: "We must totally and completely renounce our allegiance to this world and its prince, Satan".²⁴ He continues by indicating that we cannot take a bit of this world and still claim our citizenship in God's kingdom.

Insuring Lives and Property

Many forms of insurance are considered unacceptable and the Holdeman people have consistently taught against dependency on insurance. However, the policy regarding the use of insurance has changed dramatically in the one hundred years of the twentieth century. In 1909, the Church conference stated that "We believe to insure our possessions in the insurance companies of the world against fire, storm, and hail, etc. is averse to the holy patriarch's and the apostles' examples."²⁵ In carrying out their responsibility for each other, the Church created a mutual aid society to provide assistance for disasters and also to advise farmers in making investments.²⁶ Abe Unruh noted that this society is not an insurance company but rather a system for distributing aid among the brotherhood.²⁷

As recently as 1999, church leaders were still arguing against the use of insurance. In his editorial entitled "Where is Your Security", Deacon Larry Loewen states "Insurance agents are convincing many people that life insurance is a must. The argument is that it costs so little per month and, should something happen to the insured, his family would not have the immediate financial burden to worry about." Loewen explains the pitfalls of using insurance, indicating that an insurance company is "primarily interested in filling its pocket and does not have a genuine concern for one's security." He concludes by stating "If you really want the true, unshakeable security, God must be first in your life."²⁸

In 2015, Church leaders acknowledged the materialistic pressures of modern society stating that it is important to distinguish between necessary levels of insurance, such as crop insurance, and "an insurance that seeks

---

²³ *Conference Reports*, "1896 General Conference," 11.
²⁴ Hughes, "Citizenship," 4–5.
²⁵ *Conference Reports*, " 1909 General Conference," 17.
²⁶ Hiebert, *Holdeman People*, 329–30.
²⁷ Unruh, "Mennonite Union," para. 1.
²⁸ Loewen, "Security," 2–3.

advantage for gain."²⁹ Dale Koehn elaborated further on the Church's position as reported in the Mennonite World Review "Farming increasingly requires crop insurance, and farmers felt pulled in two directions — either follow their church or follow their livelihood. Koehn said the focus is to keep reliance on God but allow space for agricultural producers to operate in today's economy."³⁰ This more realistic approach is also gaining traction with government insurance programs. The General Conference of 1956 was noncommittal regarding Social Security, however a few years later in the 1959 Conference, the Church decided that its "institutions be given the right to make these benefits available to their personnel".³¹ In a continuing trend to allow more freedom of choice, the General Conference of 1974 has left it to individual conscience on whether or not to accept Medicare Plan B.³²

Managaing a Business

The ethics of managing a business can create a dilemma for Holdeman people. Ethical principles can quickly deteriorate in an atmosphere absent of religious faith. In writing about Mennonite ethics, Abraham Toews poses a question for conservative Mennonites: "Why isn't it right for us to do what others are doing?"³³ Deacon Ed Isaac responds to this question and provides guidance on business principles, suggesting that a clear distinction must be made between managing a business enterprise and the worldly profit motive.³⁴ He recommends that business operations should be confined to "a size that fits into the locality". If operations provide a good living, then one should question the need for expansion, especially when it might put others at a disadvantage.³⁵ Isaac recommends 1 Tim. 6:6–8 as a guidepost — *But godliness with contentment is great gain. For we brought nothing into this world, and it is certain we can carry nothing out. And having food and raiment let us be therewith content.*

Pursuing Higher Education

Education beyond the basic skills of reading, writing, and arithmetic has always represented a threat to the Holdeman Church. Through many painful experiences, the Church has acknowledged that those who receive higher

---

[29] *Conference Reports*, "2015 General Conference," 144.
[30] Huber, "Holdeman Mennonites," para. 12–13.
[31] *Conference Reports*, "1959 General Conference," 86.
[32] *Conference Reports*, "1959 General Conference," 107.
[33] Toews, *Problem*, 9.
[34] Isaac, "Sound," 4–5, 7.
[35] The Holdeman small business model emphasizes hard work and personal relationships, placing severe restrictions on unlimited expansion. See Smucker, "Gelassenheit," 228–31.

education frequently do not become members or are excommunicated.[36] As Boynton writes in her ethnography of the Holdeman people, youngsters in public schools were increasingly exposed to temptations they fouund difficult to resist.[37] To combat these threats, the General Conference of 1967 gave permission to congregations to establish their own primary schools and a few years later the Conference of 1974 stated "we do not approve of attending public schools beyond grade eight".[38]

In reading the letters of the *Messenger of Truth*, it is apparent that many do obtain high school equivalency through the GED (General Education Development) program or continuing with home schooling. However, there are many cautions in the later issues of *Messenger of Truth* as in Minister Paul D. Wenger's letter to members:[39]

> The world sees as foolishness that we do not approve of its system of higher education. Education is a highly honored god of this world, but it does not bring righteousness to mankind. It belittles the plain teachings of the Scriptures and has brought false doctrine into many churches. . . . May we always keep the vision of a humble Christian life and see the awful folly of choosing the perishable things of this world.

Nonconformity and separation from the world is evident in these admonitions and cautions about education, the use of computers, the Internet, and insurance. Yet, Holdeman missions in countries such as Mexico, Nigeria, India and the Far East represent an enthusiastic evangelism and a movement away from their iconoclastic European culture.

Engaging in Missionary Work

Missionary work has in many ways integrated the Holdeman people into diverse cultures, exposing them to a wide variety of living styles and presenting a picture in stark contrast with their efforts to separate from the world.[40] Their mission endeavors have followed John Holdeman's advice "that God would spread the gospel into all the world, that it should be preached to every tongue, language, and people."[41] In the General Conference of 1921, several ministers were chosen to spread the gospel, thus initiating an emergence from centuries of social isolation and commitment to anarrow ethnic identity.[42]

---

[36] Hiebert, *Holdeman People*, 450.
[37] Boynton, *Plain People*, 174.
[38] *Conference Reports*, "1967 General Conference," 106.
[39] Wenger, "Wise," para. 12.
[40] Hiebert, *Holdeman People*, 281–82.
[41] Hiebert, *Holdeman People*, 344.
[42] *Conference Reports*, "1921 General Conference," 27.

Today, mission work by the CGCM demands much of the Church's financial and personal resources. Minister R. J. Klassen notes "The mission fields are crying for ordained help, not only for two year terms, but for winter revivals and/or counsel for several months at a time. The schedule is exhausting and the work demanding. The financial gifts of the American churches are not there. There are language and cultural barriers not easy to overcome or understand."[43] Minister Ron Wohlgemuth spells out the personal and financial issues in his editorial "The Cost of Discipleship" noting that the present day mission program "has presented a challenge to us to dig deeper into our bank accounts, as well as in seeking for laborers."[44]

This missionary zeal presents an odd conundrum for the Church of God in Christ, Mennonite. While encountering people of many different cultures, they are also at risk of opening up questions about their own conservative life style. The work to improve lives in the poor countries of the world might suggest that they are becoming citizens of the world, not unlike the apostle Paul who used his Roman citizenship to proseletyze among the pagans and establish the early church.

The Question of Citizenship

If one separates from the world, he or she is indicating that they are not willing to take responsibility for any of the world's woes. However, taking a nonresistance stance requires a government and the citizenry to grant the non-resisters certain privileges such as not participating in the military. How does the non-resister give back to society and what is his or her civic responsibility? In peaceful times, these questions do not create controversy among the non-Mennonite citizenry. However, in today's world with multiple threats of war, gun violence in cities and schools, 1000s of people dying from drug overdoses, and millions of immigrants wanting to enter the United States, the non-resister may be called to give back to society for the privileges granted to them.

The apostle Paul found benefits in being a citizen of the world.[45] As Joireman writes, Paul, while claiming to be a citizen of heaven, frequently made use of his Roman citizenship in order to stay alive and continue building the Christian church.[46] Thus, it appears that Paul not only valued his Roman citizenship but also used it effectively to advance the purposes of the emerging

---

[43]Klassen, "Living Sacrifice," 4.

[44]Wohlgemuth, "Discipleship," 3.

[45]In spite of statements in Acts, scholars still claim that there is considerable uncertainty regarding Paul's citizenship. See Paul's claim in Acts 22:28 — The tribune answered, "It cost me a large sum of money to get my citizenship." Paul said, "But I was born a citizen."

[46]Joireman, "Anabaptists," 82–84.

Christian church. As indicated in Philippians 3:20 (*But our citizenship is in heaven, and it is from there that we are expecting a Savior, the Lord Jesus Christ*), Paul clearly thought of heavenly citizenship as the most important but he still engaged with the world to render benefits for his church.

Apostle Paul's view of citizenship is perhaps one of the most difficult concepts for worldly people to understand. In discussing citizenship, Hershberger cites a metaphor used by an anonymous writer of the second century A.D.[47]

> The soul dwells in the body, but does not belong to the body, and Christians dwell in the world, but do not belong to the world . . .

In his classic work published during World War II, Guy Franklin Hershberger poses rhetorical questions. Is nonresistance and separation an "aloofness adopted for the purpose of helping society or is it to save one's own religion?" "Does not the Christian owe something to his community and to the state?" Hershberger asks: ". . . would it not be even better [for the Christian] to wield the power himself, for then it would surely be used aright"? Hershberger's answer is that in the great majority of cases "the love of power for its own sake seems to eventually become so dominant as to vitiate its use for righteous purposes."[48] He supports this view by citing cases where the Quakers sold their peace principles to gain power in the government. Hershberger concludes that the Christian can render society a greater service by remaining aloof.[49]

However, remaining aloof is difficult in a world where the forces of totalitarianism will likely rise again to threaten the world. Reinhold Niebuhr, perhaps the most anti-pacifist religious writer of the twentieth century, clearly states the opposing view. "The Christian must lay aside the pure Christian ethic and play his part in the struggle for the overthrow of the forces of evil."[50] In contrast, Hershberger offers a more nuanced response; the mission of the nonresistant Christian is not a political one rather it is a curative one to bring healing to human society.[51]

The people of the Holdeman Church do give back to society, helping in ways that are consistent with their philosophy of life to bring healing to society. Their work in disaster relief began in 1947 when they rushed to assist the people of Woodward, Oklahoma in recovering from a deadly tornado. Many members of the church traveled to Woodward to help clean up the destruction and rebuild. Equipped with tools and considerable skills in building, some 150 to 200 men traveled from Kansas and Oklahoma communities to assist the cleanup effort. Out of this initial response emerged a conference agency

---

[47] Hershberger, "Citizenship," 276.
[48] Hershberger, "Citizenship," 278–79.
[49] Hershberger, "War," 197–98.
[50] Hershberger, "War," 298.
[51] Hershberger, "War," 199.

known as Christian Disaster Relief. Although these disaster initiatives are motivated by charitable and humanitarian impulses, the Church clearly sees the work as an opportunity to evangelize.[52] In the curative process of helping disaster victims, the Church works for the spiritual welfare of their fellow men, hoping that many will see the Gospel light.[53,54]

In 2016, the editor of the *Messenger of Truth* posted an article entitled "Alien Citizens" that provides a candid assessment of Holdeman citizenship.[55]

> Our spiritual loyalties are to our heavenly homeland whose obligations we hold superior to all others. Nothing must deter us from giving it the best of all our assets and talents. From our heavenly country, we expect our dividends and eternal reward. Our earthly citizenship is but a pilgrimage. If the secular government provides us with benefits, we will gratefully and unworthily accept, yet knowing that we are not fully entitled to them. It is not in our place to demand our rights.

This honest appraisal suggests that the Holdeman people have acknowledged that they will not exert effort in helping to improve the world and they accept the consequences of this stance. Although their mission and disaster work clearly is beneficial to those receiving this aid, an underlying purpose is to evangelize in addition to the humanitarian objective.

Liberal philosophers will continue to debate the question of citizenship. However, many scholars agree that there are different ways of being a good citizen in a democracy and we should be wary of imposing a single model on society. As in Cohen's study of the Amish, we might also suggest that the Holdeman commitment to their communities, their mission work , and thoughtfulness regarding business transactions are of civic importance and can be recognized as a legitimate form of citizenship.[56] One might suggest that multiple forms of citizenship become even more important in today's pluralistic and somewhat fragmented society.

---

[52] *Conference Reports*, "1956 General Conference," 71.
[53] Hiebert, *Holdeman People*, 362–64.
[54] Giesbrecht, "Enduring Church," 210.
[55] Church of God in Christ, Mennonite, "Alien Citizens," para. 8.
[56] Cohen, "Amish," 65.

CHAPTER ELEVEN

The Holdeman People Today

HE TWO WORLD WARS created social and institutional challenges for the Holdeman people. The aftermath of these cataclysmic events left the Holdemans with many new and sometimes painful experiences resulting from military demands and integrating with a non-Mennonite world. These conservative Mennonites were confronted with an existential conundrum — how to take advantage of what society had to offer while also maintaining their separation from the world.

In rejecting much of what is offered in the modern world, the Holdemans hold tightly to their traditions while also making compromises, seemingly a necessity in order for members to live comfortably in today's world. However, these compromises have led some to speculate that the Holdemans are experiencing a gradual and incremental whittling away of their identity, perhaps ultimately resulting in their demise as a singular people. Religious subcultures are subject to disintegration if they are not able to cope with increased secularism and the technological advances of modern society. Typically it is the youth who are the innovators and advocate for change while challenging traditions of the Church.

The pages of the *Messenger of Truth* reveal the troubled state of mind by many authorities in the Church. Minister Keith Wedel expresses his concern in a note on family values. Youth "may begin to think that the thoughts or convictions of their parents or those who are older are old-fashioned."[1]

---

[1] Wedel, "Family," 2–3.

A Father's Day editorial expresses alarm and foreboding about the independence of the youth in the Church:[2]

> The church has not escaped the notice of a spirit of independence that has taken the children and young people of society by seemingly irresistible power. There is a level of unprecedented youth independence, aided and abetted by almost unlimited communication and monetary means. All this is not making for spiritual or happy and contented youth in our homes. It actually is causing a lot of tension that traditional Mennonite life has eschewed.

The Holdeman people's Anabaptist "cousins", the Amish and Hutterites, are all experiencing these pressures and dealing with them in different ways. The Hutterites, living in highly controlled communities, have been fairly successful in combatting worldliness. Regarding technology, they claim that "Nothing is too modern if it is profitable for the colony."[3,4] In a striking example of diversity in their communities, a small group of Amish men publicly campaigned for George W. Bush's re-election in 2004.[5] In contrast, the Holdeman Church resists the embrace of technology and eschews involvement in the political world. Minister Gladwin Koehn states the concern brought about by the many innovations and inventions in the world. "But we must remember that the Scriptures clearly say these are deceptive times, meaning that Christians will need to keep a guard on how they think about an evil environment."[6]

An Ethnic Community

An ethnic group is a category of people who identify with each other based on similarities such as common ancestry, language, history, culture, nation, or dialect.[7] The traditions, culture, and practices of conservative Mennonites all contribute to what has been called "peoplehood". an awareness of an underlying unity that makes an individual feel part of a group.[8]

In a relatively short time, the Mennonites of Prussia and Russia transformed themselves from a religious group into a distinct ethnic and folk group, identified by both genetic and cultural traits.[9] The Anabaptist ide-

---

[2]Church of God in Christ, Mennonite, "What Hath God Wrought," para. 11.
[3]Hostetler, *Hutterite Society*, 297.
[4]Hiebert, *Holdeman People*, 501.
[5]Nolt, *History*, 335.
[6]Koehn, "Shut the Back Door," para. 9.
[7]See, for example, https://en.wikipedia.org/wiki/Ethnic_group.
[8]See the Merriam-Webster Dictionary at https://www.merriam-webster.com/dictionary/peoplehood.
[9]Francis, "Russian Mennonites," 101–07.

ology and Dutch heritage were the initial catalysts for the establishment of the Mennonites in Holland. Bound by the strictures of the Groningen Old Flemish Society, the Dutch-Prussian Mennonites segregated themselves into largely isolated, rural communities in Groningen and Przechowka and later in the region of Volhynia. In this process, the people of the Groningen Old Flemish became the Ostrogers of Volhynia and, ultimately, the core group who created the Church of God in Christ, Mennonite (CGCM). The Holdeman forbears lived for some one hundred years as Ostrogers, eking out a living in an impoverished environment absent any well-defined formal religious structure. In a transformation of several hundred years, we see the emergence within the Ostrog communities of a relatively few family names of Dutch-Prussian origin, further evidence of an ethnic group in the making.[10,11] The three elements — the Anabaptist ideology, the Dutch-Prussian heritage, and the Ostrog environment – led to the creation of a unique culture and a people who readily accepted John Holdeman as their leader when they arrived in America.[12]

It is an interesting conundrum that the mission and outreach of the CGCM, beginning gradually in the 1930s, has led to involvement with people radically different in ethnic background. The initial impetus for mission work originated with John Holdeman's desire to convert members of the "decayed church" to the true church.[13] Redekop has clarified how missionary outreach tends to dilute ethnic solidarity. As a result, some of the more conservative Anabaptist groups such as the Hutterites do not do any outreach.[14] In her study of the Mennonites in the Paraguayan Chaco, LaRocque writes that "the degree of ethnic solidarity is inversely proportional to missionary outreach."[15] Certainly, the CGCM mission work is gradually diminishing their ethnic solidarity as can be noted by the increasing appearance of surnames that are not associated with a Dutch-Prussian heritage.[16] For the CGCM, it is likely that many of the newcomers resulting from mission work would not claim to

---

[10] There is a strong correlation between frequency of surnames in the Przechowka communities of Prussia and today's Holdeman communities. See the frequencies from the author's database of Holdeman people - Table 1 in Appendix Two (Page 160).

[11] Using surnames for ethnicity classification has been shown to be effective in other disciplines. See Mateos, "Review," 243–63.

[12] The sketch in Figure 15 was drawn by Allan Eitzen. I have reproduced the image from Clarence Hiebert's book *The Holdeman People: The Church of God in Christ, Mennonite, 1859-1969*. The sketch is the very first page in Hiebert's book. Permission to use this sketch has been granted by Professor Dirk Eitzen, son of Allan Eitzen. Also, William Carey Publishing holds the copyright for the Hiebert book and has granted permission to use the sketch.

[13] Hiebert, *Holdeman People*, 342–43

[14] Redekop, "Anabaptism," 144–45.

[15] LaRocque, "The Ethnic Church," 212.

[16] A text analysis of baptisms and marriages in the *Messenger of Truth* clearly shows an increasing number of surnames emanating from third world countries.

be ethnic Mennonites.

Are the Holdeman Mennonites losing their sociological shape and what dimensions of separateness are still effective within this community? It is clear that they no longer are geographically separated from non-Mennonites in their communities. Economically, they are being pulled inevitably into the business practices and technology of modern commerce. A text analysis of some eighty years of the *Messenger of Truth* reveals that there are an increasing number of church members who have received high school diplomas. In his study of institutional and ideological aspects of three American Mennonite ethnic groups, Nolt comments that the lingering markers of Mennonite separatism are in decline.[17] In an analysis of five Mennonite denominations, Kaufman and Driedger found that more education, increased earnings, and engaging in a multiplicity of occupations has led to members of these groups becoming more diverse.[18] For the Holdeman people, the social, cultural, and religious dimensions of a centuries-old ethnicity are gradually and subtly changing in a modern world.

Figure 15: *A Sketch of a Young Holdeman Family*

As social context changes, religious groups are faced with redefining who they are, constructing new bridges in the process.[19] Obviously, the Holdeman people have much communication with "outsiders" and, if not for certain distinguishing dress characteristics, they could easily blend in with others in the rural communities of the Great Plains. Unlike many Amish groups, the Holdemans drive cars and pickup trucks that are a normal part of the rural landscape in America. Similarly, their homes and farms are indistinguishable from their non-Mennonite neighbors. Members retain the wearing of the beard for men and the devotional head covering for women. Their churches are found on the outskirts of small towns and in the rural countryside. As with other Mennonite communities, they will use the Scriptures to guide

---

[17] Nolt, "Two-Kingdom People," 485–502.

[18] The five denominations included Brethren in Christ Church, Evangelical Mennonite Church, General Conference Mennonite Church, Mennonite Brethren Church, and Mennonite Church. The study did not include the Church of God in Christ, Mennonite. See Kaufman and Driedger, *Mennonite Mosaic*, 22, 154.

[19] Driedger, *Mennonite Identity*, 24–30.

their daily lives, however this behavior will be blended with the teachings and writings of John Holdeman and the guidance of ministers editorializing in the *Messenger of Truth*. Although perhaps not as a conscious action, they will continue to act out the Anabaptist vision in their religious practices.

In studying the the Mennonite "identity crisis", scholars are concluding that members are having difficulty finding the "good" in being a Mennonite.[20,21] Some have proposed definitions for who can be considered "Mennonite", suggesting that you must be a member of an established Mennonite church while others believe that those of Mennonite heritage comprise an ethnic group regardless of religious affiliation.[22,23] Yoder asks "Is Mennonite identity shaped by belief and commitment to scriptures or explained by social and material factors?" He answers this question by asserting that Mennonites understand themselves as people who are obedient in scripture, in belief, and practice — the Bible is central to Mennonite identity not unlike the Jewish people.[24]

The Holdemans are faced with a dilemma that has emerged from a rapidly moving, modern, technology driven society. The introduction of worldly influences has eroded much of the identity that evolved from living in the eighteenth century in Prussia and the nineteenth century in Russia. Outsiders may have viewed the Russian Mennonite communities as stable, static, and secure. However, this outward appearance of stability belies a more turbulent environment within the church. As the immigrants found more permanent homes in America, the nationalist and ethnic associations that were absorbed along the migration routes have largely disappeared. The gradual blending of these people into a secular culture could be a harbinger of an ending process in which their group identity ultimately disappears.[25,26]

Living in the Modern World

The Holdeman people exist in a cultural enclave, isolated from much of the nastiness in this world. In addition to the Bible, their principles of faith and doctrine are embodied in documents that are some 400 years old — the *Schleitheim Confession*, the *Dordrecht Confession*, and the *Martyrs Mirror*. The writings of Menno Simons and John Holdeman have defined more specifically their relationship to the world and the authority of the

---

[20] Redekop, "Mennonite Idenity Crisis," 87–88.
[21] Redekop, "Sociology," 173–74.
[22] Juhnke, *People*, xi.
[23] Kroeker, "Introduction," 90.
[24] Yoder, "Role," 77–82.
[25] Gans, "European ethnicity," 418–20.
[26] Gans, "Symbolic Ethnicity," 1–3.

church. Today, the letters of leaders and parents in the *Messenger of Truth* provide the modern guidelines for living according to these aging documents.

Life is basic and serious and one can easily be distracted by the temptations of a capitalist economy. Our increasingly secular and materialistic society seems overwhelmed with pettiness and self-indulgence. Deacon Ed Isaac warns about this materialism that has saturated the world's outlook on life, suggesting that we are under orders to hold so lightly to everything we own that we can give it up without pain.[27] The Holdemans continue to express a simple life style in their plain clothing, the wearing of the beard, and the devotional head covering. Behavior is evidenced in a sober countenance so that "jesting, joking, and pleasure seeking are not part of our lives."[28] Deacon Henry Penner writes about the pitfalls of laughter, repeating a saying that a Christian will smile and giggle but a fool will laugh out loud.[29]

Holdemans believe that the paraphernalia of the modern world detracts from the religious spirit. They reject visual art and symbolic imagery in their church buildings, hoping to empty out the "mundane clutter of the world in order to create a purified space for a worshipful encounter with God and the sacred". In this simplicity, one can see the influence of the Anabaptist radicals of the sixteenth century in which Conrad Grebel advocates for a much simplified worship service, devoid of music and images.[30] In Holdeman church buildings, there are no musical instruments, no plants, no banners, and no cross.[31] There are no mottos, no posted scripture verses and no graven images of any kind.[32] In this sparseness, the clock is the only visual focal point in the severely plain interior.[33] These prohibitions extend to holidays where popular holiday symbols such as Christmas trees and Christmas cards are forbidden.[34]

---

[27] Isaac, " Security," 4–5.
[28] Koehn, "Sobriety," 5, 7.
[29] Penner, "Laughter," 7–8.
[30] Weaver, *Becoming Anabaptist*, 44.
[31] Janzen, "Form," 337–38.
[32] It is in their ban of images that one can see a four hundred year unbroken chain from the early Anabaptists to the Holdeman people. In the October, 1523 Zurich council disputation, the following statement was made: "the use of images was discussed and roundly denounced by all participants." See Estep, *Anabaptist Story*, 16.
[33] Janzen, "Keeping Faith," para. 55.
[34] Janzen, "Help Us Think," 219–20.

Worldly people living in close proximity to their Holdeman neighbors recognize and appreciate their simple and basic way of life as summarized by Clarence Hiebert:[35,36]

> Today many people have a high regard for their Holdeman neighbors because of their loyalty, consistency of purpose, and self-giving expressions of love. Farmers know that Holdeman neighbors will be present and helpful in times of difficult circumstances. Those needing devoted care in times of illness often prefer Holdeman nurses because of their genuine and tireless conern for people. Holdeman babysitters are wanted for their affection for children. Many people dealing with Holdeman men in business are assured that they will meet their payments, and Holdeman business men are trusted for their fairness in business deals.

Yet, the Holdeman people are continuously challenged in their daily practices and the policies of the church to remain a people apart from the world.

Drifting into the Secular World

There are a variety of reasons for defining and maintaining a group identify.[37] For conservative Mennonites, perhaps the most pressing need is to resist the threat of assimilation into modern society. As John Holdeman cautioned in the mid-nineteenth century, we continue to live in a time of "many novel inventions and alien teachings".[38] In today's world, there are ominous forces in society that pose serious threats to the Holdeman peaceful way of life. Autocrats are on the rise in the world as evidenced in many of the countries in Eastern and Western Europe, making it more difficult for minority groups to thrive and prosper. Over the past several centuries, the conservative Mennonite response to these nationalistic movements was to emigrate. But migrating to another country to avoid restrictive government policies or a hostile citizenry is an unlikely option in the twenty-first century. As we have seen in the Prussia of the nineteenth century, Mennonites finally acquiesced and decided that participating in the military was a reasonable compromise with the government. During World War II, Mennonites fought with and against Hitler. If a group decides to separate from the world in order to live a more righteous, Christian-oriented life, what can be their response to the leaders who are bent on imposing their will on citizens? The

---

[35] Hiebert, *Holdeman People*, 495.
[36] Hiebert, *Holdeman People*, 433.
[37] Winland, "The Quest," 110–13.
[38] Holdeman, *Mirror*, 11.

Holdeman Church exerts much effort in resisting these threats that are so pervasive in today's world.

Ministers are constantly warning their congregations about the subtle "drift", a euphemism for assimilation that all members need to guard against. The many avid genealogists in Holdeman communities is evidence of their interest in and desire to maintain a certain group identity. Yet, there will always be a need to enter the environment of others, hoping to feel secure in the process. In their unique capacity to adapt, the Holdemans will continue to encounter conflict with society as they strive to remain separate from the world. Today, these more conservative Mennonites are confronted with a dilemma — how to retain their identity and remain separated from the world while also facing pressures to integrate into the modern social fabric.[39,40]

The Holdeman people of the twenty-first century retain social and symbolic boundaries that serve to provide a degree of separation from the world and reinforce their identity. Even today, after several centuries in which their settlements were repeatedly uprooted, the descendants of the Groningen Old Flemish can still be thought of as an ethnic community that shares a common Dutch-Prussian-German ancestry. However, this small, marginalized group is gradually emerging from this ethnic isolation, hoping in the process to maintain their adherence to the doctrines of nonresistance and nonconformity while also cautiously embracing what the world has to offer.

As they make prudent compromises, these plain people[41] are seeking out occupations other than farming. Given the costs to purchase land and opportunities from increased assimilation, many CGCM communities no longer have any farmers.[42] Although rural communities are still preferred, many are taking on the proprietorship of local hardware and grocery stores. Women might be found working in a hospital or assisted living facility as a registered nurse or nursing aid. They avoid the entanglements of labor unions and strongly discourage any work on Sundays.[43] Their guiding principle is to focus on vocations that aid people and preserve the simple way of life.[44]

For the Holdemans, religion embraces the whole of life and is an expression of their identity. Social interactions are exemplified by seriousness and

---

[39]Toews, "Mennonites," 227–28.

[40]Krahn. "Mennonite Names," 36.

[41]Barclay identifies members of the Church of God in Christ, Mennonite as "plain people" in which women are required to wear a black bandanna to cover their heads and men are obliged to wear a beard and are not permitted to have neckties. See Barclay, "Plain People," 140.

[42]Bradley, "Anti-Fashion," 10.

[43]In the general conference of 2003, the Church has reiterated its opposition to labor unions indicating that participation "would cause us to be unequally yoked to the world and would compromise our nonresistant faith". See *Conference Reports*, "2003 General Conference," 133.

[44]Hiebert, *Holdeman People*, 477.

sobriety while fulfillment comes from raising a family, maintaining a well-kept household, and striving for agricultural productivity and success in small businesses. Sunday afternoons are occasions for friends and relatives to socialize and for families to keep up-to-date on the events of the past week. Yet, there is an overriding concern by ministers and members alike about the "the drift" into worldly society. In a recent editorial, Deacon Fred Schrock uses a ship metaphor with its anchor, rudder, and sails to warn against the drift. If we are not properly anchored, "We are subject to the whims and influences about us; we are drifting."[45]

The Holdeman editors who contribute to the *Messenger of Truth* have eloquently expressed their concern for the future of the Church. Their editorials are threaded with knowledgeable references to both the Old and New Testaments. In reading these articles, one is reminded of C. Henry Smith's description of the early Anabaptists which has resonance for how we see the Holdeman people today: "No other people during the reformation knew the contents of the Bible as did the Anabaptists."[46]

In ruminating about the future of the Church, Minister Joe Isaac cites apostle Paul's admonition to the elders of the church at Ephesus, noting that it is important to examine the strengths and weaknesses of the church.[47] The church is strong "inasmuch as the members walk in obedience to the Word and Spirit and deal with worldliness." However, the threat of "Amalek" (worldliness) may be the greatest from within the church.[48] The Amalek is a monster with a number of heads – covetousness, permissiveness, pleasure seeking, and sufferance. This monster might be equated to the influence from the multiple, diverse cultures one finds today in American society. Isaac cautions against the carnal style of life that includes fancy homes, stylish clothes and exotic hairdos, concluding "We are in mortal, hand-to-hand spiritual combat with this Amalek. It is a battle to the death."[49] The weapons in this battle include editorializing, counseling, revivals, a strong disciplinary system, and finally excommunication and shunning.[50] In confronting the Amalek monster, the editors repeatedly warn against the "drift toward worldliness", urging ministers, parents and all members to study the cause

---

[45] Schrock, "Drift," 2–4.

[46] Smith, *Story*, 21.

[47] See Acts 20:28 — *Keep watch over yourselves and over all the flock, of which the Holy Spirit has made you overseers, to shepherd the Church of God that he obtained with the blood of his own Son.*

[48] The Amalekites have been characterized as the archetypal enemy of the Jews and "Amalek" is considered to be a symbol of evil, representing atheism and the rejection of God. See "Amalek", *The Free Encyclopedia*, https://en.wikipedia.org/wiki/Amalek.

[49] Isaac, "Take Heed," 2–4.

[50] In order to purify the Church, there was an extensive effort to excommunicate members in the 1970s. See https://www.youtube.com/watch?v=eVXcNWh5Twg.

and "remedy it by acknowledging their mistakes."[51] The challenges in seeking these remedies is illustrated in a survey by Clarence Hiebert, revealing that the Church of God in Christ, Mennonite in comparison to other Mennonite groups disapproves at a 100 percent level of movies, television, modern dress fashions, smoking, drinking, and all dancing.[52]

Will members be able to withstand the rigors of church discipline? Mervin Johnson sounds an ominous warning:[53]

> Living by tradition, of course, does not satisfy the inward man, and finally a generation arises that sees very little merit to these shallow followings of the ancient traditions. They begin to ask questions like "What's wrong with that?" They come to view the traditions as restrictions and a hindrance to their happiness. Thus, very slowly, the traditions that were established in the beginning era of true spirituality begin to fall by the wayside until what is left is a happy-go-lucky, go-as-you-please church that can hardly be identified with the early spiritual body that it once was.

The disciplined approach to life with many prohibitions creates a picture of a joyless people. Hiebert speculates on what might be options for disenchanted Holdeman people who are looking for a different religious life.[54] While individuals may join other denominations such as the Baptists or the General Conference Mennonites, the group as a whole might associate with the Beachy Amish Mennonites[55] or possibly drift into mainstream evangelical Protestantism. Others who are disturbed by the inroads of worldliness and want to hold fast to traditions may seek relocation to isolated areas in Mexico or South America where there are fewer worldly temptations. In response to the more liberal leanings, schismatic groups have arisen that sought more orthodox approaches, suggesting that beards shouldn't be trimmed and it was not good to have a lawn around the house that was indicative of prideful behavior.[56]

---

[51] *Conference Reports*, "1959 General Conference," 144.
[52] Hiebert, *Holdeman People*, 449.
[53] Johnson, "Traditionalism," 7, 9.
[54] Hiebert, *Holdeman People*, 499.
[55] The Beachy Amish differ from the Old Order Amish in that they allow the use of electrical conveniences, tractors, automobiles, and meeting houses. This group has also instituted Sunday school. This modernization is likely to have some appeal to Holdeman Mennonites. See Beachy, "Beachy Amish," 254.
[56] Hiebert, *Holdeman People*, 310–17.

Anabaptism Preserved?

We have examined how the Holdeman people have separated themselves from the world, avoided civil government, and practiced nonresistance. Although these humble people could probably claim the label of being Anabaptists, this label is unlikely to have any affect on their way of life. Have these conservative Mennonites preserved the Anabaptist principles first articulated in the sixteenth century? In answering this question, one must acknowledge that Anabaptism is never a finished product and is always in a state of change and reformulation. The Holdeman Church presents one form of contemporary Anabaptism, one that is faithful to the historical precedents established in the sixteenth century. These precedents are not absolute and other versions are simultaneously being created based on different historical and spiritual experiences.[57] The writings of John Holdeman, the editorials in the *Messenger of Truth*, and the Church of God in Christ, Mennonite (CGCM) Conference reports shed light on this final question.

Baptism

The rite of baptism is no longer a political issue and governments in the West do not require citizens to follow a particular faith. John Holdeman does not mention Anabaptism in the *Mirror of Truth* nor is it cited in the church conference reports. However, this rite of baptism is clearly defined in the Holdeman *Confession of Faith* in which it is stated that "we consider all baptisms which are not officiated by the true ministers [meaning members of the Church of God in Christ, Mennonite] of the Gospel unevangelical."[58] They adhere to the Anabaptist principle of "believer's baptism" which is expressed in the first article of the *Schleitheim Confession* as *Baptism shall be administered to all who have been instructed and give evidence of repentance and a change in life . . .*[59]

Nonconformity

Returning to the practice of nonconformity, it is useful to restate one of Michael Sattler's principles — *Separation is needful from all evil and wickedness which Satan has planted in the world.* Minister Errol Wedel reminds us about the pitfalls of living in a society of affluence and great lawlessness. Although we may enjoy the social life, he cautions us to "guard

---

[57] Weaver, "Anabaptist Vision," 14–16.
[58] Hiebert, *Holdeman People*, 397.
[59] Horsch, *Mennonites in Europe*, 72.

against being involved in social activities that take the place of true spiritual nourishment."[60] Reuben Koehn is more specific about the pitfalls stating that pleasure resorts and competitive sports are where the pride of life becomes active. He suggests that football, basketball, baseball and most other modern sports "are not part of the Father but of the world." His advice for success lies not in loving the world and, thereby, not being conformed to the ways of the world.[61]

Nonresistance

Given the relative peace in the Western world, the nonresistant man has little to resist. As a consequence, the Holdemans have had to reinterpret what it means to be nonresistant. Members have shared their thoughts on this issue in recent letters to the *Messenger of Truth*. Nathan Johnson believes that practicing nonresistance in everyday life is most important. It is a good thing to portray a nonresistant attitude toward state and national laws including local laws for traffic, hunting, and fishing.[62] Rylan Koehn suggests that a Holdeman person cannot hold firmly to the doctrine of nonresistance if playing a game on the phone involves simulation of war games and killing.[63] Others mention how one should respond to an aggressive driver or to someone who has not paid a debt. Minister Jake Bartel summarizes how members should view their practice of nonresistance: "The sayings of Jesus also contain specific teachings on nonresistance in every area of life. Be it towards brother, friend, enemy, foreigner, or whatever differences of opinion may occur, we are to be peacemakers."[64]

A Message for the World

We have examined in detail the pillars of the Anabaptist doctrines — adult baptism, nonresistance, and nonconformity. Oddly enough, it is the adherence to nonresistance and nonconformity that have forced the conservative Mennonites to engage with the world in order to practice their religion. The oath, the ban, and the shared ministry are also part of modern Anabaptism but are clearly more inwardly focused, having little effect on relationships with the external world.

The Mennonite diaspora has resulted in the modern descendants of the Anabaptists taking up many different creeds and vocations. We live

---

[60] Wedel, "Sacrifice," 2–3.
[61] Koehn, "Love," 1–3.
[62] Johnson, "The Kingdom," para. 6.
[63] Koehn, "Dangers," 8–9.
[64] Bartel, "Hearing," para. 15.

in a world with millions of immigrants and religious refugees. From the Russian Mennonites' lives of the early twentieth century, we can begin to understand the physical deprivation and emotional trauma that migrants from the war-torn countries of the twenty-first century are experiencing. The moral dilemmas of the practicing Mennonite are evident in a desire to be patriotic and support the nation while also maintaining freedom of conscience.

For the Holdeman people, the experience in America has been a challenge to acclimate to a dynamic and pluralistic society. As one of the most conservative Mennonite groups, they have held tenaciously to Anabaptist principles, separating from the world while also making prudent compromises to accommodate modern life. Looking into the future, the demands of citizenship and the impact of nationalist movements are reshaping what it means to be Mennonite where civic and governmental pressures are more prevalent and Mennonite identity has become much more diverse. The symbols of the Holdeman heritage — the unique forms of dress, common surnames, rural communities, Plattdeutsch — were all a means of identity but are now much less evident. The Holdemans take solace and comfort in being a church of small numbers. They are not likely to view modernity as an opportunity, perhaps rather a more destructive force that is contrary to living a life of moderation and simplicity. Amidst this chaotic world, the Holdemans have held steadfast to God-given norms — humility, modesty, temperance, generosity, contentment, sincerity, peaceable living, honesty, and reverence for life.

How can one be in the world but not of the world? In the New Testament passages of John 17:14–16, Jesus affirms that his disciples are "in the world" but "not of the world. These statements represent both a paradox and a dilemma for members of the church in deciding how to exist on the continuum between social activism and isolation from civil society. The secular world will likely see these people living life while remaining largely indifferent to the travails of those outside of their community. Political and social forces will continue the pressure on conservative Mennonites to integrate into the non-Mennonite world, raising questions of identity and how, or if, to assume more responsibility for the problems that are plaguing our society.[65] The line between personal responsibility and society's problems will become even more blurred. In his essay on the obligations of Christians, Edward Yoder points out that we do have responsibilities to both the state and the community.[66] On the one hand, as Yoder notes, "there is no ground in the teachings of Jesus . . . for any extreme form of isolation".[67] Yoder poses a question, Does God ask Christians "to work directly, or indirectly, or not at all, at improving

---

[65] Urry, *Mennonites*, 257–63.
[66] Yoder, "Obligation," 104.
[67] Yoder, "Obligation," 109.

the world and the conditions in it." The dilemma for the Holdeman people is to find their place in this continuum and to honor their responsibilities to society while also not being of the world.

CHAPTER TWELVE

Epilogue

E BEGAN THIS NARRATIVE by posing a question about the preservation of Anabaptism and speculating about what message for society is represented in the life of conservative Mennonites. The more progressive Mennonites in the United States have dropped the teaching of nonconformity and have "melted into the mainstream of American cultural life."[1] In contrast, there is ample evidence that the Anabaptist principles embodied in the *Schleitheim Confession* have been preserved in the practices of the modern Anabaptist descendants — the Holdeman people. A short recap of our narrative history will bring the reader to the final questions that are yet to be fully explored.

Early in the sixteenth century, a few dedicated radicals launched the Anabaptist movement in Zurich, Switzerland. Conrad Grebel, Felix Manz, Georg Blaurock, and Michael Sattler were urban leaders and radicals in Switzerland, challenging church authorities to demonstrate how the Scriptures supported infant baptism. These committed reformers and their co-religionists rejected infant baptism and sought to live a primitive Christianity based on the New Testament, hoping to create a church composed solely of earnest believers. They insisted on Church reform and rejected the Catholic sacraments, advocating that the state should not dictate the religion of the people. No other series of events during the Reformation so thoroughly signified a break with the Catholic Church. For the Church and the Holy Roman Empire, any deviation from established doctrine was considered a crime, punishable by death. For these early Anabaptist revolutionaries, their ministries and lives were soon cut short in martyrdom, exile, or premature death from illness.

The Anabaptist movement spread rapidly from Switzerland to Germany and the Netherlands. The movement took on many different forms and it can be argued that in Dutch Anabaptism we see the sharpest rejection of historic Christianity. The Dutch Anabaptists believed with other radicals of

---

[1] Bush, *Two Kingdoms*, 148.

the time that the established church had fallen and could not be reformed. In pursuing a radically different vision, the Anabaptists of different persuasions were all labeled as heretics.

The Anabaptist sickness resulted in many diversions before Menno Simons was able to unite the Dutch into a group that became known as the Mennonites. In the Netherlands, persecution drove these early adherents to the northern provinces and eastward to Danzig and the Polish lowlands. Fearing the long arm of the authorities, Menno and his followers retreated into the countryside, often holding services in the forest or in private homes. As a result, Menno's people gradually moved to rural communities, out of the way of the authorities, undertaking livelihoods of farming and agricultural pursuits.

In the early seventeenth century, a meeting in Middelstum, Groningen between the Flemish and Old Flemish resulted in the preachers of the country churches breaking away to form the Groningen Old Flemish Society. As we have recounted, this group insisted on strict maintenance of both doctrine and practice. By the early eighteenth century, thirty-three congregations of the Groningen Old Flemish were active of which three were found along the Vistula river in Royal Poland — the Przechowka communities. These rural Dutch people brought both agricultural and water management skills with them and after several generations they had cleared the swampy lands along the Vistula. Unfortunately, conflicts with kings, bishops, and the local citizenry made life difficult for the Mennonites, resulting in a stay of only about one hundred years in the Prussia of the Frederick kings.

The most impoverished and conservative of the Groningen Old Flemish took advantage of Czarina Catherine II's offer for German immigrants to settle the vast plains of what today is the modern state of Ukraine. A small group who became known as the "Ostrogers" settled in the region of Volhynia. Once again, they lived for less than one hundred years in Czarist Russia, rejecting military service and emigrating to the Great Plains of America in the 1870s. In America, they found John Holdeman's Church of God in Christ, Mennonite most compatible with their beliefs and life style.

From our earlier chapters, the reader is familiar with the religion and culture of the modern day Holdeman people. This small group, consisting of some one hundred congregations in the continental United States, has steadfastly adhered to nonresistance and separation from the world. However, the Anabaptist legacy leaves the Church of God in Christ, Mennonite with emotion-laden questions. What happens when the forces of modernity descend upon a small, close-knit, conservative religious group? Religion, family, community, education, and culture are all transformed, often subtly, as faith and practice bend to the pressures of a modern world. Nonconformity and living apart is made more difficult by the loss of bonds formed from a

Dutch-Prussian ethnic heritage and common immigrant experiences. Will the Holdeman people be able to sustain their way of life as the threats from modernity intensify? Can their way of life serve as a model for a better way of living in a secular world?

The message the Holdeman people offer to worldly people is not explicit and still lingers like the morning mist on a summer day, making it difficult to clearly discern the fuzzy images. Will our contemporary civilization draw inspiration and guidance from these modern Anabaptists? Although separation from the world may cause some distrust in worldly people, it behooves us to listen more closely to what their way of life has to tell us.

Guy Hershberger poses a challenge for the conservative Mennonite way of life: "A light cannot witness to the way of truth unless it stands where it can be seen and unless it shines in the darkness."[2] Hopefully, some of the light will shine through in the words of this text. Peaceful living, humility, honesty, refusal to take up arms, and living within moderate means — all of these could benefit the world by finding more prominence in a violent and war-torn society.

---

[2] Hershberger, *War*, 200.

APPENDIX ONE

The Kansas Ostrogers: Antonofka to Lone Tree

RESEARCHERS AND SCHOLARS HAVE WRITTEN much about the Russian Mennonites who settled in south Russia - the communities of Chortitza and Molotschna.¹ However, there is a paucity of literature about the journey of a small group who migrated from Przechowka in Prussia to the region of Volhynia, near the city of Ostrog, (now part of the modern state of Ukraine) and settled in the communities of the Karolswalde circuit. In Przechowka and associated congregations the Old Flemish found refuge and temporary residence after migrating from Holland in the seventeenth century.

A reoccurring theme in the previous chapters has been the emergence of a small group of people with a Dutch-Prussian background who became the Ostrogers of the nineteenth century and the Holdeman people of the twentieth century. The Ostrogers were the descendants of the conservative Groningen Old Flemish, a congregation that originated in seventeenth century Holland. Krahn has indicated that of some 567 Prussian Mennonite names, at least 500 can be traced to the provinces of the Low Countries.² The Dutch-Prussian congregations of the Old Flemish were small and, as one example, the community of Schönsee in 1719 numbered only about forty-eight baptized members.³

Because of their traditions of nonconformity and separation from the world, the Ostrogers established communities in which few outsiders gained entrance and there was little contact with the more progressive Mennonite groups. In this appendix, we narrow the focus to these close-knit group of Ostrogers, telling the story of families and how a small number of surnames,

---

[1] See, for example, David G. Rempel with Cornelia Rempel Carlson. *A Mennonite Family in Tsarist Russia and the Soviet Union: 1789 - 1923.* Toronto:University of Toronto Press, 2002. and James Urry. *None but Saints: The Transformation of Mennonite Life in Russia.* Hyperion Press Limited, 1989.
[2] Krahn, *Dutch Anabaptism*, 220.
[3] Zijpp, "Schönsee," 475.

found in the Groningen Old Flemish congregation of the seventeenth century, are still dominant in the Holdeman communities of the twenty-first century.[4]

Parallel Lives

Part of the framework in this text relates to the enduring relationships among a small group of Dutch-Prussian Mennonites. This phenomenon is supported by demonstrating the connected kinship relationships that have persisted over several hundred years. In a name analysis, Hiebert found that the family names of Koehn, Jantz, Schmidt, and Unruh were the most prevalent in the Holdeman communities of the 1970s.[5] In what follows, we trace two of these interconnected families — the Jantz's and Schmidts — from Przechowka in the late seventeenth century to the Polish-Russian villages in Volhynia and from there to the Great Plains of America, settling in Lone Tree, Kansas. The patriarchs of these two families are Casper Schmidt (*prz786*) and Cornels Jantz (*prz514*), both born in the late seventeenth century in Prussia.

The parallel lives of the descendants of Casper and Cornels are depicted in Figure 16. Casper Schmidt's son, Michael Schmidt (*prz793*), was born 29 December 1694 in Konopat (also Kunpat), a small village which together with Przechowka formed a congregation of the Groningen Old Flemish. In the year 1719 Konopat, located just a few miles west of Przechowka, had a total of fifty-two residents.[6] Michael's son and grandson, both named Jacob, were born in the Prussia of the eighteenth century. Henry Schmidt, the great-great grandson of Casper, (born 14 July 1807 in West Prussia) is likely the same Henry Schmidt who is referenced in the Lileva village located near Karolswalde (see Map 6), suggesting that Henry probably left the Przechowka community as a child or young adult. Henry's spouse, Anna Marie Schmidt, born 14 November 1808 died in Lone Tree, McPherson County, Kansas in 1888.

As with the Schmidt family, we see the first four generations of the Jantz family all having PRZ designations, indicating they were born in one of the Przechowka communities situated along the Vistula river in Royal Poland (Figure 16). We know that Cornels Jantz (*prz514*), his wife and several children died in the plague, however his son, Jan (*prz519*), was one of the survivors.[7] A second Cornels, the son of Jan, was born 5 December 1739 in Schönsee (*prz528*) and married Trincke Ratzlaff (*prz160*).[8] The son of

---

[4] Goertz, *Jantzes*, 20–21.
[5] Hiebert, *Holdeman People*, 149–50. See note no. 6.
[6] Duerksen, "Konopat(h)," 222.
[7] Pankratz and Unruh, *Church Records*, 19.
[8] The reader will note that birth dates in the first generation are typically in the late

Cornels and Trincke, David Cornels Jantz (*prz1136*), was born 2 April 1794 in Jeziorka, a village located west across the Vistula river from Schönsee. David's son, Benjamin D. Jantz, born 24 April 1824 in Karolswalde, had a daughter Helena, born 8 April 1860 in Ostrog, and who married Benjamin H. Schmidt.

The lives of these two families come together in the sixth generation in which Benjamin H. Schmidt marries Helena Jantz. Benjamin H. Schmidt, born 7 September 1839 in Poland, Russia, never had a chance to live a normal life in one community. Benjamin was only thirty-four years old when he and his first wife, Helena Becker, emigrated to the United States on the *S. S. City of Montreal*, arriving on November 27, 1874 with four children - Jacob, Samuel, John, and Peter.[9] These four children from his first wife were all born in Antonofka, Poland, Russia. This family settled in Lone Tree and had several more children before Helena Becker passed away on 10 September 1879. Benjamin then married Helena Jantz in 1880, born 8 April 1860 in Antonofka, and had many more children. Apparently some time between the birth of Joel in 1894 and Lydia in 1896, the Benjamin Schmidt family moved to Pauls Valley, Oklahoma.[10] Benjamin lived in Pauls Valley for a little over twenty-five years, passing away on 10 May 1902. His second wife, Helena Jantz, passed away on 19 March, 1947 in Chickasha, Oklahoma. Some of Benjamin's siblings remained in Kansas and helped to establish other CGCM congreations. Henry H. Schmidt, brother to Benjamin H. Schmidt, born 9 July 1848 married Eva Jantz, born 5 March 1850. Henry and Eva moved from Lone Tree to Halstead, Kansas in 1881 and joined the Grace Mennonite congregation of the CGCM. Henry was ordained a minister by John Holdeman in March, 1882.[11]

The Kinship Trail

The beliefs and endogamous marriage practices of the conservative Mennonites has resulted in a small group of families remaining connected throughout several centuries and multiple migrations through the countries of Western Europe. Although there were many trials and tribulations during the 400 years of migrations, there is also a personal story that is revealed in the data

---

seventeenth or early eighteenth centuries and that female names retain the Dutch ending — Ancke (Anna) and Trincke.

[9] Haury, *Index to Mennonite Immigrants*, 39.

[10] A brief history of the Pauls Valley congregation is given in Gospel Publishers, *Histories of the Congregations*, 457–58. The congregation was disbanded in the fall of 1902 and moved to Chickasha because the land was poor and the group was experiencing some problems with their Indian neighbors. Because of the open range, crops could be damaged by livestock that was not properly tended.

[11] *Centennial Anniversary*, "Grace Mennonite Congregation," 9.

that has been recorded over these many centuries. We can, in fact, trace the ancestry of specific individuals from settlements in Przechowka of the 1700s to Antonofka, to their boarding of the *S.S. Vaderland* and to their initial settlement in one of the Canton sections of Lone Tree Township.[12,13]

The richness of these connections can be seen in several examples, illustrative of the different family names that keep reappearing in the Dutch-Prussian ancestry. Portraits of individual lives also reveal how the Dutch-Prussian groups and the Ostrogers dealt with adversity, organized their congregations, and endured a hazardous journey across the Atlantic. By looking at individual lives and a few of the most common surnames, we can see how families have worked together, lived together, and traveled together over a span of some 400 years.

In 1535, Hendrick Gijsbrechts was apprehended in West Friesland for not obeying the commandments of the Roman Church. When asked if he had been re-baptized, Hendrick answered in the affirmative and was sentenced to death.[14] Early in the seventeenth century, we find Heinrich and Peter Giesbrecht in the Dutch villages of the Danzig werder.[15] Abraham Giesbrecht was the Schulze (mayor) of the village of Scharfenberg in the Danzig lowland. In south Russia, Jacob Giesbrecht was one of the first members of the Mennonite Brethren Church.[16] Some one hundred years later on August 1, 1945, we encounter a Giesbrecht family on the Dutch border near Maastricht as they fled the Soviet Union. In this group there were six members of the Giesbrecht family: parents Jacob and Susanna, both age thirty-nine, and their children, Peter, Maria, Susanna and Lena.[17]

Sijbrant Jansz was an Anabaptist martyr who was beheaded on June 7, 1535 at Hoorn, Holland along with two other men. Several months earlier, Catholic theologians had tried unsuccessfully to make these men recant but they remained steadfast in their convictions. As result, the Court of Holland ordered them to be executed without delay.[18] Although these executions became more frequent and began to arouse Dutch citizens to protest, Sijbrant has another significant connection to our story. It is likely that Sijbrant's descendants led to a popular surname in today's Holdeman communities as is evident in the occurence of "Siebrandt" in Table 1 of family names, Appendix Two - page 160 .

Andreas Siebrandt and his wife Eva Unruh traveled on the *S. S. Vaderland* with their seven year old son, Andreas. This family settled on section twenty-

---

[12] Unruh, *Helpless Poles*, 162–163.
[13] Juhnke, "Historical Concepts," 26–27.
[14] Van Braght, *Martyr's Mirror*, 443.
[15] "Werder" is a German word for land surrounded by water.
[16] Penner, "Giesbrecht," 516–17.
[17] Homan, "We Have Come," 41.
[18] Zijpp, "Sijbrant Jansz," 526.

one in Lone Tree and the young son Andreas married Elizabeth Jantz who was the daughter of Benjamin D. Jantz (*id=142191*). Benjamin was the son of David C. Jantz (*id=14219, prz1136*) who was born in 1794 in Jeziorka, West Prussia.

Jonas C. Koehn was born in Lone Tree on October 15, 1885. Jonas' father, Cornelius, and his first wife, Maria Becker, and family are listed on the ship board list of the *S. S. Vaderland*.[19] Cornelius Koehn and wife Maria settled on section fifteen in Lone Tree Township.[20] Jonas married Amanda Schmidt (b. June 5, 1890) who was the daugher of Helena Jantz (*id=1421918*) and Benjamin H. Schmidt (see Figure 16). As with the Siebrandt family, we can also trace the lineage of the Koehn family back to Przechowka where we find the grandparents of Cornelius Koehn, Heinrich Koehn (*prz604*) and wife Ancke Ratzlaff (*prz148*), listed in the Przechowka Kirchen Buch.[21]

The Koehn (Köhn) family name was very popular among conservative Mennonites. The name was first recorded in 1681 in the Danzig church records.[22] However, some 150 years earlier, we find Antonius von Köhn, an early Anabaptist leader, working in the Lower Rhine region. He was known as "pious Antonius" and had communications with the Dutch Anabaptists. In 1542, Antonius was ordained by Menno Simons and took part in a conference in Emden, Germany.[23] Today, the Koehn family name remains perhaps the most popular surname in the Holdeman community (see Table 1 of Appendix Two).[24]

As cited earlier, William Wiggers was brought to a castle in North Holland near Schagen, imprisoned for eight days and then beheaded for practicing his Anabaptist faith.[25] The Wiggers family name is not found on any of the passenger lists compiled by David Haury nor does it appear in the church records of the Groningen Old Flemish Society.[26] As is the case with the Holdeman surname and other Swiss Mennonites, the Wiggers family likely found their way to America in the eighteenth century, many years before the mass migrations of the 1870s.[27]

The family name Nachtigal (Nachtegaal) and its American variants (Nightengale, Nightingale) is a Dutch-Prussian Mennonite name that originated in the Netherlands. This name was found in the eighteenth century, specifically

---

[19] Haury, *Index to Mennonite Immigrants*, 41.
[20] Mueller, *Church and Family Records*, 16.
[21] Pankratz and Unruh, *Church Records*, 21, 11.
[22] Krahn, "Koehn," 211.
[23] Koolman, "Antonius von Köhn," 133–34.
[24] In research on Holdeman family names, this author found that the Koehn surname has the highest frequency count in two years of text from the newsletter *Messenger of Truth*.
[25] Van Braght, *Martyr's Mirror*, 442.
[26] See Haury, *Index to Mennonite Immigrants*.
[27] In an interesting footnote, we find a Hotel Wiggers in the small community of Wüstenfelde, Germany, a village where Menno Simons spent his last seven years.

in the Prussian communities of Jeziorka and Schönsee. There are some sixty Nachtigal names listed in church records of the Groningen Old Flemish Society of Przechowka.[28] In the early nineteenth century, some of the Nachtigal family emigrated from West Prussia to Russia.[29] Johann Nachtigal was a co-minister in the Karolswalde village of Leeleva (See the village plan in Map 6). We find many Nachtigal families on the ship board lists of the *S.S. Colina* and the *S.S. Vaderland*.[30]

The Nickel (Nichols, Nikkel) family was associated with the more liberal Dutch Frisian congregation of Schönsee in the Prussia of the eighteenth century. The Dutch *Naamlijst* identifies Peter Nickel and Jacob Nickel as ministers in Prussia during the mid-18th century.[31] There are no Nickel (Nichols) family names listed in the Przechowka Kirchen Buch or in the Alexanderwohl Mennonite Church Book of the Molotschna colony. We know that Peter D. Nikkel was born in Karolswalde on January 10, 1835. Peter's second wife was Susanna Koehn, born in Antonofka on December 18, 1835. Peter, wife Susanna, and family traveled on the *S.S. Illinois*, arriving in Philadelphia on January 28, 1875.[32] From Nichols family notes, we read that Helena and Henry E. Nichols (siblings) were born to Peter David and Susanna (Koehn) Nickel in Antonokfa, Poland, Russia.[33] Henry Nichols began his journey to America on the *S.S. Abbotsford*. While on the high seas, the *Abbotsford* collided with the *Indus*, forcing a return to London for repairs.[34] While in London, Henry, along with several children, was infected with smallpox and was transferred to a hospital ship. After recovering, Henry continued his journey to America in the company of Benjamin Unruh, Peter Becker, and Tobias Unruh.

The Wedel family name was prominent in both Prussia and south Russia and early members of the group included Benjamin Wedel and Peter Wedel. A Frantz Wedel (*prz193*) participated in the leasing of the Przechowka village in 1640.[35] Elder Jacob Wedel compiled the first known church book of the Przechowka congregation in 1784.[36] It is interesting that there are only three family names that dominate the first four generations of the Wedel family in Przechowka — Wedel, Ratzlaff, and Schmidt (Figure 17).

Peter Jantz (*prz516*), born on June 3, 1744, served the Przechowka Flemish Mennonite Church and later became an elder in the Brenkenhoffswalde

---

[28] Pankratz and Unruh, *Church Records*, 22–23.
[29] Zijpp, "Nachtigal," 805.
[30] See Haury, *Index to Mennonite Immigrants*.
[31] Krahn, "Nickel," 869–70.
[32] See Koehn, *Family Record*.
[33] See Jantz and Nightengale, *The Descendants of Peter Nichols*.
[34] Schmidt, "Passenger Ship Lists," 5–7.
[35] Duerksen, "Przechowka and Alexanderwohl," 76–82.
[36] Krahn, "Wedel," 907.

Church. Peter married Ancke Wedel (*prz242*) and served the church as elder for 34 years. He appealed to the Mennonites in Holland for aid to build a church in 1778.[37] Peter later became a Protestant minister in the state church and he died on September 2, 1810, having never made the journey to Russia.[38]

---

[37] Duerksen, "Jantz, Peter," 94.
[38] Mannhardt, "Brenkenhoffswalde," para. 1.

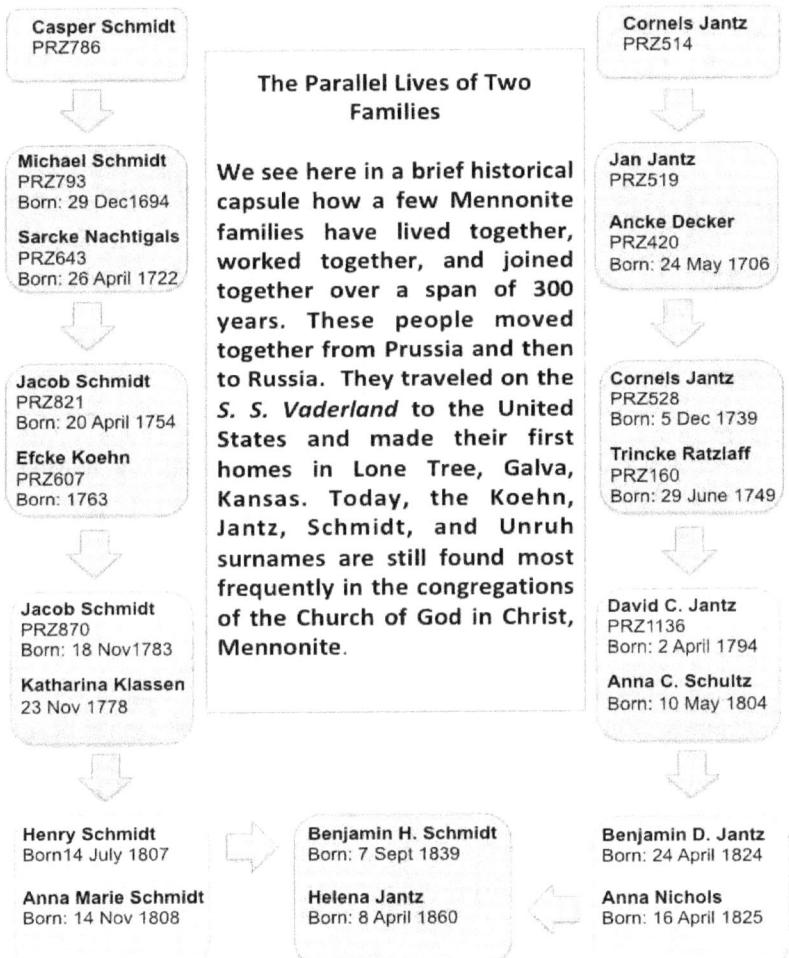

Figure 16: The Parallel Lives of the Schmidt and Jantz Families, from Przechowka to Lone Tree

APPENDIX TWO

Dutch-Prussian Family Names

HE FAMILY NAMES FOUND in the Groningen Old Flemish congregations of the seventeenth and eighteenth centuries appear frequently in the Holdeman church today. The kinship and marriage relationships provide a method for tracing the group's travels throughout Prussia and Russia. Smith cites an early study of Prussian Mennonites who were almost exclusively the descendants of the early Dutch settlers in the sixteenth century. Nearly one-half of the ten thousand Mennonites had surnames found in the first twenty-one most popular names.[1] These names were transplanted from Przechowka and, beginning in 1873 and 1874, to the Great Plains of North America.

A name analysis by Hiebert in the 1970s indicates that 662 passengers on the S. S. *Vaderland* out of a total of 708 traveled to Atchison, Kansas. Of the thirteen surnames identified in this group, the first four — Koehn, Jantz, Schmidt, and Unruh, continue to be the predominant names in the Church of God in Christ, Mennonite.[2] When members of the Kleine Gemeinde group joined the Holdemans in 1881, the community was enriched by a new set of surnames, including Esau, Giesbrecht, Goosen, Loewen, and Reimer.

In Table 1, the reader can see the distribution of surnames from data that was extracted from the author's database of some 6200 related family members.[3] This database is, in effect, an intricate web of kinship and marriage relationships.

---

[1] Smith, *Story*, 272.
[2] Hiebert, *Holdeman People*, 149–50. See note 6.
[3] The author's database has been constructed over a period of thirty years by creating a network of related people that starts with Peter Jantz in 1650 and by developing the more detailed genealogy of Peter's descendants. This database has been developed largely from published Holdeman genealogies and obituaries published in the *Messenger of Truth*.

There are twelve family names (and their spelling variations) that comprise 89 percent of the almost 5000 names that are most popular and are generally, with few exceptions, recognized today as "Mennonite". Of these twelve, the four surnames — Jantz, Koehn, Schmidt, and Unruh — comprise 64 percent of the total (see Table 1). These statistics correlate strongly with a name analysis of two years of the *Messenger of Truth* — 2017 and 2018 (see Table 2).[4] Other surnames occur less frequently such as Giesbrecht, Nichols, Wedel, and Wiggers, representing families mixed in with the larger group in their migrations throughout Europe. Many of these people emigrated from Switzerland to Northern Holland and joined their Dutch co-religionists in the migration to Prussia and Russia.

---

[4] Jantz, "Lived Religion," 13.

Family Name	Occurence	Percent	Cum
Koehn	1007	20.0	20.0
Jantz/Jantzen/Johnson	1005	20.0	40.0
Schmidt/Smith	781	15.8	55.8
Unruh	407	8.2	64.0
Becker	235	4.7	68.7
Nightingale/Nightengale	212	4.3	72.0
Nichols	192	3.9	75.9
Wedel/Wadel	163	3.3	79.2
Dirks	126	2.6	81.8
Eck	125	2.5	84.3
Buller	123	2.5	86.8
Ratzlaff	110	2.2	89.0
Holdeman	97	2.0	91.0
Loucks	46	1.1	92.1
Wiggers	42	1.1	93.2
Boehs	41	0.9	94.2
Esau	35	0.8	95.0
Yost	34	0.8	95.8
Giesbrecht	32	0.7	96.5
Penner	31	0.7	97.2
Siebrandt	27	0.6	97.8
Voth	24	0.5	98.3
Schartner	22	0.5	98.8
Friesen	21	0.4	99.2
Toews	21	0.4	99.6
Loewen	20	0.4	100.0

Table 1: Frequency of Mennonite Family Names (N=4,960)

The database of Dutch-Prussian and Holdeman people has been developed from multiple sources and is anchored in the seventeenth century with a Peter Jantz who was likely born sometime around 1650 in Holland.[5] Beginning with this Peter, we create a unique identification or ID. Each digit in the ID represents a generation and the numeric value of each digit represents the position of that individual in their family, i.e. first born is 1, second born is

---

[5] The early Jantz line has been researched by J.A. Duerksen who has indicated that Peter Jantz (*prz512*) was born sometime between 1650 and 1670 and was a deacon of the church.

Family Name	Frequency in the MOT
Koehn	1727
Unruh	656
Schmidt/Smith	636
Toews	424
Jantz/Johnson	404

Table 2: Frequency of Mennonite Family Names in the Messenger of Truth, 2017–2018.

2, etc. An example will help clarify this methodology. David C. Jantz has an id of 14219. Since there are 5 digits, this indicates that David C. is in the fifth generation, dating from the first known Jantz (i.e. Peter Jantz born in 1650). We construct the ID as illustrated in Table 3.

Where families have more than 9 children, the method continues by using the alphabet. So, for example, in the seventh generation Caroline Jantz (wife of Henry C. Koehn) was the 10th born in her family and therefore has an ID of 142191A, the "A" indicating that she is the 10th born.

Ancestor	Generation	Position	ID
Peter Jantz	1	1	1
Cornels Jantz	2	4	14
Jan Jantz	3	2	142
Cornels Jantz	4	1	1421
David Jantz	5	9	14219

Table 3: Genealogy Numbering System

A Snapshot of Surnames from Przechowka

The following images provide the reader with a sampling of the families of the Groningen Old Flemish communities and how a very few surnames keep reappearing through the various marriage and kinship relationships.

Readers will note that there is one Slavic surname referenced in Figure 16 (Appendix One) of which we have some significant details. The Ratzaff family was the largest in the Przechowka congregation and apparently began with a soldier who had been discharged and wanted to join the congregation. In order to join, he had to use a common subterfuge, traveling first to Holland to be baptized and then returning to Prussia as a Mennonite.[6] The early family groups in Prussia reveal the prominence of the Ratzlaff surname (Figures 17, 18, and 19). In each of the figures, Hans Ratlaff (*prz25*), born January 1, 1661 has sons — Hans (*prz35*), Peter (*prz36*), and Jeorgen (*prz38*).

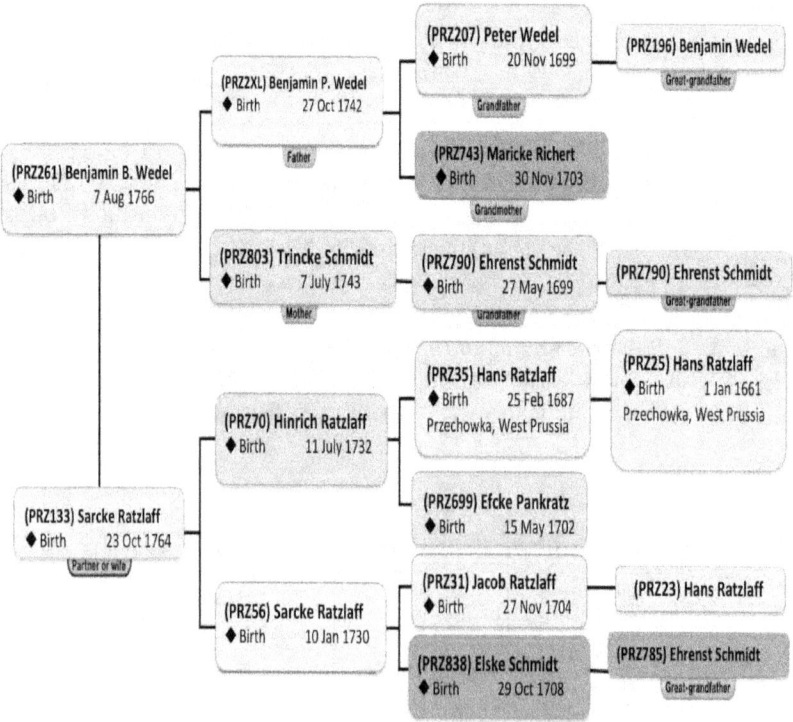

Figure 17: *The Ratzlaff, Richert, Schmidt, and Wedel Families of Przechowka*

---

[6]Pankratz and Unruh, *Church Records*, 3.

The Unruh (Unrau) family name was one of the most widespread throughout Prussia and is listed 92 times in the Kirchen Buch (Figure 18).[7,8] The Unruh surname represents about eight percent of the family names in the author's database of Holdeman people. We find among the Unruhs of the early eighteenth century a practice discussed earlier in which non-Mennonites could travel to Holland, be baptized, and return to Prussia as a member of the Old Flemish congregation (see page 43). A Lutheran, Maricke Nöfcken (*prz951*), followed this practice and later married elder Abraham Unrau (*prz949*). One of the most notable of the Unruh family is Tobias A. Unruh who led the Ostrogers to America in the 1870s (see page 78).

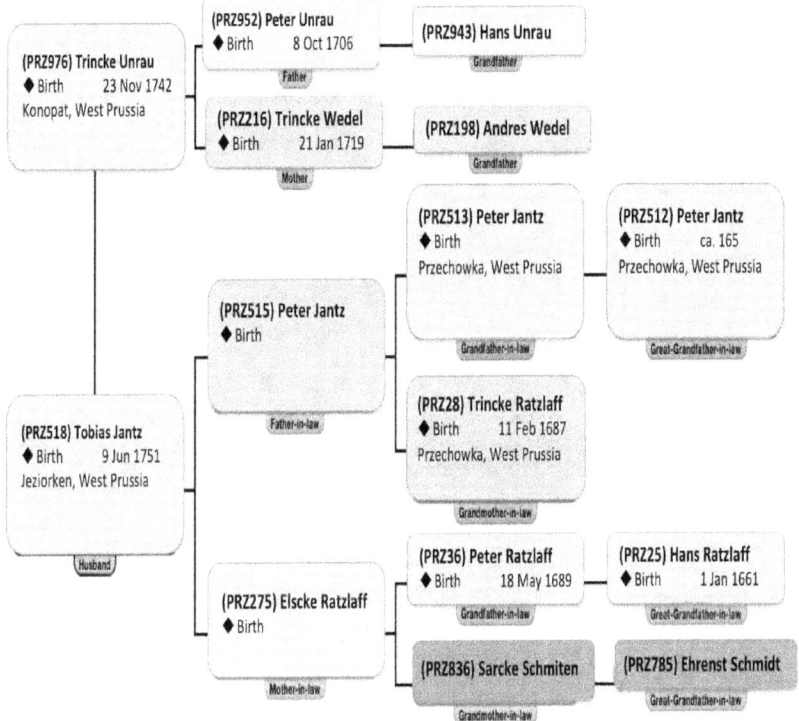

Figure 18: The Unrau (Unruh), Jantz, Ratzlaff, and Schmidt Families of Przechowka

---

[7] Unruh, "Unruh," 784–85.
[8] Pankratz and Unruh, *Church Records*, 28–30.

Although the Becker family name is not of typical Dutch-Prussian origin, the surname accounts for almost five percent of the names in the author's database of Holdeman people. The Becker family name appeared in the Old Flemish congregations of Przechowka (Figure 19). In the accounting of the eighteenth century, forty-five Beckers are listed in the Kirchen Buch.[9] In 1556, a Peter Becker was the founder of the Anabaptists of Pomerania, a region that is now mostly included as part of Poland.[10]

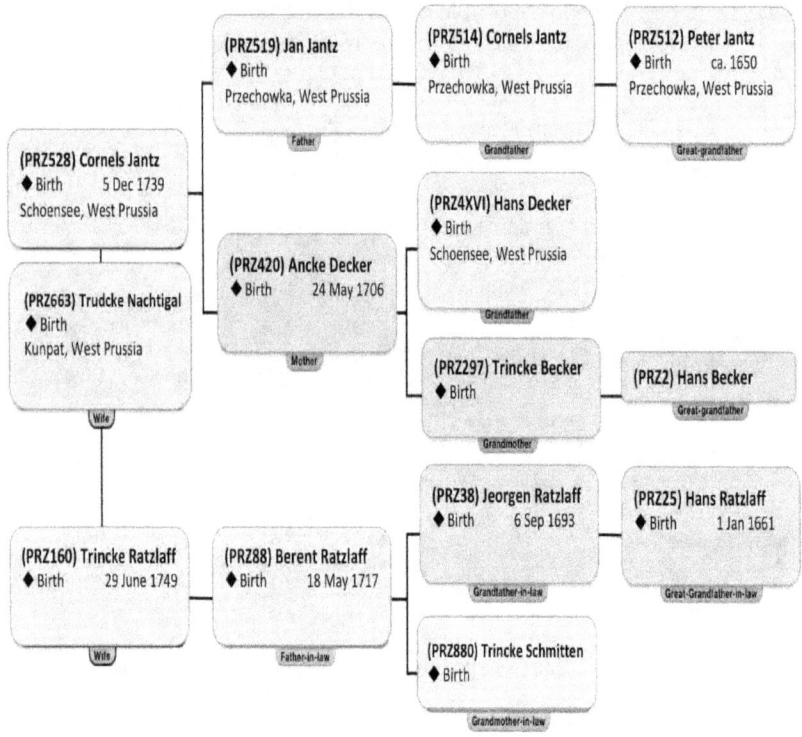

Figure 19: The Becker, Jantz, Ratzlaff, and Schmidt Families of Przechowka

---

[9] Pankratz and Unruh, *Church Records*, 14–15.
[10] Heyden, "Becker, Peter," 259.

APPENDIX THREE

Holdeman Congregations in the United States

ROM ITS EARLY BEGINNINGS with just a few churches in Kansas, the congregations of the Church of God in Christ, Mennonite have grown steadily. Virtually all of the churches that were established during John Holdeman's ministry were peopled from the Russian immigrant settlements. By the end of World War I in 1918, there were about 1,400 members in the various Holdeman churches.[1] In 2010, the estimate of total membership worldwide was 22,779.[2]

As membership and congregations increased, the church decided to establish districts — the Eastern District, extending west to the Mississippi river; the Western District extending to the Pacific coast; and the Northern District including all of Canada.[3] Today, estimates indicate that the number of congregations world wide is approaching two hundred. The following maps provide a visual display of how wide spread the church is in the United States. The number of congregations in the United States stood at 102 based on the *Histories of the Congregations*, published in 1999 by Gospel Publishers.

---

[1] Hiebert, *Holdeman People*, 243.
[2] See the Association of Religion Data Archives at www.thearda.com.
[3] Koehn, *Histories*, 12.

| PART TWO | APPENDIX THREE | Congregations |

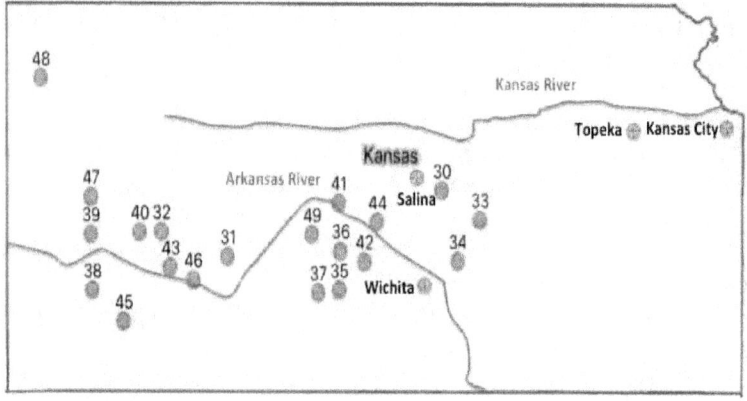

Key to Locations:
32. Cimarron, 33. Eden-Burns, 34. Emmanuel-Fredonia, 35. Garden View-Halstead, 36. Gospel-Moundridge, 37. Grace-Halstead, 38. Grant-Ulysses, 39. Lakin, 40. Living Hope-Ingalls, 41. Lone Tree-Galva, 42. Meridian-Hesston, 43. Montezuma, 44. Morning Star-Durham, 45. Plains, 46. Salem-Copeland, 47. Scott City, 48. Sharon Springs, 49. Zion-Inman

Map 8: Congregations of the Church of God in Christ, Mennonite in Kansas (map by the author).

Key to Locations:
1. Cedar Crest, Faunsdale, Alabama, 2. Southern Star, Geiger, Alabama, 6. Gentry, Arkansas, 7. Three Rivers, Dumas, Arkansas, 14. Walnut Hill, Florida, 15. Sarasota, Florida, 16. Harmony Springs, Avera, Georgia, 17. North Georgia , Bowersville , Georgia 18. Pine crest, Stapleton, Georgia, 51. Delta, Transylvania, Louisana, 52. Highland, DeRidder, Louisiana, 56. Brooksville, Mississippi, 57. Clarksdale, Mississippi, 58. Okolona, Mississippi, 59. Leland, Mississippi, 60. South Haven, Macon, Mississippi, 61. West Point, Mississippi, 71. Lighthouse, Grifton, North Carolina, 87. Cumberland Mountain, Monterey, Tennessee, 88. Pleasant View, Lobelville, Tennessee

Map 9: Congregations of the Church of God in Christ, Mennonite in the Southeast United States (map by the author).

PART TWO   APPENDIX THREE   Congregations

Key to Locations:
3. Desert View Mennonite, Yuma, Arizona, 4. Mountain Valley, Willcox, Arizona, Alabama, 5. Sun Valley, El Mirage, Arizona , 8.Glenn, California, 9. Livingston, California, 10. Winton, California, 11. Bartlett, Colorado, 12. High Valley, Center, Colorado, 13. Mesa View, Montrose, Colorado, Georgia 19. Buhl, Idaho, 20. Canyon, Hazelton, Idaho, 21. Grand View, Bruneau, 22. Mountain View, Bonners Ferry, Idaho, 23. Treasure Valley, New Plymouth, Idaho, 24. Valley View, Filer, Idaho, 69. Albuquerque, New Mexico, 80. Evergreen, Scio, Oregon , 98. Columbia River, Othello , Washington, 99. Rainbow Valley, Tonasket, Washington

Map 10: Congregations of the Church of God in Christ, Mennonite in the Western United States (map by the author).

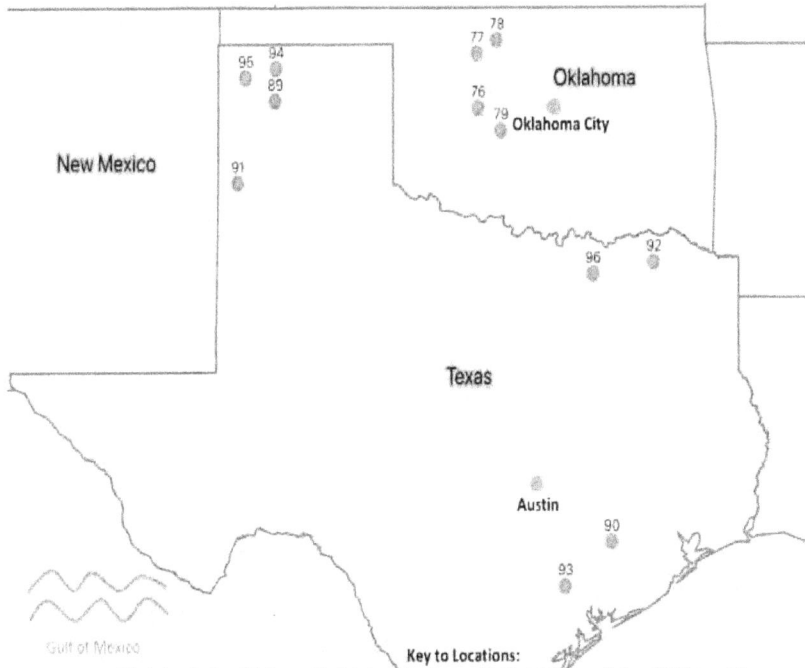

Key to Locations:
76. Cedar, Hydro, Oklahoma, 77. Fairview, Oklahoma, 78. Pleasant View, Goltry, Oklahoma, 79. Plainview, Chickasha, Oklahoma, 89. Country Side, Dalhart, Texas, 90. El Campo, Texas, 91. Farwell, Texas, 92. Red River Valley, Detroit, Texas, 93. Southern Hope, Victoria, Texas, 94. Texhoma, Texas, 95. Texline, Texas, 96. West Haven, Brookston, Texas

Map 11: Congregations of the Church of God in Christ, Mennonite in Oklahoma and Texas (map by the author).

PART TWO　　　　APPENDIX THREE　　　　Congregations

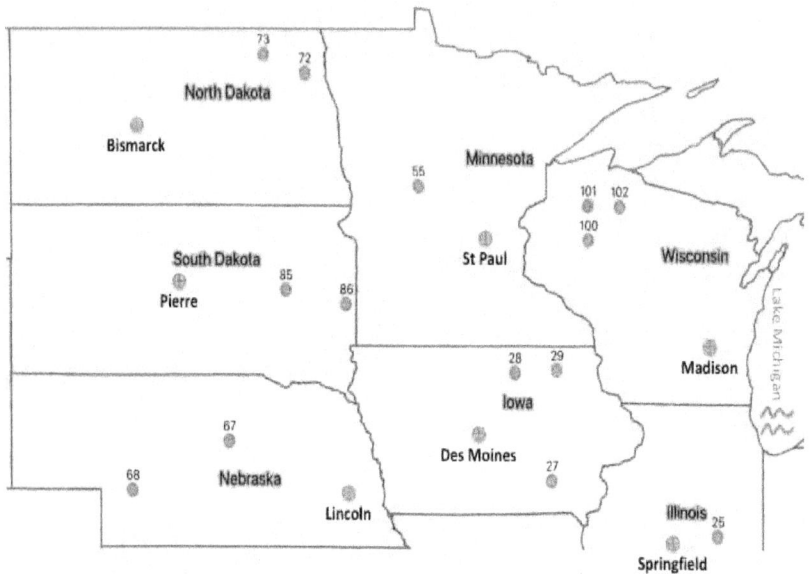

Key to Locations:
25. Prairie, Arthur, Illinois, 27. Bloomfield, Iowa, 28. Heartland, McIntire, Iowa, 29. Lime Springs, Iowa, 55. Lake Haven, Starbuck, Minnesota, 67. Cedar Hills, Greeley, Nebraska, 68. Golden Plains, Madrid, Nebraska, 72. Grafton, North Dakota, 73. North Unity, Langdon, North Dakota, 85. Faith, Iroquois, South Dakota, 86. Rolling Plains, Ward, South Dakota, 100. Barron, Wisconsin, 101. Gospel, Almena, Wisconsin, 102. Hillcrest, Barron, Wisconsin

Map 12: Congregations of the Church of God in Christ, Mennonite in the Upper Midwest of the United States (map by the author).

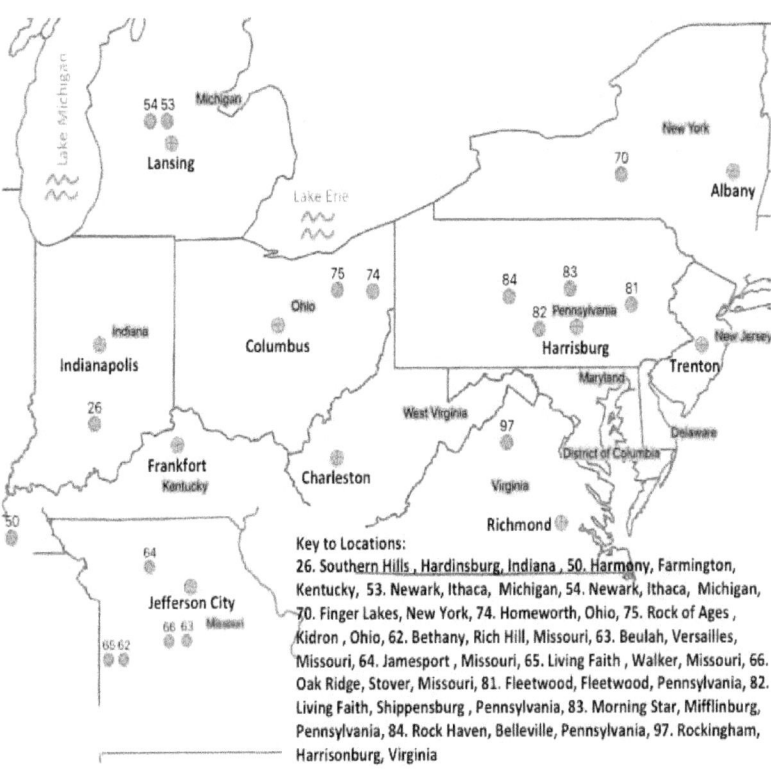

Map 13: Congregations of the Church of God in Christ, Mennonite in the Northeast of the United States (map by the author).

Abbreviations

ALX   *Alexanderwohl Church Book*

CGCM   *Church of God in Christ, Mennonite*

JMS   *Journal of Mennonite Studies*

ME   *Mennonite Encylopedia.* Scottdale, PA: Mennonite Publishing House, 1959.

ML   *Mennonite Life*

MQR   *Mennonite Quarterly Review*

MOT   *Messenger of Truth*

PRZ   *Przechowka Kirchen Buch*

Bibliography

Ammerman, Nancy. "Studying Everyday Religion: Challenges for the Future." In *Everyday Religion: Observing Modern Religion Lives*, edited by Nancy Ammerman, 219-38. New York: Oxford University Press, 2007.

Applebaum, Anne. *Red Famine: Stalin's War on Ukraine.* New York: Doubleday, 2017.

Asprey, Robert B. *Frederick the Great: The Magnificent Enigma.* New York: History Book Club, 1986.

Audi, Robert. "Religious Convictions and Secular Reasons." In *The Ethics of Citizenship: Liberal Democracy and Religious Convictions*, edited by J. Caleb Clanton, 59–91. Waco, TX: Baylor University Press, 2009.

Barclay, Harold B. "The Plain People of Oregon." *Review of Religious Research* 8 no. 3 (1967) 140–165.

Barrett, Lois Y. "PART II: Anabaptist Europe in the Seventeenth Century." *ML* 66 (2012).
https://mla.bethelks.edu/ml-archive/2012/anabaptist.php.

Baylor, Michael G. *The Radical Reformation.* Cambridge: Cambridge University Press, 1991.

Beachy, Alvin J. "Beachy Amish Churches." In *ME* I: 254.

Becker, Brandon. "What is Good," *MOT* 116 no. 16 (2018) 1–12.

Belk, Fred Richard. *The Great Trek of the Russian Mennonites to Central Asia, 1880 - 1884.* Eugene, OR: Wipf and Stock Publishers, 2000.

Bender, Harold S. "The Anabaptist Vision". *MQR* 18 no. 2 (1944) 67–88.

———. "The Anabaptist Vision". *Church History* 13 no. 1 (1944), 3–14.
http://www.jstor.org/stable/3161001.

———. "Dunker, Dunkard", In *ME* II: 109.

———. *Menno Simons Life and Writings: A Quadricentennial Tribute, 1536 – 1936*. Moundridge, KS: Gospel Publishers, 2004.

———. "Nonconformity," In *ME* III: 890.

———. "Sattler, Michael". In *ME* IV: 427.

———. "State, Anabaptist-Mennonite Attitude Toward", In *ME* IV: 615.

Bender, Harold S. and Smith, C. Henry. *Mennonites and Their Heritage: A Handbook of Mennonite History and Beliefs*. Scottdale, PA: Herald Press, 1964.

Biesecker-Mast, Gerald. "The Persistence of Anabaptism as Vision". *MQR* 81 (2007) 21–42.

Biesecker-Mast, Gerald. "Towards a Radical Postmodern Anabaptist Vision". *Conrad Grebel Review* 13 (1995) 55–68.

Birckholtz-Bestvater, Marie. "My Mission as an Artist." *ML* 9 no. 2 (1954) 53–55.

Blanke, Fritz. "Anabaptism and the Reformation". In *The Recovery of the Anabaptist Vision: A Sixtieth Anniversary Tribute to Harold S. Bender*, edited by Guy F. Hershberger. Scottdale, PA: Herald Press, 1957.

Boese, J. A. "The Story of the Mennonites at Avon, South Dakota." *ML* XV (1960) 29–43.

Boese, Ken. "Die Andre Kant." In *Church Records of the Old Flemish or Gröingen Mennonisten Societaet in Przechowko, West Prussia*. Tranlated by Lydia Pankratz and Anna M. Unruh. Goessel, KS: Mennonite Immigrant Historical Foundation, 1980.

Boynton, Linda Louise *The Plain People: An Ethnography of the Holdeman Mennonites*. Salem, WI: Sheffield Publishing Company, 1986.

Bradley, Linda Arthur. "Anti-Fashion as a Social Boundary Marker Among Holdeman Mennonite Women." *JMS*.

Burkholder, John Richard. "A Perspective on Mennonite Ethics." In *Kingdom, Cross, and Community: Essays on Mennonite Themes in Honor of Guy F. Hershberger*, edited by John Richard Burkholder and Calvin Redekop Scottdale, 151–66. PA: Herald Press, 1976.

Burkholder, Lawrence J. "Nonresistance, Nonviolent Resistance, and Power." In *Kingdom, Cross, and Community: Essays on Mennonite Themes in Honor of Guy F. Hershberger*, edited by John Richard Burkholder and Calvin Redekop Scottdale, 131–37. PA: Herald Press, 1976.

Bush, Perry. "The Solidification of Nonresistance: Bluffton and World War, 1917-1945." *ML* 55 no. 1 (2000). https://mla.bethelks.edu/ml-archive/2000mar/bush_article.html.

Bush, Perry. *Two Kingdoms, Two Loyalties: Mennonite Pacifism in Modern America*. Baltimore: The Johns Hopkins University Press, 1998.

Church of God in Christ, Mennonite. "Alien Citizens." *MOT* 114 no. 17 (2016) 1–12.

Church of God in Christ, Mennonite. "What Hath God Wrought." *MOT* 109 no. 12 (2011) 1–12.

Clanton, J. Caleb. *The Ethics of Citizenship: Liberal Democracy and Religious Convictions*. Waco, TX: Baylor University Press, 2009.

Centennial Anniversary and Progrgam. "Grace Mennonite Congregation of the Church of God in Christ, Mennonite. Halstead, Kansas, 1879 – 1979." Printed in USA.

Clasen, Claus-Peter. *Anabaptism: A Social History, 1525 — 1618*. Ithaca, NY: Cornell University Press, 1971.

Cohen, Susan Ruth. "Are the Amish Good Citizens?" *MQR* 88 no. 1 (2014) 65-95.

Conference Reports - 1896 - 2015. Moundridge, KS: Gospel Publishers, Church of God in Christ, Mennonite, 2016.

Crous, Ernst. "Karolswalde." In *ME* III: 152.

———. "Nonresistance." In *ME* III: 897–906.

———. "Przechovka." In *ME* IV: 225–26.

Dirks, Milferd. "Dear Readers." *MOT* 116 no. 14 (2018) 1–12.

Driedger, Johann. "Farming among the Mennonites in West and East Prussia, 1534-1945." *MQR* 31 (1957) 16–21.

Driedger, Leo and Kauffman, J. Howard. "Urbanization of Mennonites: Canadian and American Comparisons." *MQR* 56 (1982) 269–290.

Driedger, Leo. *Mennonite Identity in Conflict*. Lewiston, NY: The Edwin Mellen Press, 1988.

Duerksen, Jacob A. "Jantz, Peter." In ME III: 94.

———. "Przechowka and Alexanderwohl: Beginnings of Alexanderwohl, Tabor, Huffnungsau and other Churches." *ML* 10 no. 2 (1955) 76-82.

Duerksen, Velda Richert and Duerksen, Jacob A. *Church Book of the Alexanderwohl Mennonite Church in South Russia*. Translated by Velda Richert Duerksen and J. A. Duerksen. Goessel, KS: Mennonite Immigrant Historical Foundation, 1987.

Durant, Will and Durant, Ariel. *The Age of Napoleon: A History of European Civilization from 1789 to 1815*. New York: Simon and Schuster, 1975.

Dyck, Cornelius. "The Place of Tradition in Dutch Anabaptism." *Church History* 43 (1974) 34–49.

Dyck, Peter and Dyck, Elfrieda *Up from the Rubble*. Scottdale, PA: Herald Press, 1991.

Ehrman, Bart D. *The New Testament: A Historical Introduction to the Early Christian Writings*. New York: Oxford University Press, 2016.

Epp, Frank H. *Mennonites in Canada, 1786 - 1920*. Toronto: Macmillan of Canada, 1974.

Estep, William R. *The Anabaptist Story: An Introduction to Sixteenth Century Anabaptism*. Grand Rapids, MI: William B. Eerdsmans, 1996.

Francis, E. K. "The Russian Mennonites: From Religious to Ethnic Group." *The American Journal of Sociology 54* (1948) 101–07.

Fricke, E. J. "Fricke, Frederick C." In *ME* II: 398.

Friesen, P. M. *The Mennonite Brotherhood in Russia: (1789-1910)*. Fresno, CA: Board of Christian Literature, General Conference of Mennonite Brethren Churches, 1980.

Friesen, Tony. "Computers." *MOT* 95 no. 25 (1996) 1–12.

Gans, Herbert. "The end of late-generation European ethnicity in America?" *Ethnic and Racial Studies* 38 no. 3 (2015) 418–29.
http://dx.doi.org/10.1080/01419870.2015.967707.

Gans, Herbert. "Symbolic Ethnicity: The Future of Ethnic Groups and Cultures in America." *Ethnic and Racial Studies* 2 no. 1 (2010) 1–20.

Giesbrecht, Ben. *The Enduring Church.* Moundridge, KS: Gospel Publishers, 2014.

Gingerich, Melvin. "Leo Tolstoy and the Mennonite Author Daniel Musser." *MQR* 32 no. 3 (1958) 234–235.

Goertz, Adalbert. *The Jantzes of Karolswalde. Mennonite Family History.* Masthof, 1993

Goertz, Adalbert. "The Marriage Records of Montau in Prussia for 1661 - 1704." *MQR 50* (1976) 240–50.

Goertz, Adalbert. *From Jeziorka, Prussia to Russia in 1804.* http://www.mennonitegenealogy.com/russia/jez.htm.

Gospel Publishers, *Histories of the Congregations.* Moundridge, KS: Gospel Publishers, Church of God in Christ, Mennonite,1999.

Gospel Publishers, "Questions and Answers." *MOT* 42 no. 14 (1943) 1–12.

Grant, Michael. *Constatntine the Great* New York: Charles Scribner's Sons, 1993.

Grimsrud, Ted. "Anabaptism for the Twenty-First Century". *MQR* 80 (2006) 371–390.

Haury, David. A. "Bernhard Warkentin and the Kansas Mennonite Pioneers." *ML* 29 no. 4 (1974) 70–76.

Haury, David A. *Index to Mennonite Immigrants on United States Passenger Lists 1872 -1904*, edited by David A. Haury. North Newton,KS: Mennonite Library and Archives, 1986.

Hershberger, Guy F. "Our Citizenship is in Heaven." In *Church, State, and Citizen: Christian Approaches to Political Engagement* editied by John Richard Burkholder and Calvin Redekop, 276. Scottdale PA: Herald Press, 1976.

———. *The Recovery of the Anabaptist Vision: A Sixtieth Anniversary Tribute to Harold S. Bender.* Scottdale, PA: Herald Press, 1957.

———. *War, Peace and Nonresistance.* Scottdale PA: Herald Press, 1944.

Heyden, H. "Becker, Peter." In *ME* I: 259.

Hiebert, Clarence. *The Holdeman People: The Church of God in Christ, Mennonite, 1859 - 1969*. South Pasadena, CA: William Carey Library, 1973.

Hiebert, P. G. and Hiebert, Clarence. "Church of God in Christ, Mennonite (CGC)." *Global Anabaptist Mennonite Encyclopedia Online*, 1989. https://gameo.org/index.php?title=Church_of_God_in_Christ,_Mennonite_(CGC)#1990_Article.

Holdeman, John. *A Mirror of Truth: A Treatise for the Instruction and Comfort of the Just and for the Conversion of the Unsaved*. Hesston, KS: Church of God in Christ, Mennonite Publication Board, 1956.

Homan, Gerlof D. "'We Have Come to Love Them': Russian Mennonite Refugees in the Netherlands, 1945-1947." *JMS* 25 (2007) 39–59.

Horsch, John. *Mennonite History, Volume 1: Mennonites in Europe*. Scottsdale, PA: Mennonite Publishing House, 1955.

Hostetler, John A. *Hutterite Society*. Baltimore: Johns Hopkins University Press, 1974.

Huber, Tim. "Holdeman Mennonites Discuss the Challenges of Entertainment." *Mennonite World Review*. http://mennoworld.org/2015/12/14/news/holdeman-mennonites-discuss-challenges-of-entertainment/

Hughes, Edwin. "Where is Your Citizenship." *MOT* 95 no. 18 (1996) 4–5.

Isaac, Ed. "Our Security - In Christ or Money." *MOT* 95 no. 12 (1996) 1–12.

———. "Sound Business Fundamentals." *MOT* 97 no. 4 (1998) 1–12.

Isaac, Joe. "Take Heed Therefore." *MOT* 97 no. 4 (1998) 1–12.

Jantz, Ronald C. "Lived Religion: The Modern World and the Existential Threat to the People of the Church of God in Christ, Mennonite." Manuscript accepted by the *Journal of Mennonite Studies* (2020) 1–24.

Jantz, Ronald C. and Nightengale, Irene. *The Descendants of Peter Nichols: From the Year 1835 to the Present*. Unpublished draft.

Janz, Jacob B. *Mennonite Life in Volhynia, 1800 - 1874*. Translated by Agnes Janz Hubert. Work Paper No. 25.

———. *Profile Of The Mennonite Kleine Gemeinde 1874*. Volume 4, DFP Publications, 1987.

Jantzen, Mark. *Mennonite German Soldiers: Nation, Religion, and Family in Prussian East, 1772-1880*. University of Notre Dame Press, 2010.

———. "Seeking out the Crevices in a Rigid Society" *ML* 66 (2012). https://mla.bethelks.edu/ml-archive/2012/seeking.php.

Janzen, John M. "Form and Meaning in Central Kansas Mennonite Buildings for Worship." *MQR* 73 (1999) 323–353.

Janzen, Reinhild Kauenhoven. "Keeping Faith and Keeping Time: Old Testament Images on Mennonite Clocks." *ML* 55 no. 4 (2000). https://mla.bethelks.edu/ml-archive/2000dec/reinhild_janzen_article.html.

———. " 'To Help Us Think of God': Iconic versus Anti-Iconic Mennonite Celebrations of Christmas and Easter in Kansas." *MQR* 79 no. 2 (2005) 207–229.

Johnson, Jesse. "Lone Tree." In *ME* III: 388.

Johnson, Mervin. "Traditionalism Versus Spirituality." *MOT* 115 no. 9 (2017) 1–12.

Johnson, Nathan. "The Kingdom of Peace." *MOT* 113 no. 7 (2015) 1–16.

Joireman, Sandra F. "Anabaptists and the State: An Uneasy Conscience." In *Church, State, and Citzen: Christian Approaches to Political Engagement*, edited by Sandra F. Joireman, 73–91. Oxford, UK: Oxford University Press, 2009.

Joldersma, Hermina and Grijp, Louis. *"Elizabeth's Manly Courage": Testimonials and Songs of Martyred Anabaptis Women in the Low Countries*. Edited and translated by Hermina Joldersma and Louis Grijp. Milwuakee, WI: Marquette University Press, 2001,

Juhnke, James C. "Except the Lord Build the House: Halstead Seminary Centennial." *ML* 38 no. 4 (1983) 4–7.

———. "Historical Concepts for MC-GC Integration: Franconia Conference Split (1847) and Russian Migration (1874)." In *Without Spot or Wrinkle: Reflecting Theologically on the Nature of the Church*, edited by Karl Koop and Mary Schertz, 26–37. Eugene, Oregon: Wipf and Stock Publishers, 2015.

———. "Mennonite Benevolence and Revitalization in the Wake of World War I," *MQR* 60 (1986) 15–30.

———. "Mennonites in Militarist America: Some Consequences of World War I." In *Kingdom, Cross, and Community - Essays on Mennonite Themes in Honor of Guy F. Hershberger*, edited by John Richard Burkholder and Calvin Redekop, 171–78. Scottdale PA: Herald Press, 1976.

———. *Vision, Doctrine, War - Mennonite Identity and organization in America, 1890-1930*. Scottdale, PA: Herald Press, 1989.

———. *A People of Two Kingdoms II: Stories of Kansas Mennonites in Politics*. North Newton Kansas: Bethel College, 2016.

Kauffman, J. Howard and Driedger, Leo. *The Mennonite Mosaic: Identity and Modernization*. Scottdale, PA: Herald Press, 1991.

Kauffman, J. Howard and Harder, Leland. *Anabaptists Four Centuries Later: A Profile of Five Mennonite and Brethren in Christ Denominations*. Scottdale, PA: Herald Press, 1975.

Klassen, Cornelius F. "The Mennonites of Russia, 1917-1928," *MQR* 6 (1932) 69–80.

Klassen, Peter J. *Mennonites in Early Modern Poland and Russia*. Baltimore: Johns Hopkins University Press, 2009.

———. "Faith and Culture in Conflict: Mennonites in the Vistula Delta." *MQR* 57 (1983) 194–205.

———. "Barriers to Emigration from Prussia." *MQR* 72 (1998) 84–95.

Klassen, R. J. "Where Is the Living Sacrifice." *MOT* 90 no. 8 (1991) 1–12.

Klaassen, Walter. "The Anabaptist Critique of Constantinian Christianity". *MQR* 55 (1955), 218–230.

Klassen, William. "Oath", In *ME* III: 3–8.

Kniss, Fred. "Against the Flow: Learning from New, Emergent, and Peripheral Religious Currents", *Sociology of Religion* 75 no. 3 (2014) 351–366.

Koehn, Clarence. "Sobriety." *MOT* 96 no. 3 (1997) 1–12.

Koehn, Gladwin. "Shut the Back Door." *MOT* 112 no. 2 (2014) 1–12.

Koehn, Mrs. Henry B. *A Compilation of the Genealogical and Biographical Record of the Descendants and Relation Circle of Henry B. Koehn, 1846 - 1955*. North Newton, KS: The Mennonite Press, 1955.

Koehn, Norma Jean. *Family Record of Cornelius P. Nichols: 1871 to 1983.*

Koehn, Reuben. "Love Not the World." *MOT* 97 no. 14 (1998) 1–12.

Koehn, Rylan. "Dangers of Technology.", *MOT* 116 no. 11 (2018) 1–16.

Koehn, Wilbur. "Technology and Faith in God." *MOT* 96 no. 5 (1997) 1–12.

Konrad, Anne. *Red Quarter Moon: A Search for Family in the Shadow of Stalin.* Toronto: University of Toronto Press, 2012.

Koolman, J. ten Doornkaat. "Antonius von Köhn." In *ME* I: 133–34.

Koop, P. Albert. "Some Economic Aspects of Mennonite Migration with Special Emphasis on the 1870s Migration from Russia to North America." *MQR* 55 (1981) 143–156.

Krahn, Cornelius. "Alexanderwohl", In *ME* I: 48–50.

———. "Anwohner," In *ME* I: 135–36.

———. *Dutch Anabaptism: Origin, Spread, Life, and Thought.* Scottdale, PA: Herald Press, 1981.

———. "Gebietsamt." In *ME* II: 441.

———. "Janzen." In *ME* III: 95.

———. "Koehn." In *ME* III: 211.

———. "Lileva," In *ME* III: 345.

———. "Mennonite Names and Places." *ML* 15 no. 1 36–38.

———. "Menno Simons". In *ME* III: 577–78.

———. "Menno Simons." In *ME* III: 579–82.

———. "Nickel." In *ME* III: 869–70.

———. "Oklahoma." In *ME* IV: 33.

———. "Poland." In *ME* IV: 199–200.

———. "Russia." In *ME* IV: 390.

———. "Siberia." In *ME* IV: 517–521.

———. "Slavgorod." In *ME* IV: 537.

———. "Slavgorod Mennonite Settlement." In *ME* IV: 540–542.

———. "Wedel." In *ME* IV: 907.

Krehbiel, Christian. *From the Steppes to the Prairies*. Mennonite Publication Office, 1949.

Krehbiel, Nicholas A. *World War I: The CO Problem*. http://civilianpublicservice.org/storybegins/krehbiel/world-war-1.

Kroeker, Wally. *An Introduction to the Russian Mennonites*. Intercourse, PA: Good Books, 2005.

Kroeker, Marvin. "Mennonites in the Oklahoma 'Runs' ." *ML* 10 no. 3 (1955) 114—120.

———. "Natives and Settlers: The Mennonite Invasion of Indian Territory." *ML* 61 no. 2 (2006). https://mla.bethelks.edu/ml-archive/2006June/kroeker.php.

Lange, Dorothea. "Abandoned Farm North of Dalhart, Texas. 1938." The Library of Congress, Prints and Photographs Division.

Lark, James. "Mennonite Brethren Church", In *ME* III: 595–602.

LaRocque, Emma. "The Ethnic Church and the Minority." In *Kingdom, Cross, and Community: Essays on Mennonite Themes in Honor of Guy F. Hershberger*, edited by John Richard Burkholder and Calvin Redekop, 208–18. Scottdale, PA: Herald Press, 1976.

Loewen, Larry. "Where Is Your Security." *MOT* 98 no. 8 (1999) 1–12.

Loewen, Royden. *Diaspora in the Countryside: Two Mennonite Communities and Mid-Twentieth Century Rural Disjuncture*. Chicago: University of Illinois Press, 2006.

Loewen, Helmut-Harry and Urry, James. "Protecting Mammon. Some dilemmas of Mennonite Non-resistance in late Imperial Russia and the Origins of the Selbstschutz." *JMS* 9 (1991) 34–53.

Lohrenz, J. H. "Mennonite Brethren Church." In *ME* III: 597.

Lohrenz, Gerhard. "Tiege." In *ME* IV: 721.

Macgregor, Jeff. "American Rhapsody." *Smithsonian* (2018) 22. https://www.smithsonianmag.com/arts-culture/american-rhapsody-180970545/.

Mannhardt, H. G. "Brenkenhoffswalde." In *ME* I: 416–17.

———. "Brenkenhoffswalde and Franztal (Lubusz Voivodeship, Poland)." *Global Anabaptist Mennonite Encyclopedia Online.* http://gameo.org/index.php?title=Brenkenhoffswalde_and_Franztal_(Lubusz_Voivodeship,_Poland)&oldid=144883.

———. "Frederick William I." In *ME* II: 386.

———. "Frederick II." In *ME* II: 1955), 383.

Mayfield, Lydia. *Halstead, The Early Years.* First Printing, 1987.

Meeks, Wayne A. *The First Urban Christians: The Social World of the Apostle Paul.* New Haven, CN: Yale University Press, 1983.

Miller, Paul D. "The Story of Jansen Nebraska." *ML* 9 no. 4 (1954) 173–175.

Momaday, N. Scott. "Revisiting Sacred Ground." In *The Man Made of Words*, 118–23. St. Martin's Press, Volume 1, 1997.

Mueller, Adam. *Church and Family Records of the Emmanuel (Canton) Mennonite Church.* Translated and Printed by Adam Mueller, 1985.

Neff, Christian. "Alexander I." In *ME* I: 44.

———. "Augsburg Confession." In *ME* I: 187.

———. "Biestkens Bible." In *ME* I: 340–41

———. "Flemish Mennonites." In *ME* II: 337–38.

———. "Ministry, Call to the." In *ME* III: 704.

———. "Napoleon I." In *ME* III: 812.

Nickel, John P. and Nickel, Gene M. *The Nikkel-Nickel Family of Prussia, Russia, America, and Canada.* Steinbach, Manitoba, CA: Printed by Derksen Printers, 1981.

Nolt, Steven *A History of the Amish.* New York: Good Books, Third Edition, 2015.

———. "A 'Two-Kingdom' People in aWorld of Multiple Identities: Religion, Ethnicity, and American Mennonites," *MQR.* 73 no. 3 (1999) 485–502.

Nolt, Steven and Meyers, Thomas J. *Plain Diversity: Amish Cultures and Identities.* Baltimore: Johns Hopkins University Press, 2007.

Pankratz, Lydia and Unruh, Anna M. *Church Records of the Old Flemish or Gröingen Mennonisten Societaet in Przechowko, West Prussia.* Tranlated by Lydia Pankratz and Anna M. Unruh. Goessel, KS: Mennonite Immigrant Historical Foundation, 1980.

Patterson, Sean. "The Eichenfeld Massacre: Recontextualizing Mennonite and Makhnovist Narratives." *JMS* 32 (2017) 151–174.

Penner, Henry. "Laughter." *MOT* 95 no. 1 (1996) 1–12.

Penner, Horst "West Prussian Mennonites Through Four Centuries." *MQR* 23 (1943) 232–45.

———. "Giesbrecht." *ME* II: 516–517.

———. *West Prussia.* http://gameo.org/index.php?title=West_Prussia.

Penner, Lester. "Dear Brothers and Sisters." *MOT* 113 no. 21 (2015) 1–12.

Plett, Delbert F. *Saints and Sinners: The Kleine Gemeinde in Imperial Russia 1812 to 1875.* Steinbach, Manitoba: Crossway Publications, 1999.

Ratzlaff Family Blog. "Location of Leeleva." http://ratzlaffhistory.blogspot.com/2013/09/the-location-of-leeleva.html.

Redekop, Calvin. "Anabaptists and the Ethnic Ghost." *The MQR* 58 no. 2 (1984) 133–146.

———. "The Sociology of Mennonite Identity: A Second Opinion." In *Mennonite Identity: Historical and Contemporary Perspectives*, edited by Calvin Redekop and Samuel J. Steiner, 173–92. Waterloo, Ontario: Institute for Anabaptist and Mennonite Studies, Conrad Grebel College, 1988.

Reimer, Gustav. "Bestvater." In *ME* I: 301.

Rempel, David G. and Carlson, Cornelia Rempel. *A Mennonite Family in Tsarist Russia and the Soviet Union: 1789 - 1923.* Toronto: University of Toronto Press, 2002.

Rydford, John. *Indian Place Names: Their Origin, Evolution, and Meanings.* Norman, OK: University of Oklahoma Press, 1968.

Sawatsky, Harry Leonard. *They Sought a Country: Mennonite Colonization in Mexico.* Berkeley, CA: University of California Press, 1971.

Schmidt, Lydia, et al. *History of Abraham Schmidt and His Descendants.* Printed in the U.S.A.

Schmidt, John F. "Michalin." In *ME* III: 667.

———. "Siebrandt, David." In *ME* IV: 523.

———. "Three Years After Date . . ." *ML* 28 (1976) 35–39.

———. "Passenger Ship Lists as an Archival Resource." *ML* 36 no. 4 (1981) 5–7.

Schmidt, P. U. "Schmidt." In *ME* IV: 465.

Schmidt, Francis M. and Caldwell, Norma J. *J. A. R. Schmidt History, Ancestry, and Descendants.* 2004,

Schrag, Martin H. "Swiss Volhynian Mennonite Background." *ML 9* (1954) 158–61.

———. "Volhynia." In *ME* IV: 844–47.

———. "Waldheim." In *ME* IV: 876.

Schrock, Fred. "Drift versus Being Anchored." *MOT* 117 no. 14 (2019) 1–12.

Smith, C Henry. *The Story of the Mennonites.* Newton, Ks: Mennonite Publication Office, 1957.

Smucker, Donovan E. "Gelassenheit, Entrepreneurs, and Remnants: Socioeconomic Models Among the Mennonites." In *Kingdom, Cross, and Community: Essays on Mennonite Themes in Honor of Guy F. Hershberger*, edited by John Richard Burkholder and Calvin Redekop Scottdale, 219–41. PA: Herald Press, 1976.

Snyder, C. Arnold. *Anabaptist History and Theology.* Kitchener, Ontario: Pandora Press, 1997.

Subtelny, Orest. *Ukraine: A History.* Toronto: University of Toronto Press, Fourth Edition, 2009.

Toews, Abraham P. *The Problem of Mennonite Ethics.* Grand Rapids, MI: Wm. B. Eerdmans Publishing, 1963.

Toews, John B. *Czars, Soviets and Mennonites.* Newton,KS: Faith and Life Press, 1982.

———. *Lost Fatherland: The Story of the Mennonite Emigration from Soviet Russia, 1921 – 1927.* Scottdale, PA: Herald Press, 1967.

———. "A Visit to Mennonite Villages in Siberia." *ML* 28 (1973) 86–90.

———. *With Courage to Spare: The life of B.B. Janz, 1877-1964*. Hillsboro, KS: M.B Publishing, 1978.
https://openlibrary.org/works/OL3592602W/With_Courage_to_Spare.

Toews, Paul. *Mennonites in American Society, 1930-1970*. Scottdale, PA: Herald Press, 1996.

———. "Mennonites in American Society: Modernity and the Persistence of Religious Community." *The MQR* 63 no. 3 (1989) 227–46.

Toews, Peter. "Report of Investigations." *MOT* 97 no. 10 (1998) 4.

Unruh, Abe J. *Great Grandfather's Diary*. Tranlated by Abe J. Unruh.

———. *The Helpless Poles*. Grabill, IN: Courier Publishing Company, 1973.

———. "Mennonite Union Aid (Church of God in Christ, Mennonite)." *Global Anabaptist Mennonite Encyclopedia Online*,1957.
http://gameo.org/index.php?title=Mennonite_Union_Aid_(Church_of_God_in_Christ,_Mennonite)&oldid=133143.

———. "Pawnee Rock Mennonites: Background," *ML* 10 (1955) 131–132.

———. "Unruh." In *ME* IV: 784–86.

Unruh, Abe J. and Thiessen, Richad D. "Unruh, Tobias A. (1819-1875)." *Global Anabaptist Mennonite Encyclopedia Online*. http://gameo.org/index.php?title=Unruh,_Tobias_A._(1819-1875)&oldid=132477.

Unruh, Abe J. and Unruh, Verney. *The Tobias A. Unruh Biography, Diary, and Family Record, 1819-1950*. Pulaski, Iowa: 1950.

Unruh, Benjamin H. "The Background and Causes of the Flight of the Mennonites from Russia in 1929." *MQR* 4 (1930) 267–281.

Urry, James. *Mennonites, Politics, and Peoplehood*. Winnipeg, Manitoba: University of Manitoba Press, 2006.

———. *None but Saints: The Transformation of Mennonite Life in Russia*. Hyperion Press Limited, 1989.

Van Braght, Thieleman J. *The Bloody Theater or Martyrs Mirror of the Defenseless Christians*. Scottdale, PA: Mennonite Publishing House, Fifth English Edition, 1950.

Weaver, J. Denny. "The Anabaptist Vision: From Recovery to Reform." *ML* 37 no. 3 (1982) 14–16.

———. *Becoming Anabaptist: The Origin and Significance of Sixteenth-Century Anabaptism*. Harrisonburg, VA: Herald Press, 2005.

Wedel, Errol. "Where Is the Sacrifice." *MOT* 97 no. 13 (1998) 1–12.

Wedel, Keith. "Family Values." *MOT* 116 no. 6 (2018)1–12.

Wenger, J. C. "Avoidance." In *ME* I: 200.

Wenger, Paul D. "Wise or Foolish." *MOT* 102 no. 5 (2003) 1–12.

Winland, Daphne Naomi. "The Quest for Mennonite Peoplehood: Ethno-religious Identity and the Dilemma of Definitions." *Canadian Review of Sociology and Anthropology* 30 no. 1 (1993) 110–38.

Wohlgemuth, Ron. "The Cost of Discipleship." *MOT* 90 no. 9 (1991) 1–12.

Wuschke, Ewald. "German Settlements in Poland and Volhynia," *American Historical Society of Germans from Russia* 13 no. 4 (1990) 50–53.

Yoder, Edward. "Conrad Grebel as a Humanist". *MQR* 3 (1929) 132–146.

———. "The Obligation of the Christian to the State and the Community." *MQR* 13 no. 2 (1939) 104–22.

Yoder, John H. *The Legacy of Michael Sattler*. Translated and edited by John H. Yoder. Scottdale, PA: Herald Press, 1973.

Yoder, Perry. "The Role of the Bible in Mennonite Self-Understanding." In *Mennonite Identity: Historical and Contemporary Perspectives*, edited by Calvin Redekop and Samuel J. Steiner, 69–82, Waterloo, Ontario: Institute for Anabaptist and Mennonite Studies, Conrad Grebel College, 1988.

Yoder, William. "Mennonites are Strongest in Siberia." Moscow: *Russian Evangelical Alliance* (2010). http://www.anabaptistwiki.org/mediawiki/index.php?title=Mennonites_are_Strongest_in_Siberia.

Yost, Jed. "Filters." *MOT* 116 no. 15 (2018) 1–12.

Zijpp, Nanne van der. "Dirk Philips." In *ME* II: 65.

———. "The Early Dutch Anabaptists". In *The Recovery of the Anabaptist Vision: A Sixtieth Anniversary Tribute to Harold S. Bender*, edited by Guy F. Hershberger, 69-81. Scottdale, PA: Herald Press, 1957.

———. "Groningen." In *ME* II: 593.

———. "Groningen Old Flemish Mennonites," In *ME* II: 595–96.

———. "Jans(z), Arent." In *ME* III: 93.

———. "Jan Smit (d. 1572)." *Global Anabaptist Mennonite Encyclopedia Online*, 1957.

———. "Jeziorka." In *ME* III: 110.

———. "Nachtigal." In *ME* III: 805.

———. "Obbe Philips." *ME* IV: 9–10.

———. "Sacramentists." In *ME* IV: 398–99.

———. "Schönsee." In *ME* IV: 475.

———. "Sijbrant Jansz." In *ME* IV: 526.

Zijpp, Nanne van der and Thiessen, Richard D. "Jeziorka (Kuyavian-Pomeranian Voivodeship, Poland)." Global Anabaptist Mennonite Encyclopedia Online. http://gameo.org/index.php?title=Jeziorka_(Kuyavian-Pomeranian_Voivodeship,_Poland)&oldid=141177.

Index of Subjects

adult baptism, 24, 106
adult fare, 79
Alexander I (1801-1825), 55
Alexander II (1855-1881), 55
Alexanderwohl, 52
Alles, Derk, 34
Amalek monster, 141
American Relief Administration, 71
American Revolution, 117
Amish, 102, 132, 134
Amish communities, 83
Amsterdam, 23, 43
Anabaptism, 3, 17–19
Anabaptism Scale, 26
Anabaptist movement, 17–19
Anabaptist principles, 3
Anabaptist sickness, 34, 93
Anabaptist vision, 26
Anabaptists, 18, 23
ancient civilization, 5
Antonofka, 54, 58, 60, 63, 66, 78
Anwohner, 60, 63, 70
Apostle Paul, 107, 130
apostle Paul, 2
Arents, Jan, 40
artificial intelligence, 124
Atlantic voyage, 78
avoidance, 3, 109
Avon, South Dakota, 82

Baltic Sea, 50

ban, 8, 63, 108
baptism, 143
Baptist Church, 75
Baptist Germans, 78
Beachy Amish, 142
beard, 109, 123
Becker, Peter, 164
Biestkens Bible, 95
Bird-in-Hand, 81
Birkholtz-Bestvater, Marie, 45
Bishop of Kulm, 43, 47
Bishop of ulm, 35
Black Blizzards, 89
Black Kettle, 87
blacksmiths, 60
Blaurock, Georg, 21, 106
Bolsheviks, 69, 70, 72
Braun, Ivan I., 73
Brenkenhoffswalde, 49, 50
Brenkenhoffswalde Church, 156
British Zone, 75
business model, 128
business principles, 128

cabinet builders, 60
Camp Funston, 118
Canton, 153
Canton Church Book, 84
Canton, Kansas, 68, 83
capitalist economy, 138
card playing, 63

Index of Subjects

carnal weapons, 19
Catherine II, 64
Catholic authorities, 24
Catholic bishops, 43
Catholic Church, 33, 44
Catholic king, 22
Catholic persecution, 33
Catholic pope, 93
cell phone, 124
cell phones, 124
Charles V, 14, 33
charter of privileges, 55
Cherokee Strip, 85
Cheyenne Indians, 87
Chickasha, 86
Chickasha, Oklahoma, 87
Chief Black Kettle, 87
Chortitza, 54
Chortitza colony, 55, 96
Christian Disaster Relief, 132
Christian society, 19
Christmas trees, 138
Church of God in Christ,
        Mennonite, 3, 98, 109
citizenship, 2, 130–132
civil government, 126
civil society, 145
Civil War, 82
Civilian Public Service, 118
civilization, 5
Claesz, Jan, 23, 40
collective tax, 47
collectivization, 74
Communism, 68
Communist Revolution, 98
Communist state, 73
competitive sports, 144
computers, 125, 129
Confederation of Warsaw, 44
conscientious objectors, 118
conservative Mennonites, 5
Core beliefs, 17

Cornelisz, Adriaan, 115
Cossacks, 120
Council of Zurich, 106
Court of Holland, 153
Crimean War, 56
crop yields, 64
cultural enclave, 137
cultural history, 3
Czar Alexander I (1801-1825), 52
Czar Alexander II, 14, 64, 77
Czar Nicholas I, 50
Czaress Catherine II, 48, 49
Czars of Russia, 55

dairy farming, 38
Dante, 19
Danzig, 35, 43, 44, 50
Danzig werder, 153
David Holdeman, 83
de-kulakization, 73
death penalty, 106, 121
Deckkert, Johann, 62
Denk, Hans, 109
Derks, Alle, 34
desolate prairies, 82
dictatorship, 70
dikes, 44
Dirks, Benjamin, 59
disaster relief, 131
discipleshipde, 26
Dnieper River, 50
Dordrecht Confession, 115
Driesen, 59
drought, 71
Dunkers, 117
dust bowl days, 89
Dutch Anabaptists, 30
Dutch Anabpatists, 94
Dutch bibles, 38
Dutch Mennonites, 35, 43
Dutch windmills, 45
Dutch-Prussian Mennonties, 5
Dyck, Elfrieda, 74

190

Index of Subjects

Dyck, Peter, 74

economic conditions, 74
economic contributions, 17
economic decline, 70
educational isolation, 63
Eichenfeld, 70
Ekaterinoslaw, 53
Emperor Charles V, 30
endogamous marriage, 46
Erasmus, 106
Ethical principles, 128
ethnic group, 134
ethnic identity, 113
ethnic isolation, 140
evangelism, 129
excommunication, 101

Fürstendorf, 60
Fairview, Oklahoma, 84
famine, 71, 74
Far East, 129
farm implements, 78
federal prisons, 115
Florence, Kansas, 83
folk group, 134
foot washing, 8, 35
forestry service, 68
Fort Leavenworth, 118
Frederick I (1701-1713), 41
Frederick II, 47, 48
Frederick the Great, 47
Frederick William I, 47
Frederick William II, 37
Frederick William III, 57
Fricke, Frederick C., 100
Friedensberg congregation, 63
Friesen, Dietrich, 75
Friesen, Tony, 124
Friesland, 29, 153
Frisians, 37
frivolous behavior, 96

Gdańsk, 35

Gebietsamt, 97
General Conference Mennonite Church, 63
German language, 38, 115
German Lutherans, 65
Gertrude (Menno's wife), 30
Giesbrecht, Abraham, 153
Giesbrecht, Jacob, 153
Gijsbrechts, Hendrick, 153
government loans, 75
grasshoppers, 83
Graudenz, 57
Great Plains, 5, 17, 158
Great Reforms, 64
Grebel, Conrad, 18, 21, 106
Groningen, 33
Groningen Old Flemish, 17, 34, 35, 140
Groningen Old Flemish congregation, 40
Groningen Old Flemish Society, 5
group identity, 122
gun ownership, 121
gun violence, 130

Halstead Mill, 87
Halstead Seminary, 87
Halstead, Kansas, 118
Harvey County, 86
head covering, 123, 136
heavenly citizenship, 131
Heinrichsdorf, 58, 62
Heretics, 17
Hesston College, 119
high school, 129
higher education, 128
Hirschler, Christian, 83
History of the Church of God, 98
Hitler, 139
Hofmann, Melchior, 32
Hohenzollern, 48
Hohenzollern rulers, 48
Holdeman Church, 83, 110, 113, 117

191

Index of Subjects

Holdeman faction, 38
Holdeman Mennonites, 20
Holdeman ministers, 111
Holdeman, John, 66, 83, 97, 98, 107, 115, 117
Holdemans, 4, 126
Holland, 24
holy kiss, 109
Holy Roman Emperor, 18, 32
Holy Roman Empire, 33
holy sacraments, 24
Hughes, Edwin, 127
Hulshof, Hendrik Berents, 39, 95
Hutterites, 102, 134

identity crisis, 137
immersion, 107
imperial edict, 30
imperial ukase, 64
India, 129
Indian Territory, 85
Indians, 82
Infant baptism, 20, 105, 106
infant baptism, 107
insurance, 127, 129
Internet, 124, 129
Isaac, Ed, 128, 138
Isaac, Joe, 141

Jablonovsky, Karol, 59
Jadwaninne, 65
Jans, Ellert, 23
Jans, Gijsbert, 23
Jans, Pieter, 22, 23
Jansz, Anna, 24
Jansz, Arent, 40
Jansz, Claes, 40
Jansz, Geertge, 40
Jansz, Sijbrant, 153
Jantz name, 39
Jantz, Abram, 63
Jantz, Benjamin T., 60
Jantz, Johann, 62

Jantz, Peter, 117, 155, 160
Janz, B. B., 71
Janz, Peter, 50
Janzen, Cornelius, 96
Janzen, Heinrich, 96
Janzen, Peter, 97
Janzen, Wilhelm W., 74
Jewish authorities, 121
Jews, 17
Jeziorka, 34, 35, 49, 53
John the Baptist, 107

Köhn, Antonius, 154
Königsberg, 47
Kansas Relief Committee, 83
Karolswalde, 58, 59, 63
Karolswalde Church Record Book, 59
Karolswalde circuit, 5, 54, 64
King August II, 44
King of Poland, 43, 47
Kingdom of Prussia, 59
Kleine Gemeinde, 3, 38, 67, 93, 96
Kleinsee, 35
Koehn, Dale, 124, 128
Koehn, Dennis, 119
Koehn, Floyd B., 119
Koehn, Henry B., 84
Koehn, Jonas C., 154
Koehn, Leonid, 66
Koehn, Raleigh, 65
Koehn, Reuben, 126, 144
Krehbiel, Christian, 82
Krimmer Mennonite Brethren, 93
kulaks, 73
Kulm, 48
Kulm Military Academy, 47, 56

labor unions, 140
Lancaster, Pennsylvania, 83
land leases, 35
land rush, 84
Lange, Wilhelm, 49

Index of Subjects

Latvia, 50
laughter, 138
Leavenworth, Kansas, 118
Leeleva, 7, 54, 62
Lenin, 69, 70
life insurance, 127
Lileva, 62
linen weavers, 60
Little Arkansas River, 87
Loewen, Larry, 127
Lone Tree, 60
Lone Tree congregation, 84
Lone Tree Township, 84
Luther, 19, 107
Luther, Martin, 17
Lutheran church, 48

Münsterites, 18, 94
Maastricht, 153
Makhnovite bandits, 70
Manitoba, Canada, 67
Manz, Felix, 18, 21, 115
Manz, Feliz, 106
marsh fever, 45
Martrys Mirror, 22
martyr accounts, 22
Medicare, 128
Menists, 30
Mennonite Brethren, 67, 93
Mennonite Brethren Church, 71, 75
Mennonite Central Committee, 71, 75
Mennonite diaspora, 144
Mennonite holocaust, 69
Mennonite identity, 145
Mennonite names, 150
Mennonite refugees, 33, 44
Mennonite sect, 23
Mexico, 129
Michalin, 41, 56, 58, 59
Middlestum, 40
migrants, 5
military conscription, 118

military exemption, 64, 77
military hospital, 118
military service, 47, 64, 116, 122
ministry, 110
Mirror of Truth, 98
missionary work, 101, 129
missions, 129
Molotschna, 54, 67
Molotschna colony, 55
Montau, 45
Montezuma, 86
moral decadence, 98
Moravia, 40
Moundridge, Kansas, 84
musical instruments, 138

Nachtigal, Johann, 62, 155
Napoleon, 48
Napoleonic wars, 57
Netherlands, 33, 43, 44
Netze River valley, 49
New Testament, 17
Nichols, Henry, 155
Nickel, Abraham, 57
Nickel, Peter, 155
Niebuhr, Reinhold, 131
Nigeria, 129
Nikkel, Johann, 72
NKVD, 73
Non-citizens, 17
nonconformity, 8, 123, 129, 143
nonresistance, 2, 17, 114, 116, 117

oath, 109
Oklahoma, 84
Old Flemish, 34
Old Mennonite Church, 119
Ostrog, 54, 82
Ostrog Mennonite Villages, 58
Ostroger Mennonites, 38, 58
Ostrogers, 56, 99, 113

pacifism, 114

Index of Subjects

Pauls Valley, 86
Peace of Augsburg, 18
Penner, Henry, 138
peoplehood, 122
Peter Toews, 97
Philip II, 14
Philips, Dirk, 34, 94
Philips, Obbe, 94, 115
photography, 124, 125
plain living, 35
Plattdeutsch, 38, 63, 76
pluralistic society, 145
polder, 45
Polish barons, 44
Polish king, 44
Polish monarch, 44
Polish parliament, 44
Polish Sejm, 44
political environment, 43
pouring, 107
profit motive, 128
Protestant princes, 18
Prussia, 46
Prussian Cabinet, 117
Prussian churches, 37
Prussian Mennonites, 75, 116
Przechowka, 34, 35
Przechowka community, 35
Przechowka families, 150
Przechowka Kirchen Buch, 40, 155
Przechowka Mennonite Church, 37

Quakers, 131

radical reformers, 106
Ratzlaff, Hans, 162
Red Army, 72
Red army, 76
Red Army medical service, 72
Red Star Line, 79
red winter wheat, 87
Reformation, 14
Reformation times, 19

Reichstaler, 47
Reichtaler, 47
Reimer, Klaas, 67, 96
religious affiliation, 137
religious authorities, 22
religious freedom, 64
religious peace, 18
Rempel, David, 70
Reublin, Wilhelm, 106
Ritter, Elizabeth, 98
Roman citizenship, 130
royal decree, 43
Royal Poland, 5, 33, 44, 47
rural Kansas, 6
Russian authorities, 63
Russian bunker, 65
Russian citizens, 69
Russian consulate, 50
Russian Czars, 69
Russian czars, 58
Russian government, 74, 77
Russian Gulag, 71
Russian language, 77
Russian Mennonite Convention, 70
Russian military, 69
Russian Revolution, 74
Russian revolution, 68
russification, 69

S.S. Abbotsford, 80, 155
S.S. Cimbria, 52, 82
S.S. City of London, 79
S.S. City of Montreal, 80
S.S. Colina, 62, 82
S.S. Hammonia, 82
S.S. Illinois, 78, 81
S.S. Kenilworth, 80
S.S. Nederland, 41
S.S. Teutonia, 52, 82
S.S. Vaderland, 60, 68, 80
Sacraments, 20
sacraments, 20, 22
satan, 114

Index of Subjects

Sattler, Michael, 21, 114
scarlet fever, 76
Schönau, 75
Schönsee, 34, 37, 155
Schleitheim Confession, 25, 114, 123
Schleitheim convocation, 109
Schmidt, Nathaniel, 118
Schrag, Dale, 65
schulze (mayor), 153
Schwetz, 53
secular government, 126
secular society, 93
Sedition Act, 120
Selbstschutz, 120
Selective Service Act, 118
Selective Service System, 119
separation from the world, 17, 114
shared ministry, 110
shunning, 3, 101, 141
Siberia, 69, 73, 75, 76
Siebrandt, Andreas, 153
Siebrandt, David, 59
Simons, Menno, 29, 30, 107, 115
single share plow, 64
Slavgorod, 75, 76
Slavic surname, 161
small pox, 76, 80
Smit, Jan, 23
social activism, 145
social media, 124
Social Security, 123, 128
south Russia, 5, 38, 56
Soviet government, 65, 70
Soviet policy, 73
Soviet Union, 71, 72
St. Augustine, 107
St. Petersburg, 64, 78
Stalin, 69, 73, 74
Stalinist purges, 73–75
Stalinists, 65
Stanislaus II Augustus, 44
stone masons, 60

swamp fever, 45, 46
swampy lands, 44
Swetz, 59
Swiss Anabaptists, 41
Swiss Brethren, 32
Swiss Mennonites, 41
Switzerland, 159

Täuferkrankheit, 34
Thomas, Helena, 78
Tiege Mennonite Brethren Church, 73
tobacco, 67
Toews, Peter, 97, 108
Tolstoy, Leo, 122
tornado alley, 89
totalitarianism, 131
Turkish war, 56
typhus, 76

ukase, 55
Ukraine, 5, 75
Ukrainian peasants, 70
Ukrainian Security Service, 73
Ukrainian war, 55
Ulysses, 86
Union of Citizens of Dutch lineage, 72
Unrau, Abraham, 163
Unruh, Abram, 40
Unruh, Tobias A., 59, 78
USSR, 73

Van Braght, Thieleman Jansz, 22
Vietnam war, 119
Vilna River, 66
Vistula, 44
Vistula delta, 43–45, 117
Vistula river, 35, 37
Volhynia, 5, 14, 62
Voluntarism, 19
Von Brenkenhoff, 49

wüste Stellen, 47

Waldensians, 19
Waldheim, 60, 62, 78
war bond drives, 115
Warkentin, Bernard, 87
Waterlanders, 33
Wedel, Elder Jacob, 155
Wedel, Errol, 143
Wedel, Jacob, 37
Wedel, Peter, 52
werders (deltas), 44
West Prussia, 77
White Army, 70
Wiedertäufer, 19

Wiens, Peter, 75
Wiggers, William, 22, 154
William I, 116
windmills, 44
Witmarsum, 29
World War I, 69, 118
World War II, 65, 139

Yankton, Dakota Territory, 62
Yantz, Jacob, 79

Zurich Council, 18
Zwingli, Ulrich, 17, 26